GOOD NIGHT, EVERYBODY
...and Be Kind

Dennis Anderson

Xcommunication

X-communication
1002 North Thirteenth Avenue East
Duluth, Minnesota 55812
218-724-2095
www.x-communication.org

Good Night, Everybody...and Be Kind

Text by Dennis Anderson

Content and Copy Editing by Scott Pearson

Proofreading by Kerry Elliott

Cover and interior layout and design and
additional copy editing by Tony Dierckins

Cover photo by Jeff Frey and Associates

Photo of Dennis Anderson and friends
on page 251 courtesy of the *Mesabi Daily News*

Photo of Dennis Anderson and Arne Odegaard on page 254
courtesy of the *Pine Journal* (formerly the *Cloquet Pine Knot*).

All other photos courtesy of the author

First Edition 2005

05 06 07 08 09 10 • 5 4 3 2 1

Library of Congress Control Number: 2005921221

ISBN: 1-887317-28-7

Printed in the United States of America

Good Night, Everybody

…and Be Kind

For those who mean so much to me:

Judy, my wonderful wife, who has been my life partner since January 15,
1966, and who has never lost faith in me or what I could accomplish;

My children, Sally Jo, Cindy, Jodi, and Christian, and their
phenomenal spouses, Rob, Jesse, Jason, and Aerin;

My beautiful grandchildren, Alyssa, Autumn, Taylor, Amelia, Jacob, Andrew,
Emily, Cameron, Cassie, Conner, Cooper, Grace, and, the youngest, Aubrie;

My mom and dad, Florence and Arthur Anderson, who wanted to
read this book, but passed into eternity before it was finished—
how I wish my typing fingers would have moved faster;

Judy's mom and dad, Gloria and Warren Huot,
whose gift of their daughter was the gift of my life;

And to the thousands of you who tune in each
night at six and ten to catch up on the news.

∞

This book could not go to press without a thanks to some special people:

My publisher Tony Dierckins, whose time, effort and guidance were
motivating factors in seeing this publication to fruition; my editor
Scott Pearson, whose wisdom and talent kept the flow of the book on
track; to Kerry Elliott, whose proofreading skills were beyond value;
and to all others at X-communication who had any hand in
the publication of *Good Night, Everybody...and be Kind.*
It's been a great experience.

— *Dennis Anderson*

CONTENTS

PREFACE

What compels a person to write a book? Any number of things I guess, not the least of which is the urge to tell a story. I have a few things to say about the great Northland and those of us who inhabit this little corner of the globe. Perhaps you will find your town, your neighbor, or even yourself somewhere on these pages. After all, I've been reporting about you and where you live for more than forty-three years.

Taking on a project of this size while still juggling a career and a few others things on the side was no easy task. Perhaps "task" is the wrong word. A task is more like a chore, and although writing this manuscript has been a challenge, it was also great fun.

When ABC's Sam Donaldson wrote *Hold on, Mr. President*, he had the luxury of taking time off from work to type his memoirs. He had wanted six weeks, but in the end he got every other Thursday for two months. I felt safer asking for no time off—I've been working on my book for ten years and I didn't think management would allow me to stay home that long and still get paid.

Writing this has forced me to dig through boxes of private files, public records, and scribbled notes that make no sense to others. But, to be honest, much of what is on these pages has been gleaned from memory. It is accurate and true to the best of my recollection.

My broadcast journalism career began on December 1, 1961, while I was still a senior in high school. Yup, I started young. Back in the 1960s, the world didn't have *Eyewitness News*, *Action News*, *60 Minutes*, *20/20*, *Dateline*, or *Nightline*. There was no CNN, no All News Channel.

CNBC and Fox weren't around. There were no television satellites in 1961, and stories were shot on film, not videotape. It sometimes took days to get "breaking news" pictures on the air. Let's face it, early television wasn't much more than radio with an occasional picture of a person or event thrown in for good measure. If an anchorman (no anchorwomen at that time) was a carry-over from radio, imagine the surprise when you got a chance to see what he looked like after listening to his voice for so many years. Radio allowed us to put whatever face we wanted on the voice in the box. Television became a lot more revealing and a lot less forgiving. Still, I find it interesting that I am recognized as much for my voice as for my face.

It's been said that you can tell a lot about a man by what he reads. Well, there is plenty to read in my home. The following periodicals are an indication of some of my interests: *Minnesota Monthly, Home Theatre Magazine, Architectural Digest, Trains, Flying, Time, Newsweek*, and *U.S. News and World Report*. Monthly bills from five separate book clubs offer further testimony to my love of reading, mostly histories and biographies. People and the history they create fascinate me like nothing else. Perhaps that's why I'm a journalist.

But journalists are not historians. Writing history is better left to someone else. Instead, we are men and women who report on the events of the day, which become history.

More than one journalist has called this craft a "sacred trust," which indeed it is. Journalists can quickly turn the public against them if they are not cautious; we cannot run slipshod. I hope we never lose the sense of dignity that must accompany this profession. What we do is for the public good, to report facts and ignite comment and debate. But we are also not a callous bunch who leave our hearts at home when we leave for work in the morning—we too feel the emotions of an event and hurt when others are hurting.

The biggest sin a reporter can commit is getting the story wrong, or having it so slanted that it heavily promotes a certain stand or direction.

That does not mean it's necessary for a reader or viewer to "like" a story; journalism isn't about likeability. It's about truth and accuracy, and when they are thrown out the window, we've endangered what we are all about. Every serious journalist at one time or another catches flak, but that doesn't mean their stories are wrong or slanted. It means they have struck a nerve, and journalism should strike nerves. It's journalists who sensationalize for the sake of sensationalism who strike a nerve with me. One of the best motion pictures ever cranked out of Hollywood was Orson Welles' *Citizen Kane*. It's a movie of lost objectivity by newspaper publisher John Foster Kane, who tampered so much with truth that he destroyed himself in the process.

We have all seen and read examples of sleazeball journalism: stories that fail to express both sides of a debate; stories that incite then fall short in addressing how the issue can be tackled; stories that pique someone's interest with an overblown headline, then don't deliver the goods; stories that contain more opinion than fact; stories that have little truth beyond the opening line; and stories that evoke fear without justification. We in journalism talk a great deal about the public's right to know. If you're going to believe what we tell you, we in this business must guard against being seduced by self-importance. I've seen surveys that rank us below used car salesmen, and that's no slam on them.

This book is not my attempt at the final word on journalism. Rather, it is a chance to say some things I'm not capable of voicing on the nightly news; an opportunity to take you behind the scenes of where I have lived, how I have lived, and what I have done. This profession has offered intellectual and emotional rewards. It has given me a chance to go places, do things, and meet people that would not have been possible in any other line of work. For me, there is no better place I could have spent the past four decades. Mine is the best job in town, a front seat to the news. The good Lord willing, it isn't over.

Perhaps this book will help you get to know me a little better. On the television screen you get only as much as I want to give. The same is true here, of course—but since you paid good money for this book, you'll get a little more. You're going to spend time walking through my childhood and into a career that has been a wonderful ride through history. I will give you a front-row seat into some of the biggest stories I've broadcast and introduce you to the people I've met in more than forty-three years on the air.

Have fun reading.

— Denny Anderson
September 27, 2004

TELEVISION, THEN AND NOW

When television first came out, many people thought it was nothing but a passing fad. Holy cow, were they wrong. There are now nearly four hundred television markets in the United States, ranging in size from millions of viewers in some markets to just a few thousand in others. Obviously, the vast majority of television stations exist outside huge metropolitan areas, so most of us get our news from small- and medium-market TV. Duluth is market number 139, just about smack dab in the middle. New York City is the largest market, while Minneapolis-St. Paul, our good neighbor to the south, is number thirteen.

WDIO-TV is the youngest of the original three Duluth commercial television stations (FOX-21 has recently joined the network affiliates). Built at a cost of $600,000, the ABC affiliate signed on the air for the first time on January 24, 1966, getting started just before the February ratings period.

Frank Befera, the owner of WMFG-Radio in Hibbing and WHLB-Radio in Virginia, spearheaded the drive to form Channel 10 Incorporated. Actually, another group of investors began building a different Channel 10 company in Duluth a few years earlier. Unfortunately for them, they started building before getting FCC approval, which is a no-no in the world of radio-television. The new Channel 10 got the license and changed Twin Ports broadcasting.

With Befera at the helm, several investors came aboard, breaking ground in the fall of 1965. Not too many people in the broadcast industry believed Befera and his boys could make their completion date, but they did. The work was done under the guidance of chief engineer George Woody. Barking orders with his West Virginia drawl, Woody, as he is called, got his staff cracking and did the impossible. Their first broadcasts were a little shaky, but they were on the air.

Seven months after their initial sign-on, the station opened its doors to the public for an open house, with thousands of people from across the Northland getting their first look at the inside of a television station.

WDIO was unique from the start, making a strong commitment to news. Dick Gottschald was hired away from WEBC-Radio to become Channel 10's first news director. Dick had distinguished himself as an award-winning radio newsman, and while TV is different from radio, Dick's heart and soul were in news.

Dick Wallack was hired to anchor the news, Jack McKenna came back to Duluth from the Twin Cities to be the station's weatherman, and Lauren "Sandy" Sandquist became the station's booth announcer and first sportscaster. It didn't take long to hire a sports director by the name of Doug Duncan, with Sandy remaining on payroll to fill in at sports when needed and to record many of the station's commercials and station breaks. Some of those breaks were actually done live in those days.

Aside from the tremendous talent that had been hired, all with many years of broadcast experience, the station introduced color news film right from the start. By 1967, WDIO went full color, something today's audience takes for granted.

There wasn't a beginner on the staff. Management wisely knew that only experienced talent would grab the attention of viewers. After all, Channel 10 was the new kid on the block with no track record. Within a year, the station's prestigious ten o'clock news had become number one in ratings, a distinction it has never lost.

Here's something else you may find interesting. WDIO was built with its transmitter in the same building as its studios, with heat from the transmitter recirculated to heat the building.

Also in 1967, Channel 13 went on the air in Hibbing as Channel 10's satellite operation. WIRT-TV is a fully licensed television station in its own right, and it is used to transmit the Channel 10 signal into a vast part of the state that otherwise couldn't get our coverage. That makes for a strong reach for WDIO's programming and news.

∞

Suffice it to say, I wasn't hired right away. In fact, economics kept Channel 10's staff down to just a couple dozen people in those early years. Stu Stronach was hired away from a Duluth radio station and became WDIO's first real investigative reporter. Stu, who died a number of years after he retired to an electricity-free farm south of Superior, was an award-winning investigator the likes of which this market hasn't seen since.

He was bold in his work. Cunning would be more like it—a Mike Wallace of Duluth. Stu would disappear for days, checking into the newsroom first thing in the morning and late in the afternoon. The hours in between would be spent snooping like a bloodhound. There is a degree of secrecy in how we gather certain information, which means we often rely on informers ("Deep Throats"). Many stories would not get on the air without secret sources. But even then, everything we air is checked. When Stu finally had his information, his interviews lined up, and his sources confirmed and triple-checked, he would call for a photographer to begin filming his story.

Dick Nordvald of WMFG-Radio in Hibbing was WDIO's first Saturday night newscaster, and Steve Johnson, a weekday Channel 10 general assignment reporter and Action Line editor, delivered the Sunday night news. Nordvald favored radio over television and he held the Saturday slot for just a year. His leaving gave me the chance to pick up the Saturday broadcast prior to my 1968 move to work at Fargo's Channel 11. Then in October of 1969, Channel 10 hired me full time, putting my foot in the door for the eventual anchor chair, which came unexpectedly.

With Dick Wallack seemingly well entrenched in that chair, I had no thoughts of knocking him off his perch. Dick is a good fifteen years older than me, so he had a maturity that I still lacked, plus he had become a well-liked fixture in the five years he was on Channel 10.

So it came as a surprise when Dick told management that he was bailing out of WDIO to take a similar position at Channel 6, then known as WDSM. He accepted Channel 6's offer for more money and gave his notice. That was in the spring of 1971, and right off the bat WDSM made a big mistake. Rather than put Dick immediately on the air, for whatever reason they saved him until that fall. About midsummer they began an ad campaign called "Dick's on 6."

Their campaign fell flat. You see, they waited too long and our audience had already gotten used to me. WDIO manager Frank Befera got a glowing letter from business giant Jeno Paulucci saying how much he preferred me over Wallack. It was a tremendous compliment from Jeno, a letter I still have in my archives. If Jeno felt that way, hopefully others did.

Also, Channel 6 used an odd-looking modernistic painting of Dick in their newspaper and billboard ads, rather than a photograph of his familiar face. That didn't work either. It wasn't the same face that people had grown accustomed to on the screen. To put it simply, Wallack didn't take his audience with him, and Channel 10 was thrilled.

Befera told me that never in the history of television (up to that time), had an anchor left one station to go to another in the same market, and taken the audience. It goes to show that popularity has a brief life span. It's more than the newscaster; it's also the organization, and WDIO's news department was first class. Dick continued on Channel 6 for several years, later as a producer. He's retired now and we don't see each other often, but it's a treat on those rare occasions.

∞

Anchors my age were groomed in a different era, when news content came before all else. I'm old enough to have formed my on-air persona before consultants and talent coaches became a part of my industry. I dare wear a toupee and a moustache. In all my extensive travels, I can't think of seeing another anchor with facial hair, at least not since the 1970s. Walter Cronkite had a thin moustache the entire nineteen years he anchored for CBS.

Fashion and trend-setting will have to be left to someone else. You should know that I wear a full suit each night on the news, not just a coat and tie with jeans or shorts on the bottom half out of camera range.

I like to believe that this journalist came from the old school, the likes of Edward R. Murrow and his cadre of talent. Now don't get me wrong, I'm not trying to put myself in their league, but we have a shared philosophy. News is a public trust, it has to be. This industry is the protector of truth and needs to be worked by women and men who can be trusted to watch over it carefully.

Sadly, much of the media has gotten away from hardball journalism, the investigative stuff. Ed Murrow was a remarkable reporter who understood that TV could take us to places like no newspaper. That's what attracted me to this business, the ability to transport the listener and the viewer right to where the story is unfolding. They can see it and hear it as it's happening. Old newspaper men used to say they had ink in their veins. Modern TV journalists have electronic gadgets flowing through their arterial systems.

News-gathering is a demanding craft requiring us to weigh decisions carefully, not recklessly as some of you would believe. These decisions are often made after spirited debate in the newsroom, with the ultimate decision left in the hands of the news director. That's how it should be: give and take by reporters, producers, anchors, and news management. Some of the staff, myself included, may not agree with the final decision about how a story will be reported or look on the air, but we have our say and recognize that the news director takes final responsibility.

Our current news director is Steve Goodspeed, a man who takes his job seriously and puts in far more than forty hours a week. He is a man of impeccable morals and insists upon fairness and balance in each and every story. He was first hired by me, when I was Channel 10's news director back in the 1970s. Steve left after a few years and was rehired when Joel Anderson left us in the early 1990s. We got Steve from KMSP, Channel 9, in Minneapolis, where he worked as a general assignment reporter. He is a talented storyteller and writer, and is continually working with reporters to help them hone their skills. Steve is a constant reminder that there is no substitute for accuracy.

∞

WDIO has been sold twice in my time, the first time to Harcourt Brace Jovanovich Publishing, in the early 1970s. The publishing giant held on to the property until 1987, when it was sold to Hubbard Broadcasting of St. Paul. Harcourt Brace Jovanovich (HBJ) had talked of plans to buy other broadcast properties, but WDIO was their only TV station. Frank Befera, WDIO's founder, president and general manager was to become the president of HBJ's broadcast wing, something that never materialized.

Both buy-outs had staff talking about possible layoffs and job consolidations, fears that were laid aside once the purchases were made. It is natural for staff to fear for their future, to wonder what new owners would do with the place and with the people—even middle-management personnel wondered if they still had jobs. Once we heard it was the Hubbard family interested in buying out HBJ, we breathed a sigh of relief. I told the staff, "Even if I'm not personally included in Hubbard's plans, this is good for WDIO."

Here's why. First and foremost, the Hubbards are a broadcasting family with a long legacy. Stanley Hubbard is an innovator, like his father, who took early television and moved it into what we now take for granted. His KSTP in the Twin Cities is the flagship station of Hubbard Broadcasting, which remains family owned and operated and includes TV stations in New York, New Mexico, and, of course, Minnesota. Mr.

Hubbard and his late father brought much technical know-how into the industry, taking it from early color all the way to satellite technology.

Secondly, the Hubbards had the financial means to improve WDIO's technology. And that they did. Within a short time, Hubbard Broadcasting bought state-of-the-art tape machines, editing equipment, satellite and microwave live trucks, a new transmitter for Duluth (and Hibbing's WIRT), and other needed capital improvements.

And thirdly, the Hubbards have integrity, bringing their family values into the larger family of those who work for them. It has been a good marriage between them and WDIO. Mr. Hubbard himself sent me a kind letter of congratulations when the University of Minnesota Duluth honored me with the Chancellor's Award in 2003, given for my accomplishments in furthering the cause of good journalism.

Chapter 1

CHANNEL 10 VS. THE POLICE

It was around midnight on a March evening in 1971 when the police scanner alongside my bed crackled loud enough to awaken me from what should have been a full night's sleep. The Duluth police dispatcher was sending officers to a possible burglary in progress at the Ski Hut on the corner of Eleventh Avenue East and Fourth Street.

Somewhat reluctant to leave my warm bed, the news instincts I had honed over the years told me to get dressed and check it out, since the Ski Hut was just around the corner from our Third Street apartment. So in the dead of night, I slipped out of the house wearing just enough clothing to ward off the late-winter chill. Armed with nothing more than curiosity and a Bell and Howell 16mm news camera with spotlight, I arrived on the scene about the same time as the first police squad.

Within moments the place was alive with officers scanning every wall of the building looking for a door through which the burglars might escape. These weren't quiet interlopers. We put our ears up against the back wall of the Ski Hut and could actually hear the intruders rummaging around inside, oblivious to the long arm of the law waiting for them. Since my camera spotlight was much brighter than their flashlights, I offered the police the use of my light. Together we walked around the building looking for any possible means of escape.

Minutes later the officers made a rush through the front entrance and quickly had two young burglars in tow, handcuffed and ready for the trip downtown. That's when I turned my spotlight back on and lifted the camera to my eye. This would be captivating news film of two men just captured and being walked to a waiting police car. Very routine, or so it seemed.

"No pictures," bellowed Sergeant Richard Gunnarson. I thought to myself, *He can't stop me from taking pictures,* so I kept filming. "No pictures," Gunnarson commanded again, but, not wanting to lose the scene, I kept my finger on the camera trigger. At that point, Gunnarson came up to me and put his hand on the camera lenses, forcing the camera down to my chest and demanded one more time, "I said no pictures!"

"You can't stop me from taking pictures," I retorted, while the sergeant kept a firm hand on the camera.

Again he insisted, "I said there will be no pictures. Give me the camera." Keep in mind I was standing on a public sidewalk watching a public event take place, with one or two other spectators now on the scene taking this in. Eventually, one of them became my best witness.

After refusing to give my camera to the sergeant, Lieutenant Alexander Lukovsky walked over and likewise insisted on my surrender of the camera. Headlines in the next day's *Duluth News-Tribune* said it all: "Duluth Police Seize Camera." The Associated Press news wire service picked up the story, which put it in every newsroom in the country.

> Duluth (AP)—Camera and film used by a television newsman were confiscated by police while making an arrest at a Duluth sports shop Monday, station WDIO-TV said. Dick Gottschald, WDIO news director called the incident a 'threat not only to television news casting, but to other media as well.' Gottschald said the matter was referred to the station's attorney. As station sources outlined the incident, Dennis Anderson, a WDIO reporter was at the scene of a break-in at a ski shop early Monday. He was outside the shop on public property, taking pictures as police took a man from the shop. An officer, Sgt. Dick Gunnarson, told him to stop filming the scene, Anderson said. When Anderson refused to do so and declined to turn over his camera as police ordered, the equipment was taken from him forcibly, he said. No charges were

filed against Anderson. Gunnarson, reached for comment declined to go into specifics of the incident, 'until such time as we get a ruling from the city attorney.' The officer said possible charges are pending that Anderson had interfered with the duties of a police officer.

As Lukovsky had put the camera in his squad car he told me, "You can have it back in the morning." I got the impression that he was trying to defuse the situation. Perhaps he was thinking that Gunnarson had erred, but chose not to go against him. Whatever the reason, I got the distinct impression that he wasn't too comfortable taking the camera.

The next day news director Dick Gottschald went down to police headquarters and was given the camera and film. Meanwhile, city attorney Dan Berglund told Gottschald that it had not yet been decided whether charges would be brought against me. After three days of sweating out a possible warrant for my arrest, no charges were made. That's because I didn't interfere with the police; they interfered with me.

A couple of days after the camera confiscation, the Duluth police department had gone to work on what I call damage control. Appearing on KDAL-Radio's *Anthony Answers* talk show hosted by Dick Anthony, Lukovsky and Gunnarson claimed I had no right to film the arrest of any person at any time. They told their listeners they would prevent me from doing so in the future and they would arrest me if I ever again attempted to photograph another arrest.

WDIO general manager Frank Befera, Gottschald, and I got together in Befera's office to listen to and tape record the radio show, and as the program got going we couldn't believe what we were hearing. Ten days after the confiscation, we filed suit. As you can imagine, we were incensed by what happened and the incident became fodder for a long list of news stories across the state and region. A great deal of mail poured in over the ensuing weeks supporting our lawsuit against officers Gunnarson and Lukovsky. We saw their action as a blatant attempt to control the news, and that was something we were not going to put up with. We made it clear in our lawsuit that the two officers had deprived me and WDIO of our constitutional rights.

We went to trial and a federal judge agreed. U.S. District Judge Phillip Neville ruled that the seizing of the news camera and film violated the First, Fourth, and Fourteenth Amendments of the United States Constitution. Judge Neville added that "police have no right to arrest or seize and hold any of the equipment of a reporter working on public property or in other places where the public is generally permitted."

The judge's ruling was victory for the people. Judge Neville made it clear that "when news people are engaged in lawful coverage of newsworthy events, police have no right to arrest them or take any of their equipment, providing the news people are not breaking the law or interfering with police."

To top this off, the police department had first agreed to return the camera on condition of prior review of the film by police. They thought the burglars might have been juveniles. In other words, they wanted to view the film to determine whether it should be shown on the news.

Can you imagine that? They wanted to make a journalistic decision that they had no right to make. Police as editors—I don't think so. They do not have the right to determine what is printed in the paper or shown on television. God help us if they do. If the burglars had been juveniles and we put their faces on television, that would have put my butt in the sling. It's not up to the police to make that determination.

I have a great deal of respect for police officers. I did then and I do now. They work under exceedingly tough conditions, and they are called upon to make snap decisions. Every police chief has to deal with a variety of personalities in his or her department, union issues, a finicky public, unruly officers, the media, the mayor, and the daily fight against crime. I am proud that one of my sons-in-law is a Duluth police officer and another works in corrections as a St. Louis County jailer. Usually I have gotten along quite well with the men and women in blue. They have a difficult job at best, but they, like the rest of us, must carry out their profession within the confines of the law. The law was broken when they confiscated my camera.

This wasn't the end of our running battle with the police department that year, and it got national attention from a publication that went into millions of homes—*TV Guide.*

In November 1971, eight months after my camera and film were confiscated, *TV Guide* correspondent Neil Hickey wrote a story he called "Hassle in Duluth. A TV Station and Police Lock Horns."

In the article, then-mayor Ben Boo responded to the confiscation saying, "The primary concern here was the safety of the police officers. I see their point." Police Chief Milo Tasky said, "The officers believed the light being used endangered them unnecessarily, and I support them one hundred percent." It should be noted that those statements given to Hickey were made prior to the judge's ruling against the police.

The article went on to report how the Minnesota Civil Liberties Union "jumped" on the side of the TV station, as Hickey put it, "declaring the camera confiscation a 'serious violation of the First Amendment.'" Plus, we got more support.

The chairman of the Freedom of Information Committee of Sigma Delta Chi, which is a national journalism society, told *TV Guide* that the society could only "view with disgust" the action of the Duluth police officers.

Then, as *TV Guide* reported, "the police struck back hard." The Duluth police union, Local 107, issued a strong statement against WDIO Television, a statement signed by union president and police officer Eli Miletich, who later became police chief. Many months before Judge Neville's ruling in our favor, the union denounced WDIO for what they called "a subtle and deliberate attempt to ridicule, intimidate and discredit members of the Duluth Police Department." They said WDIO was "muckraking," and "disguising it as news."

And the police union didn't stop there. It was at this point they blasted a shot across our bow. The union resolution signed by Miletich went on to say, "Be it further resolved that the police union go on record as urging our membership and their entire families and concerned friends and acquaintances not to patronize the commercial sponsors of WDIO news." A copy of this resolution was sent to advertisers buying time on Channel 10 in an effort to hit us in the pocketbook.

That's when the Minnesota Broadcasters Association, during their meeting in Mankato, passed a resolution condemning the police department for attempting to restrict news coverage. Their resolution deplored police for urging sponsors not to advertise on WDIO.

Then it became a game of cat and mouse. The station claimed police were trailing WDIO staff by waiting near the studios on Observation Road to catch them in minor traffic violations. Near his home, Dick Gottschald was tagged for speeding, going what he said was just a little over the speed limit.

Police claimed the station was following them in news cars hoping to catch them on film committing some infraction. *TV Guide* put it well: "For awhile the squad cars and TV cars were chasing each other's tails around Duluth, in a kind of Marx Brothers game of tag."

Mayor Ben Boo told *TV Guide* he thought WDIO, as a young television station, was coming on strong with "some sensationalism to get the public's attention." The mayor did say he didn't personally approve of the police union's attempt at an economic boycott against WDIO's advertisers. By the way, there was almost no economic impact from the boycott. Channel 10 sales manager Duane Eastvold reported not a single advertising contract was lost.

Roy Karon, the short-lived news director at KDAL-Television (now KDLH), told *TV Guide* that WDIO made "too big a fuss" over the camera confiscation. I will admit that the battle with police that year didn't hurt the ratings. The March Neilsens gave Channel 10 a fifty-six percent share of the audience.

As I put this chapter to rest, I must say again that I have nothing but high respect for the Duluth Police Department. The whole thing got out of hand from the very moment of the Ski Hut burglary. I personally know a good number of local police officers, and the majority of the local force is comprised of dedicated, hard-working men and women, several of whom have given their lives to serve and protect.

Chapter 2

IRON RANGE ROOTS

Mom and Dad seemed to have a marriage that was one of commitment—both took their wedding vows seriously and without reservation. They were married on July 6, 1939, in a church parsonage in Eveleth. Dad's mother bought them a beautiful mahogany bedroom set which is in our master bedroom to this very day. They weren't ones to express their love for each other verbally, at least not that we kids were able to hear. That was done more privately. Yet their love was shown by how they treated one another and us children, mostly with respect, although there were moments when Dad gave us a paddling on the butt. He was the disciplinarian, not Mom.

I came into the world at 9:39 on the morning of January 18, 1944. World War II was raging. Adolf Hitler had tightened his grip on Europe, trying to transform the world into his thousand-year Reich. D-day was still five months away, and even then it took another ten months for the Allies to reach Berlin, where Hitler killed himself. Thousands of troops were dying in the Pacific, where the Japanese wouldn't surrender until President Truman dropped the second of two nuclear bombs. World War II officially ended with the signing of an instrument of surrender on September 2, 1945, when I was twenty months old.

Dad was thirty-one when I was born, and now the father of two children. He worked for the Oliver Iron Mining Company, a war-necessary industry, digging as much iron ore out of the ground as needed for tanks, bullets, and anything else the boys overseas required to defeat the enemy.

Mom was a twenty-seven-year-old stay-at-home woman, much more common in those days. Arthur and Florence Anderson had their first son.

My parents weren't content to give me just a single middle name, so they stuck me with two, Arthur and Robert for my dad and uncle. Eventually, I considered changing my name to Art Roberts for radio purposes, but a popular announcer was already using that name on a 50,000-watt Chicago station that reached into northern Minnesota. So the more ethnic sounding Dennis Anderson stuck. I'm not disappointed.

It didn't take long for Mom to give birth, once she got to the hospital. The records show that I got my first glimpse of daylight an hour and forty-nine minutes after checking in. All mom's births were that way—fast—including, sadly, the four miscarriages she suffered. The last was a full-term boy they named Duane, born dead just hours after I was sent to a week-long school patrol camp in Brainerd. That was 1955, and our family had been looking forward to another addition. My sister Donna had preceded me into this world by four years, and my brother James popped his head out two years after me. Doctors told my folks that they were lucky to have three kids who survived.

My brother Jim came into the world just when whooping cough invaded our household, striking my sister Donna and me. The medical name for whooping cough is pertussis, a bacterial disease that causes cold-like symptoms and often develops into coughing fits. It was not what Jim needed as an infant, and he managed to avoid the bug. Jim waited extra days in the hospital before Donna and I ended up staying with Grandma and Grandpa Lind for six weeks, so our baby brother could come home. Quarantine signs were hung outside our grandparents' house, a common practice in those days when highly contagious illnesses struck; there was even a hospital in Virginia called "the pest house."

For the first six months of my life, we lived in a tiny stucco-covered house in Virginia's Williams Addition neighborhood. Mom and Dad rented that little house for $27 a month plus heat and lights, which sounds cheap by today's standards. But wages were also next to nothing for an iron miner, and Dad thought he would give it two years then find another job. He ended up staying with the Oliver Iron Mining Company and later the Minntac Plant for thirty-seven years. Dad always wondered if he made a mistake when he turned down a job as a mail sorter in a railroad post office car, known as an RPO.

In July 1944, my parents bought a white clapboard house, the first and only home they would ever own, from the Salo family. It was just one block from the stucco house. Dad's mother Caroline would often baby-sit, and each Sunday Grandma would walk the mile or so to our house for dinner, then spend the afternoon. Mom's mother, Ida, lived just a few houses away, so we saw her daily either at her place or ours. She became something of a second mother, and her death at age ninety was a painful loss.

Our new house was nothing fancy, mind you—just a story-and-a-half with a living room, kitchen, a single bath, small den, two upstairs bedrooms, and a basement. And you know, that house changed little over the next decade. Dad was making enough money to feed us, but not to decorate the place. I wouldn't say we grew up having little in the way of food or clothing, at least not that I was aware. We never heard our parents argue about a lack of money, not once. We didn't have many extras, but if we were poor, I didn't know it. Eventually though, the house got new asbestos shingles and a large porch which brought the basement entrance into the house.

One day my brother and a couple of friends joined me in a game of cops and robbers, which ended when I fell into the six-foot-deep foundation of that new porch, striking my head on the cement. The board we used to span the excavation was far too narrow for the tricycle I was riding, and that tumble got me a trip to the clinic with a concussion. The saving grace was a quart of root beer a friend brought over later that afternoon, and it was all mine.

∞

Many people don't realize it, but Minnesota has three Iron Ranges, the most familiar and the largest being the Mesabi Range. It meanders from Virginia to just east of Grand Rapids. The other two are the Cuyuna, the smallest, and the Vermilion. The Vermilion Range is about forty-five miles long, stretching from just north of Virginia to Winton, near Ely.

The possibilities for growth and prosperity must have seemed endless throughout much of this region one hundred years ago. Farms were settled in Wisconsin and Minnesota, and the dairy industry took hold. Many large dairy farms provided fresh milk and cheese to waiting customers (the Johnson Brothers' Dairy served our family needs).

According to the 1907 book *The Virginian*, in June 1893, a brush fire burned out of control southwest of the village of Virginia. Pushed along by strong winds, the fire moved into the village. Less than an hour after the first building was hit by flames, the inferno had reduced the entire town to ash. Some folks left forever, their homes and all other earthly belongings destroyed. Others refused to give up and stayed to rebuild their town, which was incorporated in February 1895.

Seven years after the first fire leveled Virginia, tragedy struck again when a second fire roared through the city's business district, thanks to sparks from the Moon and Kerr Lumber Company's shavings burner.

Undaunted, Virginians rebuilt once more, this time using brick and mortar, and constructed a main street that today retains the architectural flavor of the old city. By 1920, Virginia was the fifth largest city in the state.

Virginia was very much a mining town during my childhood, with the sound of ore trains and freight trains piercing the air night and day. Steam locomotives still ruled railroading, hauling long ore drags out of the pits to the nearby crusher. The Duluth, Missabe & Iron Range Railway's big Yellowstone Mallets pulled the longer consists to Duluth and Two Harbors, where the ore was dumped into boats for the trip to the eastern steel mills. These were mammoth steam engines, big 2-8-8-2s that snaked their way through the forests down to Lake Superior.

Minnesota's first ore train made its journey sixty years before my birth, pulling its load to Agate Bay, which in 1887 became Two Harbors.

Northern Minnesota's timber industry still exists, although it pales in comparison to what was harvested to feed the Virginia & Rainy Lake Lumber Company, the largest white pine mill in the world. The big mill was located right in the heart of Virginia, using Silver Lake and Virginia Lake (now called Bailey's Lake) to float its logs up to the saws for cutting, as much as a million board feet a day. Think of that. This was a major employer for the area, with 1,300 men drawing paychecks. The funeral home my brother owns in Virginia used to be the mansion in which the lumber company's superintendent lived. By the time I was born, just one of the lumber company's giant slab burners was left standing, along with a single storage shed.

Passenger trains still chugged in an out of town, using depots on both ends of Virginia's main street. On the west end of Chestnut Street stands the ornate Duluth, Winnepeg & Pacific depot, now used as a bank. The east end of Chestnut hosted the DM&IR depot, a more nondescript building that was torn down years ago.

My first train ride came in kindergarten, a short hop to Iron Junction and back, taken by the entire population of James Madison School. Grandpa Frank Lind, my mother's dad, was the school janitor; he died in 1948, a year before the start of my education. That was also the year Mom and Dad took us to Hibbing to see President Harry Truman on his famous Whistle Stop Campaign, which I don't really remember.

And it was 1948 when tragedy indirectly struck our family with the murder of my brother's godfather. Years before Dad met Mom, he befriended the Makela family of Meadowlands. Emil Makela and his wife Sylvia eventually became such close friends that my parents asked them to be godparents to my brother.

We visited the Makelas often, and each trip to their small farm was a treat. What city kid doesn't love a day on a farm, with a chance to play in the hay, ride the horses, and explore the nearby woods? My sister and brother and I savored every chance we got to play with the Makela boys, Wilfred and Richard, who we called Dickie. They lived in a little white house perched on a knoll overlooking their barn and pasture land.

∞

On the afternoon of Saturday, January 31st, 1948, the Elmer Town Board met to consider, among other things, an off-sale beer license for thirty-two-year-old Joe Contanzi, who operated a small store in Elmer, about five miles north of Meadowlands. They were meeting in the Elmer school, a small wood structure with a teacher's apartment upstairs.

It was there, in their first order of business, that the board turned down Contanzi's request for a beer license. This was the second time the license was denied, despite an earlier okay from Sheriff Sam Owens and the county attorney. Contanzi apparently became outraged. He allegedly went out to his truck and came back inside with a 30-30 deer rifle and started shooting. When the smoke cleared three people lay dead, including my brother's godfather, and a fourth man was wounded.

Newspaper accounts in the *Duluth News-Tribune* tell how thirty-year-old Frank Svoboda, the town clerk, was shot first. Emil, who was thirty-five, tried to escape the room, but moments later he lay dead just inside the threshold of a door he had beaten through with his hands. Emil was the president of the town board and had been hit with two bullets.

The *News-Tribune* reported that Contanzi aimed his rifle at sixty-year-old Albert Dupac, a board member and the town supervisor, who fell dead between a row of desks. Another bullet struck sixty-year-old Louis Ringhofer in the arm, who survived by faking death.

The only member of the town board to escape a bullet was thirty-five-year-old Albert Bernsdorf, who managed to get outside and hide behind a snow fort made by kids in the school yard. Sheriff Owens told the newspaper that "at least a dozen shots" had been fired, with "bullets tearing into desks and blackboards."

Contanzi drove off in his truck, and news of the shootings spread fast. Some folks even formed a posse armed with guns, volunteering to help find the shooter. It turned out that Contanzi drove a couple miles from the school house to the home of Hjalmer Carlson, a seventy-year-old bachelor who knew him. The posse moved in to surround the house and found Contanzi's body outside in the snow. Black-and-white crime-scene photos, which county sheriff Ross Litman allowed me to see, show Contanzi lying in the snow, dead of an apparent self-inflicted gunshot wound.

The *Duluth Tribune* reported that Contanzi had told Carlson what he had done, saying he had written a message to his wife and a note for Sheriff Owens.

My folks learned of the shootings in the morning paper, and within minutes they packed their car and drove to Meadowlands. Emil's death had a profound impact on my parents. Even though their pain softened over the years, what happened on that late January day never really left them. They kept newspaper accounts of the shootings tucked away, ironically in an old army surplus ammunitions box, and every once in a while Dad would pull them out and reread them, shaking his head. He and Mom lost a good friend that day, and they made certain to keep their friendship solid with the Makelas until their own deaths. Wilfred and Dickie came to Mom and Dad's funerals a half century later.

Chapter 3

MINNESOTA WINTERS

Anyone who lives in Duluth-Superior knows that the Twin Ports doesn't have a real spring. Temperatures are kept cool (often cold) by off-lake winds, and we seem to get our share of rain right through June. Each spring, especially in March, our neck of the woods can get nasty ice storms. Snow isn't unusual in April, and not too many years ago we had a ten-inch snowfall on the first of May. July and August provide us with a narrow window of opportunity for warmth, and even that isn't guaranteed because of the big lake. Once fall arrives, the beauty of our colored leaves doesn't last long, with one good wind stripping the trees bare. I may not have said it first but I've often joked that the Northland has nine months of summer and three months of bad sledding. If it sounds like I'm not a good pitchman for the Chamber of Commerce, that's not my intent. I love Duluth and our up-north style of life. While I will always carry an affection for the Iron Range, especially the city of Virginia, where I was born and raised, Duluth has been home since 1969, and that won't change. My family is well entrenched here, and some day my bones will rest in a Duluth cemetery. But I'll tell you for certain, before that day these bones will spend retirement winters in much warmer climates.

∽

It was early on Saturday morning, March 23, 1991, when I awoke and flipped on KDAL-Radio for the morning news. The announcer was talking about a television broadcast tower that had fallen during the night. I made a quick call to WDIO management at home to get more details, then I called KDAL and for the next several minutes they had me on the air talking about what I knew.

Banner headlines in the next day's *Duluth News-Tribune* read, "Spring Storm Shows its Muscle." The paper's story appeared above the front page fold and featured a large picture of me talking on a cell phone while standing in front of the fallen tower. It had twisted into something that resembled a roller coaster, snaking its way around the TV station and barely nicking the corner of the building.

It's amazing the tower didn't fall on the station itself, which would have effectively put us off the air for a long time. The engineer on duty that night had left the building just twenty minutes earlier, and while getting gasoline several blocks away, he saw a large flash in the direction of the TV station but didn't know what had happened.

Police blocked Observation Road from both ends fearing other towers could fall under the heavy weight of all that ice still clinging to those superstructures.

We had immediate decisions to make. With no broadcast tower, there could be no signal transmitted unless someone came to our assistance. Fortunately, Duluth TV stations enjoy great relationships with each other, especially in times of emergency. We are fierce competitors, but when the chips are down all the stations are willing to help.

WDSE, Public Broadcasting's Channel 8, allowed us to use their signal the first few nights, before we were able to get an antenna installed on their tower so we could resume broadcasting. Until then we had to videotape our newscast at five o'clock, then run the tape over to the Channel 8 building at UMD. They played that tape on their air at six o'clock, while we did a live newscast in our building for those who watch on cable. While we couldn't use our transmitter without a tower, we were still able to provide cable service without interruption. Then we repeated the sequence for the ten o'clock news.

It meant double duty for everyone, putting a lot of pressure on the staff and our resources, but it also meant we didn't miss a beat. Not a single newscast was lost.

By the middle of May, WDIO signed up with Kline Towers of Columbia, South Carolina, to build a new state-of-the-art tower. It was built in New Hampshire and trucked to Duluth in sections, the first piece put in place on October 14, seven months after the old tower fell. The last piece was put up thirteen days after the first.

Once the steel was standing, the wiring had to be installed and the antenna attached at the top of the structure. All that took time, and on January 4 we were once again broadcasting on our own. It was ten months that will not be forgotten. The top of this tower rises to 2,049 feet above sea level, a bit higher than the old one, and far sturdier.

Channel 10 published a booklet of the tower collapse, called *Tower Talk '91*. It told the story through words and pictures from the night the tower fell until the new one was operational. Let's hope that doesn't happen again.

∞

Every once in a while Mother Nature throws a megastorm at us, as she did on October 31, 1991, forever known in these parts as the Halloween Blizzard—and this trick was no treat.

It started earlier in the day with just a few flakes coming down, with thousands of kids still planning to go trick-or-treating that night. By the time it ended, thirty-seven inches fell on Duluth, which took the brunt of the storm, and twenty-eight on the Twin Cities, the greatest snowfall in Minnesota history. It shattered two other records, the most snowfall in a twenty-four-hour period and the most snow in October. Folks at the National Weather Service gave it the name "Megastorm," and who could disagree?

The storm lasted four days, caused seven deaths, forced schools and businesses to close, buried cars all over town, piled snowdrifts as high as roofs, and stranded workers. Events were cancelled, and very few got out for trick-or-treating.

This is the kind of story that newsrooms live for. It had elements of everything, from cancelled weddings to babies being born. One Duluth doc had to get to the hospital on cross-country skis to deliver a baby.

I've been stranded overnight at the television station more than once while waiting out snowstorms. But this time, weathercaster Ken Chapin and I wanted to get home. So a photographer volunteered to do the driving, managing to drop me off at an intersection a couple of blocks from my house. Ken wasn't as lucky, ending up staying the night camped uncomfortably on an office floor.

I had earlier alerted my wife that there would be an attempt to get home that night, and two of my older kids volunteered to meet me at the intersection. In the time they waited for my arrival, the snow had dropped in such quantity that it took the three of us more than an hour to walk the two blocks to the house.

By morning, almost nothing was moving. Working together, our family dug out of the house by literally carving a six-foot-deep path from the door to the driveway. The snow was piled past the top of the doorway, leaving a white wall of snow when the door opened inward.

In the first newscast of the day we reported, "Pumpkins had been carved, candy was at the ready, and trick-or-treaters were all set for their annual sojourn into the night." By the time ghosts and goblins were to start on their appointed rounds, the Megastorm had begun and few got out.

No matter what the weather, the news must go on. A member of the station's sales staff drove his snowmobile to my home to get me to the television station. He was the only one on staff who had a machine, and he played taxi-driver that day and the next. Even that was a struggle, trying to navigate over drifts that stood like miniature mountains trying to block our travel. It looked bleak out there, almost a white-out and so very deserted. Nothing moved. (Another time, a police officer with a four-wheel drive vehicle got me to work. He was dispatched to my home from his regular patrol in my neighborhood and got me to the television station. I ended up spending the night there, stranded. That happened three or four times over the years, before the station bought a fleet of four-wheel-drive vehicles.)

Yet life does not stop for a blizzard, and neither does death. A Duluth funeral director got stranded while driving from a Park Point nursing home with a body in the car. The hearse got stuck on the way back to the mortuary, and before long it was buried beneath the snow. A cross country skier's ski pole hit the top of the hearse as he slid along, and he took time to find out what he had struck. When he found the vehicle, its driver had almost succumbed to carbon monoxide poisoning.

We had story after story to tell, each one as different as the people involved, all of whom were trying to deal with the raging blizzard as best they could. This storm tested our mettle, and we kept the story going for days.

∞

There has long been a rivalry between International Falls, Tower, and Embarrass as to which town is Minnesota's coldest. While the Falls has the official honor of being "the nation's ice box" (it was featured in car battery commercials in the 1970s and parodied in *Rocky and Bullwinkle* cartoons as "Frostbite Falls"), Tower and Embarrass are often much colder. On February 2, 1996, Groundhog Day, no groundhog in his right mind would have ventured forth. That was the morning the state's all-time record cold temperature of fifty-nine degrees below zero was broken when the mercury fell to sixty below in Tower.

An equipment failure in Embarrass may have kept that community from bottoming out even lower, and some questioned if the reading in Tower was valid. But, speculation or disappointment aside, the record stands and folks in Tower will be forever proud that their temperature was cold enough to make a miser's heart feel warm.

I happened to be attending a funeral in Cotton that morning, about thirty-five miles north of Duluth, where the temperature was fifty-two below. Duluth had thirty-nine below, falling just two degrees shy of its coldest day ever. It was forty-four below that morning in Hibbing, fifty-three below in Embarrass, forty-seven below in Bemidji, and the so-called nation's icebox, I-Falls, was a balmy forty-five below.

Channel 10 weathercaster Collin Ventrella and I were bantering back and forth on the air about the freezing temperatures, and a part of that conversation was picked up by ABC News in New York. Our cold weather dialogue was broadcast over the network, and several days later I started getting mail from several parts of the country and one from a viewer in New Zealand, a former Duluth man.

Many who wrote couldn't believe people actually live in Northern Minnesota, and some wanted to know what sixty below felt like. How do you describe it? After a while cold is cold.

Most of the cold weather stories we put together had to do with the effect it had on people, some of whom kept their cars running almost continually for fear they would freeze up and not start again. Others told of sitting by the woodstove all night, while two or three hearty folks actually camped outside in tents in Tower and Embarrass. Another couple spent the night in an igloo they dug into the side of a large snow bank.

TV and radio stations from all over the country called our newsroom for live reports from bundled up reporters having a little fun with this Arctic blast. One experiment was repeated several times for different stations, and that was the tossing of water into the air to see if it came back down in the form of ice. The smaller drops did.

Meanwhile, folks we interviewed in Tower wore their newfound fame like a badge of honor, happy to be getting all the national attention. One fellow told us he pounded nails with a frozen banana.

There was one thing to be said about the cold snap—the crime rate dropped. The frigid Friday also meant no school, and towing companies were running hours, if not days, behind. Not much moves when it's forty-five to sixty below. There weren't any local deaths attributed to the cold; ironically, temperatures in the mid-nineties in the summer of 2001 claimed several lives in Duluth. We're apparently more accustomed to cold than to heat.

∽

Not all storms are about the weather, such as the stormy week I had in February, 1970, when it seemed as if the gods didn't like me. The week started off with a car accident, which damaged my new Oldsmobile. The next day my wife miscarried twin boys. Twenty four hours later, I froze an ear while filming a late-night fire in below-zero temperatures. Then a day or so later, with Judy and our two-year-old daughter Sally now in Virginia, staying with Judy's parents for a few days, the entire ceiling let loose in my little girl's bedroom. Plaster and lathwork crashed down into her crib, which would have killed or seriously injured Sally, had she been home. What a week. The ceiling collapse even made the United Press wire service, and I got letters from people in various parts of the country who once lived in the Northland.

∽

One winter, Jack McKenna, his wife Marge, sportscaster Bill Stefl, his wife Ruth, and Judy and I made a trip to the Ely sled dog races. We were guests of Mayor Jack Grahek and his family, and we stayed at the Grahek's lake place, which was equipped with a sauna that had been fired up for our use.

Jack, Bill, and I were inside wearing our swimming suits, leaving the wives outside. All of a sudden we heard someone in the room that leads into the sauna, and it sounded like Judy. We could also tell that she was running water, and we figured that she was about to open the door and throw cold water on us. So, we got the bright idea to take off our suits and wait for the door to open. Sure enough, it was Judy. Just as she was about to toss a bucket of ice cold water in our direction, she realized we were naked. She got so startled, she slipped on the concrete floor, and the bucket of water landed on her. Screaming from the sudden and unexpected bath she got, and from the sight of us sitting naked as jaybirds on the bench, she ran outside and into the cold. Ah, poetic justice.

Chapter 4

GROWING UP

Dad came home with a surprise one day in 1951, a gift for mom that turned out to be a present for the whole family. It was a magnificent floor-model radio, a Philco brand that was and still is a fine piece of furniture. It stands about three feet tall and back then its wood cabinet emitted a rich mellow sound. The tubes are now long blown, but there will be a time when it plays again. It graces our home in Duluth alongside another cabinet radio that belonged to Grandma and Grandpa Lind. That radio is a Stromberg-Carlson and in beautiful shape, although also silent for now. I used to go to Grandma's house and lay on the floor with my head up against the speaker, letting *The Green Hornet* take me away.

Just a day or two after dad brought the radio home, Jim decided to get a little creative with a paint brush. The three-year-old artist got a bucket of white paint and proceeded to put a new finish on it. Luckily mom spotted Jim's talents almost immediately and with a rag, a little turpentine, and a lot of elbow grease she got the paint off. Jim never again attempted to play Rembrandt.

Without realizing it at the time, that radio may have helped me fall in love with broadcasting. You see, I spent hours lying on the floor with my chin cupped in my hands listening to my favorite shows in that pre-television era. Those of you who didn't live through those marvelous days of entertainment radio really missed something, and it's difficult now to understand the impact radio had on the world. FDR used radio for his "fireside chats," calming a frustrated nation unsure if its sons would return from the battlefield. It was a voice that brought the reality of world events into the home. But it was also the first kind of home entertainment that allowed its listeners to forget the cares of the day, at least for a little while. It created a stable of stars who helped us laugh when we were down.

The same was true for me. Radio was a wonderful escape, with shows like *The Lone Ranger, Stella Dallas, Gangbusters, Fibber Magee and Molly, Inner Sanctum, Big John and Sparky, The Jack Benny Show*, and Don McNeil's *The Breakfast Club*. And there were newscasters like Lowell Thomas, Edward R. Murrow, Eric Sevareid, Charles Collingwood, Winston Burdett, Howard K. Smith, Westbrook Van Voorhees (the voice of *The March of Time* on Mutual Radio), and Alex Dreier. Dreier anchored the 7:30 morning news, an NBC radio broadcast I rarely missed while dressing for school. It amazed me that he could hook up with reporters around the world and their voices would come into my home, in my room. Dreier had a long and distinguished career with both NBC and ABC radio before moving over to television in Chicago, then on to Los Angeles. He even played a newscaster in the movie *The Boston Strangler*. In some fashion, Dreier had a big influence on my becoming a newscaster. I can still hear the cadence of his baritone voice delivering those early-morning newscasts. He was eighty-three when he died in 2000.

And there was always a movie playing at one of the local theaters, the State, the Maco, and the Granada. Every Saturday was serial day at the State. Hundreds of kids would line up to have our summer passes punched by the ticket taker, then settle down to watch the serial. Each episode ended with a cliffhanger, and for the next seven days we'd wonder how the hero would rescue the lady in distress, guaranteeing we'd be back every single Saturday of the summer.

We watched films about Buck Rogers and Hopalong Cassidy and others starring Roy Rogers and Gene Autry. Horror films were great—

the scarier the better. The "Tarzan" movies were my Saturday morning favorites. When the movie ended we would rush home to play Tarzan, cowboys and Indians, or cops and robbers and mimic what we had just seen on the silver screen.

Parents too loved Saturday morning movies—they would drop us off and have the next three hours to themselves. In those days you not only got a feature movie but a couple of cartoons, a Laurel and Hardy or a Three Stooges, a travelogue, a one-reeler, and a newsreel.

I fell in love with movies, and today we have an honest-to-goodness theater in our basement. It's complete with front-screen projection, a seven-foot-wide screen, velvet theater curtains, surround sound, proper lighting, and comfortable theater seating. The room is enhanced by movie posters and a popcorn machine.

It's great not having to leave the house to see a movie. Take for example Mel Gibson's blockbuster film, *The Passion of the Christ.* I didn't see it in a regular theater, not wanting to have people stare at my reaction to the highly emotional film. Instead, it was shown in the Anderson Home Theater. No effect was lost.

If I could live my childhood again, I would. While not perfect, there aren't too many things that I'd change. The Iron Range was a fun place to grow up, with the 1940s and 1950s agreeable for kids. Without television we had to make our own fun, and it took many forms. We played games well after dark, games like kick the can, hide and seek, and capture the flag. And what boy didn't have a bag of marbles to play pot, hole, and circle, hoping never to lose his favorite cat's eye? An old chum by the name of Dennis Koski went down to the state marble tournaments more than once—he was that good.

∞

There were two spooky looking buildings in Virginia that I tried at all cost to avoid as a child. One was the old power plant near the west shore of Silver Lake. It was a big, foreboding brick building with a tall smokestack and broken windows. Along an outside wall stood a small silver-colored trailer home, maybe seven feet wide and eighteen feet long, with a tiny garden. I have no idea who lived there, or even why he was allowed to be there. Was he a caretaker of this abandoned spook house, or just a squatter who plopped down his belongings and nobody cared?

Pigeons by the hundreds had made their home inside the gutted out power plant, and a couple of times my buddies and I actually got brave enough to walk inside. We didn't stay long.

The other building that gave me the willies was the home of the old Virginia Brewing Company, later the headquarters for Drieman Van and Storage. This too was a big building, reaching more than eighty feet high and close to one-hundred feet at its base, with single- and double-story additions on two sides. It was built to look almost castle-like or gothic, with a chimney reaching into the sky. I feared walking along the sidewalk that fronted the place, and usually took another, less intimidating route. Much of that building is still used today, and it also stands near Silver Lake.

∞

There was also a storm that really scared me in the early 1950s. Dad and a couple of his friends had gone fishing on Lake Vermilion, leaving Mom and us kids at home. Dad's mother Caroline was also at the house and was thinking about walking home when she noticed how dark the skies were getting to the northwest. She decided to stay put until the storm passed.

And wouldn't you know, Virginia took a direct hit. The storm dropped hail so large, and with such horizontal force, it broke every window in the house with the exception of the three on the east side of the building. Each time a window smashed, Grandma Caroline cried, "Yoy, yoy, yoy." The roof took a beating too, and tree branches were everywhere.

Once the quick-moving storm slid past town, people came out of their homes to check for damage. Others, with their electricity cut off, scrambled to find flashlights and candles.

Mom's biggest concern was Dad's safety, fearing the storm had also hit Lake Vermilion. It had, but he and his fishing buddies were fine. They had taken refuge on an island where they pulled the boat ashore and turned it over for shelter. Smart guys.

∞

Dad's father John left home when Dad was twelve, and they would see each other just once more, a dozen years later. Dad and his brother Luther forever carried the disappointment that they, along with their sister Ruth and mother Caroline, were abandoned by the man. Sadly, I never got to know my grandpa John. Never even met him.

John Anderson was born in Dalsland, Sweden, a rural place called Makeberg, Or-Soken. I've been told the word Soken means county. Little is known of his childhood except that he was the fourth son to be called John; the other three all died young. Clearly my great grandparents were determined to have a John.

He came to the United States with his parents in 1904 or 1905, and, when old enough to work, he got a job building the Duluth, Winnipeg & Pacific Railway mainline at Kinmount, Minnesota. Later he worked for the Duluth, Missabe & Northern Railway as a car inspector.

Eventually John fell in love and married the lady who would become my grandma Caroline. My father was their first child, who came along in 1912. Grandpa John made trips back to Sweden, and on one occasion he helped his nephew Carl enter the United States illegally by getting Carl false entry papers. Carl had not yet served the mandatory three years with the Swedish Army. Grandpa John got Carl those bogus papers in Halifax, Nova Scotia, then they slipped into the United States. Carl was killed in 1931, when he was kicked by a horse.

Grandpa kept traveling back and forth to Europe, so Grandma moved my dad and his siblings to Cook, to live on Mathilda Westling's farm, where they helped with the chores. On his last trip overseas, Grandpa brought his mother Marie to this country, and she lived in Virginia until her death in the early 1920s.

Grandma Caroline used to say her husband John was a "good provider and a churchgoer," but then he got his first taste of moonshine and before long Grandpa was hooked. He was working as a janitor in the St. Louis County courthouse in Virginia, where he took to consuming a quantity of illegal brew that had been confiscated in police raids on local stills. That's right, Grandpa was drinking the evidence that was to be used at trial, refilling the bottles with colored water.

Apparently no one was any the wiser, for there is no record that John was ever caught guzzling the evidence. He took another job, this one working for the St. Louis County school system, during which time he had a few dalliances that were not tolerated by Grandma. So in July 1924, with only $15 in her pocket, Grandma Caroline and Grandpa John separated, leaving her with three children to raise; my dad, age twelve, Luther, nine, and seven-year-old Ruth.

After that, Grandpa John was seen just once more by his wife and children. That was in 1930, when he contacted grandma hoping to make a reconciliation Not on your life—she wanted no part of him. Then in the spring of 1934, under the effects of alcohol, he moved to Chisholm to supervise the construction of a work camp.

We do know that Grandpa John died in Duluth, and after searching funeral home records in the late 1990s, I discovered that he was buried in Park Hill Cemetery by the Crawford Funeral Home. To this day Grandpa lies in an unmarked grave which I have visited just twice. I even asked my dad a couple of times if we should put a gravestone over his father. "Naw, that's okay," he said.

∞

One of my best childhood friends was LeRoy Anderson—same last name but no relation. After all, this is Minnesota, where you can find an Anderson or two on every city block. Along with Anderson, my childhood neighborhood was filled with families with names such as Niemi, Dasseos, Washburn, Walters, Vassau, Vak, Souinen, Pelto, Stupca, Kletkutka, Manninen, Maki, Heglund, Gentilini, and the like—a good cross section of European ancestry. Not only is the Northland a beautiful place to live, work, and recreate, but its people have a history of holding tight to their ancestral roots. We call ourselves Swedes, Finns, Koreans, Norwegians, Italians, Czechs, Chinese, French, Irish, Japanese, Polish, and any number of other nationalities, but we are full-blooded Americans, most of us born and raised in this county.

LeRoy, whom we called "Puttsy," lived directly across the street, and we were inseparable. His dad dumped a load of sand in their backyard, making a giant sandbox that attracted a steady stream of neighborhood kids. One year Santa brought me a steel Tonka road grader which saw many hours in that sandbox, and it's now tucked away on a shelf in my basement.

I helped Puttsy and his brother Warren build a boat out of marine plywood and sailed it in Kendall Lake west of Eveleth, where we occasionally camped in two-man tents. We got the daylights scared out of us while rowing that boat early one evening. A swimmer with a scuba tank surfaced at our side and grabbed on.

I once scared Puttsy with a practical joke that isn't all that funny when I think about it now. A few of our older friends built a small log cabin in a wooded area on property owned by the Duluth, Winnipeg & Pacific Railway. It was necessary to walk a half-mile of train tracks to get there, plus hike a narrow trail through the woods. It was along that trail that I hung a dummy in a tree by its neck, to look like a suicide. Puttsy wasn't amused.

My great-uncle Gust Jackson was a locomotive fireman on the DWP, and several times a year he and the train's engineer would invite me to climb aboard and ride the rails for an hour or two. Gust worked on the switch engine, which stayed in the railyards putting trains together for their runs to Canada and Duluth.

Gust was married to my grandma Ida's sister, Lena. Grandma and Lena Aronsson emigrated here from Nafverstad, Sweden (in Bohus Province), in 1910, hoping to make a little money and return home five years later. They never made it back.

Puttsy and I spent many hours in the DWP roundhouse, where the locomotives were repaired. Those big steam engines were maneuvered inside by an old-fashioned turntable. Thinking about it now, sitting here at the keyboard, conjures up the sounds and smells inside that building. Never were we kids told to leave the roundhouse or any of the railroad property—try doing that today.

If Puttsy and I weren't stringing tin-can telephones between our houses, we were building go-carts and shacks. Iron Range kids were great shack builders; get us started and we wouldn't quit. These shacks were built for sleeping, with homemade beds that hinged up against the walls when not in use. Some of them were multiroomed and two stories tall. They were built from anything we could beg, borrow, or steal. We would walk the back alleys scavenging whatever we thought was needed, taking all the scrap lumber we could find, sometimes ripping nails out of somebody's garage walls or from wooden sidewalks, which were still common. We didn't know it, but we were recycling forty years before it became vogue.

Our neighborhood gang (not a gang in today's sense) included Puttsy, Bill "Butchy" Smith, Roger Niemi, Ralph Nelson (who was our best man when Judy and I married), Charlie Luzovich, David Lindberg, Roger Manninen, Herb Anderson (see, there's that Anderson name again), Chuck Stupca, and myself. Brother Jim tagged along on occasion, but mostly he had his own buddies.

While shack building was popular, it wasn't to be outdone by rubber guns. They were carved from wood in the shape of a handgun and designed to shoot stretched rubber bands cut from old inner tubes. Remember, these were the days before tubeless tires. Rubber guns worked on the same principal as stretching a rubber band from the tip of your index finger and letting go. Red rubber stretched better than black, and it was a bonus for anyone lucky enough to find a red inner tube.

We spent hours walking through alleys and searching the back of gas stations for tubes that had been tossed away. Puttsy's uncle Hank Jensen operated a Sinclair station, actually living in a small apartment in the same building. Hank knew what we wanted, and he would save rubber for us.

We had rubber gun fights chasing each other up and down streets, between buildings, and jumping from garage roofs to chicken coops. A good rubber gun could shoot twenty feet or more and a close-up shot would sting. I suspect many of you made rubber guns.

Then there were the Hammer boys, who lived in Hopper, a tiny neighborhood on the west side of Hoover Road in what was then referred to as West Virginia, now a part of Mt. Iron. We feared the Hammers because they were older, and we would taunt them into rubber gun fights, bicycle races, and duels with homemade swords. Sometimes we would toss a fresh-packed mud ball in their general direction. If all this sounds violent, we didn't look at it in those terms. It was kids having fun without all the political correctness of today. We played hard and, you know what, not a one of us turned into a killer, a bank robber, or a thief. I don't remember any parent knocking on another parent's door to scream at them for something their kid did.

But we had other things to do than spend every day as young gladiators. Range summers were made for swimming, and Virginia's now-closed Silver Lake beach was the gathering spot for hundreds of kids. The distance to Silver Lake was an easy bicycle ride, and once or twice a day we would jump on our bicycles for the short jaunt to the lake. One friend's dad had enough money to buy him a Schwinn, the Cadillac of bicycles in those days. It was red with polished chrome fenders, hand brakes, a three-speed shift, and a headlight and generator.

Over the years I had two bicycles, both J. C. Higgins models, with the second bought by Mom and Dad for my thirteenth birthday. This was the model they called the "English Racer," which sported hand brakes and a shift. It must have set my parents back a few bucks in 1957.

Silver Lake beach had a long row of changing rooms, long deprived of a coat of paint, and the building stood by habit alone on log pilings that had been driven into the ground. There were dozens and dozens of small cubicles, each with individual doors and a wooden bench. Lucky you, if you brought your own lock and key. Kids were notorious for stealing from one another or just hiding clothes from the kid in the next booth. More than one boy or girl walked home wearing nothing but a towel and a frown.

There was a boys' side and a girls' side to that old changing house. These roomettes, half the size of a tiny outhouse, offered some privacy but not much. The walls were punctuated with knot holes. Those knot holes had another name—spy holes. And every once in a while you would hear a hoot and a holler from the girls' side as a venturesome lad would throw open the door and catch a girl half dressed or not at all.

∞

By the time we got to high school we had other interests—besides girls. The new cars came out every fall, and my friends and I would pay a visit to each car dealer in town to check out the latest designs. We'd start at Reliance Chevrolet on Virginia's North Side then work our way south to the Ford garage, where the Coates Hotel swimming pool was eventually built. We'd make it over to the Studebaker dealer in Finntown before stopping at Action Pontiac on our walk home. This was a big deal, and a lot of teenagers filled the showrooms on the arrival date of each new car. Cruising the drag was the thing to do at night, especially on the weekends, so a set of wheels was what teens dreamed of—again, besides girls.

Hanging a set of giant fuzzy dice from the rear view mirror was like flipping your tassel to the other side of the mortar board at graduation — you had made it. We'd walk around the cars for thirty minutes examining every part, every feature, and even the design, giving our approval or disdain for what the automakers had come up with. We'd run our hands over the polished surfaces of the candy-apple reds, bright yellows, and turquoises of the day. Lots of chrome on those babies, and the bigger the tail fins the sharper the car. But I'm getting ahead of myself.

∞

And while it sounds like childhood on the Range was endless fun, there were always reminders of the hard life of the iron miners like my father. Every once in a while dad would take me to the paymaster's window to collect his check. Standing in that long line with a few hundred miners and their kids, I knew that iron mining would not be my lot in life. There was no way I wanted to dig iron ore for "John Oliver," the name company employees gave to the Oliver Iron Mining Company. I had other dreams. Dirty boots, ore-stained bib overalls, a lunch pail, and a brakeman's lantern were Dad's tools of the trade. They would not be mine.

Chapter 5

BREAKING STORIES

On November 10, 1975, during the broadcast of ABC's *Monday Night Football*, the phone rang in the WDIO newsroom. On the other end of the line was a Superior woman, who told me in an excited, high-pitched voice that a ship had gone down in Lake Superior. She had been listening to what she called a short-wave radio and overheard someone talking about the sinking of an ore boat. Moments later came a second phone call from a different woman, this one in Duluth. She reported the same thing.

That's when a routine Monday night of football turned into a scramble to get the story. I dialed up the Duluth Coast Guard station where a young man acknowledged that a ship had sunk, but he could give no additional information. He suggested I call the Coast Guard at Sault Ste. Marie, Michigan, and that's where I hit pay dirt. An officer on duty confirmed a probable sinking, giving enough information to go on the air with a news bulletin.

Minutes later I was in the station's audio booth to read a hastily written script. The microphone went on, the engineer pointed a cue, and over the next minute or so, I became the one who broke the news that the *Edmund Fitzgerald* had sunk in Whitefish Bay. A vicious November storm was pounding the big lake.

That first announcement of the tragedy was audio only, with a "news bulletin" slide seen on the screen. That's because in those days studio cameras had to be warmed up, and adjusted through the use of a test pattern, for many minutes before they were ready for broadcast. Today's sophisticated cameras become air-ready more quickly.

As you might imagine, the telephones in the newsroom lit up like Christmas trees, every line flashing. We got calls from family members and friends who had loved ones on the ship, and from others who simply wanted information. Throughout the rest of the evening I went on the air with live updates as more details became known. Extra staff was called in to help gather information, not only from the Coast Guard but from newsroom wire services which we had alerted as well as shipping agents, port officials, and anyone else who knew something about the *Fitzgerald*, its history, and where it was going.

It would be the next day before we knew the total loss of life, but we did learn that the "Fitz" had been seen one moment by the crew of the ore carrier *Arthur M. Anderson*, and the next moment the big boat was out of sight.

That night, WDIO became the pipeline for feeding information to the community. The sinking of the *Fitzgerald* resulted in many stories over a period of days, as people mourned the deaths and speculated as to what caused the 730-foot vessel to go down.

The "Fitz" had left Superior a day earlier, where it took on a cargo of Iron Range taconite pellets. Some people believe her cargo shifted in the storm's heavy wave action. Others are convinced the cargo hatches had not been closed properly. Still others think the boat hit a shoal and tore her hull. Whatever happened, the *Fitzgerald* was overpowered by the seas, and she sank fast. She now rests on the bottom of Lake Superior, upside down and broken.

In his play about the sinking, *Ten November*, Steven Dietz wrote, "We get cocky with nature.... Nature is both cause and effect. It is the force against which we play our lives." The twenty-nine men aboard the *Fitzgerald* on that storm-tossed lake fought that force and lost. We learned once again that the lake can be unforgiving. As of this writing, at least one body has been sighted by divers and left with the wreckage, which is considered by many to be a consecrated grave. The men of the *Fitzgerald* became the latest in a long list of those who have gone to the bottom of the sea—and the big lakes—in ships, where they rest for eternity. God be with them.

The legend of the *Edmund Fitzgerald* is kept alive by anniversary broadcasts of what happened on that cold, windswept night, and by the haunting ballad written and sung by Gordon Lightfoot. That day in history is part of my fabric, and I've been interviewed a number of times both in this area and by Twin Cities media over the small role I played in this legend of the lake.

You need to know that I struggled that night, as I have many times, about putting something on the air so quickly. Usually we like to have confirmation from at least two or three sources; in this case the Coast Guard itself was sufficient. The struggle comes when a broadcast journalist knows full well that he or she may be informing certain people that there has been a loss of life in their family. Still, this incident was of such magnitude that I believed then, as I do today, that it was the right decision to broadcast the story when we did.

∞

Incidentally, we took no criticism for that bulletin or further reports during our night of coverage. Newspaper journalists generally aren't the first to report breaking news, so it's broadcast reporters who are often on the fence. That doesn't mean we run slipshod, carelessly breaking into programming without discussion—sometimes even argument—as we weigh the pros and cons.

Hardly a day goes by that I don't hear someone blame the news media for something. To listen to them, we are responsible for war, we are responsible for presidential behavior, we are too liberal, we are unfair to unions, we don't like nursing homes, we are insensitive, we are to blame for the priest sex abuse scandal that rocked the Catholic church. We are blamed for everything from crime to snowfall.

Here's how I look at it. It is easier to blame that little box we call a television set than to look at the real issues and at ourselves. That way people don't have to take responsibility for their own lives.

Take, for example, the gang issue in the city of Superior. A twenty-three-year-old thug by the name of Alejandro Rivera was one of three young men arrested for the murder of Carl Peterson. One of those hauled off to jail was Peterson's own son Patrick; the last of the three was David Williams.

While awaiting trial, Rivera was interviewed on the telephone by WDIO's Julie Moravchik, one of the finest reporters I've had the pleasure to work alongside. In the interview from jail, Rivera disclosed that he was the leader of the Imperial Gangsters. (They were a small group of wannabe's who sold drugs and made money for those higher in their organization's pecking order.) He told Julie that it was his gang that had firebombed district attorney Dan Blank's house at 4:30 one morning. Blank, his wife, and their three-year-old daughter escaped physical harm, but the prosecutor and the community were clearly upset.

Rivera used the interview to threaten Blank again, telling Julie on audio tape that Blank was not safe, that eventually someone would get him. We put most of that interview on the air during the ten o'clock news, touching off a firestorm of anger against our news department.

Phone calls, e-mails, and letters came into the television station by the numbers. We had touched a raw nerve in the community and viewers were clamoring. The first call came from Superior Police Chief Mark Diamond, who read Julie the riot act over the phone. She didn't flinch, not one bit. Rivera's attorney Keith Peterson called to find out if it was true that his client had spilled the beans on the air. Numerous angry viewers believed we were giving Rivera a platform to spew his hatred. Wrong! It was an obligation on our part to warn the community what gang activity can become if police don't nip it in the bud—our kids and grandkids can easily get caught up in gang life, becoming ruthless, cunning killers.

A few days later we received support from an unlikely source, the *Duluth News-Tribune*. They published an editorial entitled "Stand up to gangs, thugs." They said, "WDIO-TV has been criticized for airing the interview (with Rivera), both by authorities and by members of the public. The criticism seems misplaced.... It is better to keep these things out in the open rather than have them circulating in the rumor mill. Rivera's statements, while likely overblown, give police agencies and citizens warning that gang activity may continue and they must be vigilant." The editorial concluded, "Citizens must be ready to stand up to intimidation."

A couple of days after the brouhaha over the Rivera interview died down, some two-hundred Superior residents held a walk for non-violence. Organizers said it was a symbolic move to take back their town. They were showing gang members and other criminals that they had had enough.

The Rivera interview helped pull the city of Superior together to support the Dan Blank family, and it opened a lot of eyes to the cruelty of local gang activity. I have no regrets for the decision news director Steve Goodspeed made to put that interview on the air.

Eventually, all three were convicted of murder and locked up, Rivera without the hope of parole. Up to that time, Rivera's sentence was the most severe ever handed down in Douglas County. Even after Rivera's conviction, Dan Blank went on our air saying he would be "looking over his shoulder for a long time."

Patrick Peterson, who was seventeen when he shot his father to death, has to serve twenty-seven years in prison before he's even considered for parole. David Williams is also behind bars.

Minutes after Patrick Peterson was sentenced for his part in his dad's murder, he returned to jail, and he too called Julie Moravchik. He told her that he didn't get a fair chance to say everything he wanted to in court, claiming he was "too shaken up." He said he was "scared for my life." He told Julie, "If I hadn't done what I did, I wouldn't be here either." Peterson claimed in that interview that he had no knowledge that his father, who was asleep on the couch when he was shot, was going to be killed. "Dave Williams," he claimed, "is the one who shot my dad in the head." District Attorney Dan Blank told us, "Peterson has changed his story so many times, his testimony could not be trusted and it was thrown out."

Many of our good citizens play the ostrich game, hiding their heads in the sand so they don't have to see or hear about the problems facing our communities. We had the actual gang leader explaining what gang activity was really like, and that interview sparked debate. That's our responsibility as a news outlet. My job isn't to make people happy or to make people like me or the media. My job is to inform. News must stir public comment and debate, or we are not doing our job. Julie did hers and did it well.

It's okay if you get upset with the media. But remember, we are only the messenger. Information should sometimes strike raw nerves. It's up to you to take the information we give and use it as you will. Some of you get angry, others take action, and many are indifferent. It's that indifference that bothers me the most. Julie Moravchik boldly told a story that needed telling, and Channel 10 was courageous enough to put it on the air. Perhaps those who criticized our coverage should thank us for opening their eyes.

∞

Every other Tuesday morning finds me visiting Aftenro Home, an assisted living center across from the UMD campus, where I conduct church services. On my drive home on June 30, 1992, KDAL-Radio announcers were talking about people in Superior being evacuated because of a dangerous cloud of benzene that leaked from an overturned train car just outside the city. So I called the newsroom to see how the story was being handled, and they suggested I get right in.

It became one of those marathon broadcasts dictated by the magnitude of the story, and in this case it was huge. We went on the air with a special report minutes after I got to the studios, and stayed on the air for the next several hours.

With me in the studio and several reporters out in the field coordinating with health officials and the public, we put on what became an award-winning news special that was recognized by our peers and, more importantly, connected with the public. Our news department proved to ourselves and our audience that we were capable of broadcasting for long periods, disseminating meaningful information.

Superior police were driving though residential areas warning folks over their squad cars' public address speakers to get out of town. Then word came that the benzene cloud was drifting over a portion of Duluth, and neighborhood after neighborhood was evacuated on this side of the harbor.

We set up reporters in three locations for live broadcasts, then got another crew in an airplane for what turned out to be excellent video of the toxic cloud wafting over Superior and Duluth.

Fourteen Burlington Northern railcars left the tracks, causing one to fall off the bridge that spans the Nemadji River, near Superior. The tanker car was filled with a mixture of chemicals including benzene. Its tank was pierced when it hit the rocks below, setting the benzene free—twenty-four-thousand gallons of it in the form of a dangerous cloud.

Residents who lived close to the spill complained of nausea, headaches, fatigue, and other health problems long after the incident. It was estimated that nearly twenty-five thousand people were evacuated from the Twin Ports that day, many of them driving up Highway 53 to the Range and Highway 2 toward Grand Rapids to escape the cloud. Folks in Superior found their way to Ashland.

The story was quickly caught by the national media, putting me in the position of not only anchoring our special hours-long broadcast, but also making live reports on television stations all over the country. We started in Florida, worked up the East Coast, over to the Midwest, then on to the West Coast, and finally to Hawaii. For the next several weeks cards and letters arrived on my desk from all over the United States, written by people who had a connection to the Northland, thanking me for the story.

In August of that summer, dozens of folks jammed a town hall meeting where they complained of health problems stemming from the incident. One person said their horse and a sheep had died, and other livestock got sick. In the end, twenty-three species of wild and domestic animals had died, but there were no human fatalities. Thankfully, more than a dozen years later, we have heard of no long-term health problems.

It turned out there were defects in the rail. Six of thirteen track segments that were tested by the National Transportation Safety Board had fatigue fractures which caused the train to leave its tracks, resulting in the benzene spill that will forever be known as "Toxic Tuesday."

The evacuation of the two cities was pulled off in orderly fashion and without panic. That was part of our role that day, urging folks to remain calm and to leave town as quickly as they could. Many who didn't leave gathered in schools where they felt safe.

Downtown Duluth resembled a ghost town. City buses evacuated people, restaurants donated food, hotels put people up in their lobbies, and area hospitals addressed immediate health concerns.

Twelve years after the spill, the state of Wisconsin reached a settlement with Burlington Northern. The railroad had to pay the state $330,000 in damages, costs, and penalties, which included $220,000 for environmental damages to fish and wildlife and $85,000 for spill response costs. The final $25,000 included civil forfeitures and penalties for violating Wisconsin's air and water pollution control laws. Governor Jim Doyle called it "a fair resolution to an unfortunate incident."

∞

A good reporter acts like a tenacious bulldog, refusing to let go of a tasty bone dangled in his face. Sometimes those bones are tips called in by anonymous sources. Like the phone call I got on the afternoon of November 23, 1993, telling me that Jeno Paulucci had died. The caller told me in no uncertain terms that he had heard Jeno died of a sudden heart attack that very morning.

Reporters generally take pride in bringing a story to fruition after sniffing out details like a deputy on the trail of an escaped convict. The first thing I did was alert the six o'clock news producer of my tip. The first thing the producer said to me was, "Who's Jeno?"

Obviously, my producer wasn't from Duluth. Jeno isn't your everyday normal citizen. He's got clout in this town, or at least enough dollars to wield some clout.

The second thing I did was to bark an order to "get me all the video tape of Jeno that you can find." I have several interviews with Mr. Paulucci stored away from previous stories, and we needed to lift a sound bite for his on-air obituary. This would be the lead story, and I needed as much tape as they could find.

One of the benefits of being a newscaster in one place for so long is the connection I can make with movers and shakers that a lesser-known reporter might find unavailable. So I called Jim Tills, Jeno's right-hand man. "Jim, this is Dennis Anderson calling. I heard that Jeno died this morning."

"What!" exclaimed Tills. "Jeno's not dead. He's sitting right here next to me, not two feet away."

"What do you mean he's not dead? He has to be dead. I've got my producer rummaging through tons of old video tape. You wouldn't lie to me now?"

"Denny," said Tills, "Jeno is not dead. He's *not* dead."

When Jim Tills speaks, he tells the truth. There went the lead story. Two minutes later my phone rang. "Denny, this is Jeno. Dammit, I'm not dead." Now I'm thinking, is this really Jeno, or does Tills do a great Paulucci imitation? It *was* Jeno.

The next day Jeno's messenger hand-delivered a letter to me. Up in the left-hand corner of the envelope was a picture of the Paulucci family mausoleum and under it the words, "Longevity is our motto."

There was matching stationary inside the envelope. At the top of the letter was an even larger picture of the Paulucci mausoleum with the subtitle, "Tales from the Crypt." Jeno had gone out and printed up special stationary. He wrote:

> Sorry Dennis to disappoint some of your audience, but the rumor of my death as they say, is grossly exaggerated. However, thanks for your concern as well as your "nose for news." As an old friend and supporter, I promise to let you know before I change residence. For now I have too much to do to take time to die. Kindest personal regards.

> [signed] Jeno

Being the first to report Jeno's death would have been a journalistic coup, but announcing that Duluth's most famous entrepreneur was dead when he was very much alive would have been an embarrassment and could have damaged both my reputation and that of the station. I'm glad I made that call. And it was fun to get a ribbing from the old man himself.

Chapter 6

Mom and Dad

Mom and Dad didn't make us kids eat everything, but we had to finish whatever we put on our plates. I didn't like bread crust, so I hid it under my plate so Dad wouldn't see it. Dad hated waste; no matter what he saw me wasting, he would say something like, "Dennis, you didn't live through the Depression." I had no idea what he was talking about. To a little boy, the Depression meant nothing, but to him and others who lived through it, it was rough and never forgotten.

∞

Mrs. Marconette, who lived next door, had a marvelous Victory Garden (the name given to gardens during World War II) to help make up for the loss of many products that weren't available during the war. She had a raspberry patch that must have been ten feet by thirty-five feet, with berries hanging over the fence into our yard. I was out there with my little bucket almost daily picking a pint of plump, juicy berries. Mrs. Marconette didn't mind as long as they were eaten. She would wear a big straw hat to ward off the sun, with her berry bucket tied to her waist, freeing both hands to milk the vines dry.

The Marconettes raised chickens, something that was permitted even in the city. Their chicken coop abutted our coal shed and I used to sit there and watch the birds peck around their wire confines clucking to their hearts' content. A well-worn tree stump sat in the middle of that fenced-off area, and once or twice a week Mr. Marconette would stretch a chicken's neck across it and butcher the bird, tossing the headless chicken into the air. Bleeding profusely, it would flap its wings and jump around until it finally succumbed. Hence the old saying, "He ran around like a chicken with its head cut off." They really do.

Mrs. Marconette called me a cry baby. If my wagon's wheels would go off the sidewalk, I would cry. When mom put on lipstick, I would cry, knowing that she would be gone for awhile. Mrs. Marconette would tell mom, "Let him cry, let him cry."

It's embarrassing to tell you, but I was plagued with nightmares, and walked and talked in my sleep. The doctor told Mom to keep me away from scary movies. They didn't succeed, but the bad dreams eventually passed. Even so, mom had to keep a light on in the adjoining bedroom to help me work through a fear of the dark. She tried to convince us kids that there was nothing in the room at night that wasn't there in the day. Mom's reassuring promise was little comfort with monsters hiding someplace in the room. A teddy bear and a stuffed monkey were constant companions under the covers to ward off evil. That teddy bear is still with me, tucked safely away in a storage cabinet. Its face still has the remains of red fingernail polish, a battle wound from an afternoon of pretending to be a doctor five decades ago.

∞

With dad working shifts in the mines, we kids had to be quiet around the house so he could sleep during the day. Anyone growing up in a family where mom or dad worked shifts knows what that's all about. It's almost impossible to be quiet anywhere when you're a kid, especially in the house. You don't know how many times mom told us, "Be quiet, you'll wake your father." It was usually too late, so we'd hear dad bellow from his upstairs bedroom, "Be quiet, I'm trying to sleep."

Dad's love of fishing was contagious. At least once a week he would pack up the car with food, bamboo fishing poles, minnows, worms, Mom, Jim, Donna, the dog, a couple of neighborhood kids and me, and head off to a nearby lake. There were several to chose from within thirty miles of our front door, including Lake Vermilion, Lake Fourteen, Lake Leander, Kendall Lake, Four Mile Lake, and Pfeiffer Lake.

Most of the time we ended up on the Cook end of Lake Vermilion to shore fish for walleye in Wake-um-up Bay. If we were real lucky, we'd camp out for a couple of nights, usually on some island reached in a rented boat. I was a junior in high school when dad bought his first and only fishing boat, a sixteen-foot Alumacraft. That old boat still gets plenty of use at our cabin more than forty years after he bought it.

When I was sixteen Dad and my sister's husband, Ben Nylund, bought a chunk of land near Polly's Resort on Lake Vermilion, just across a service road from the entrance to Ludlow's Island Resort. (Now there's a first-class place. As a teenager I was fascinated by an amphibious car the Ludlow's bought for promotion. Today, Mark and Sally Ludlow operate what their family began sixty years ago.)

Dad and Ben didn't buy lakeshore property, yet their land had easy water access. Nor did they build a cabin on that land. It became a favorite camping spot, however, and on one trip our dog Stinky got stinky. The poor girl tangled with a skunk during the middle of the night.

Dad also loved Sunday drives. Nearly every Sunday afternoon, following a hearty roast beef dinner—always roast beef after church, and I mean every Sunday, with rare exceptions—with spuds, gravy, and a vegetable, we would jump in the car and go someplace. Sometimes it was a drive to Cherry and over to Hibbing, taking Highway 37, which dad called the Hibbing cutoff. We'd return to Virginia through Chisholm, Buhl, and Mountain Iron, then stop at the Tastee Freeze for nickel ice cream.

Other Sundays saw trips to Ben's parent's farm just south of Cook, on Highway 53, where Ted and Eva Nylund raised their family and a few head of cows. Curtis, Beatrice, Gary, and Karen are Ben's brothers and sisters, all of whom helped their parents keep the farm going while Ted also worked in a mine and supplemented that income by operating a private sawmill on his land.

If it wasn't a drive to Cook, the car would almost automatically head for Tower, where old friends Lila and Albert Jonason had a small farm. Dad didn't alternate much between those three destinations, somewhat of a creature of habit. Maybe that's why my kids say to me, "Dad, you're so predictable." It's contagious.

∞

My father's sudden death by heart attack on March 26, 1991, hit me like a ton of bricks. He and Mom had spent much of his last day at Mitch and Ann Lomsak's home in Britt, then went out for supper. Once they got home Mom finished her ironing, then Dad volunteered to put the ironing board away in the porch. When he came back into the kitchen he sat down and said he was "feeling strange." He fell dead against my mother moments after she called for an ambulance. His quick and unexpected death ended their nearly fifty-two years of marriage. It was a blow to the entire family, and more than three-hundred people turned out for Dad's funeral at Gethsemane Lutheran Church. Weeks later a paramedic told me he thought they were going to have two victims at the house that night, my mother had been so distraught.

You would have loved my mother Florence. She was a gentle lady, filled with happiness and never short of a smile. Perhaps I got my signature television sign-off from Mom's example of kindness. She never said a bad word about anyone. Best of all, her love for others was unconditional.

Mom may have been a housewife, but she also found things to do to get out of the house. She frequently worked as an election judge at the nearby James Madison School. I wasn't sure what an election judge did at the time, but I knew she put in a full day where people voted. And she liked it, volunteering year after year.

She also joined a singing group in 1952, which lead to the scare of my young life. She and seventeen other young women became members of the James Madison School PTA Mothers' Chorus, and they ran into trouble on their very first out-of-town singing engagement. They had driven to Duluth on a rickety old bus to sing with all the other PTA Mothers' Choruses in the state. What happened that cold October night haunted me for years. I thought we had seen the last of Mom, not a good feeling for an eight-year-old.

The ladies didn't get very far after they boarded their bus for the return trip to Virginia. That old crate broke down just eleven miles north of Duluth, leaving them stranded for most of the night, and we had no idea what happened.

With the motor conked out, the only heat they could generate was by singing, and the colder it got the louder they sang. Their driver told a passing motorist to notify the bus company back in Virginia that they needed help and to send another bus. Remember, communications wasn't what it is today, and many folks simply didn't have telephone service.

An hour passed, then another. One song turned into a dozen, then two dozen. Before they were done, they had sung the night away and with no audience to appreciate their talent.

Eventually a trucker stopped and he actually pushed their bus all the way to a restaurant then known as the South Gateway, at the intersection of Highways 53 and 37. Traffic was light at that hour, with no thought of a four-lane expressway for another dozen years. Their good Samaritan refused a financial offer for his generosity, and as he swung his rig around to return to Duluth, they sent him off with a resounding rendition of "For He's a Jolly Good Fellow."

The Gateway's owners lived above the restaurant and opened the place for the stranded women, feeding them doughnuts and hot coffee until help finally arrived. But there was one more snafu in the tale they lived to tell about; it was a taxi that came to get them, not another bus. So the cab driver ended up pushing their bus the rest of the way into Virginia.

WHLB-Radio sportscaster Armundo DeYonnes also wrote a column for the *Mesabi Daily News* called "Range Roundup," and his story of the stranded women made them local celebrities.

The women were safe, Mom was back with us, Dad was relieved, we kids were spared, and their singing career took off like nobody's business. The *Mesabi Daily News* listed the women, including my mother: Mrs. Arthur (Florence) Anderson, Mrs. Walter (Frannie) Scott, Mrs. Matt (Clara) Niemi, Mrs. Paul Sersha, Mrs. Woodrow Carlson, Mrs. Elmer Haug, Mrs. Gust (Grace) Josephson, Mrs. Ben Majeski, Mrs. Oswald Salmi, Mrs. Anthony (Florence) Alimenti, Mrs. Mandrup Skorseth, Mrs. Roy Kirkman, Mrs. Eino Aristo, Mrs. Jack Luzovich, Mrs. J. O. West, Mrs. Curthiss Hammer, Mrs. Howard (Harriet) Lindberg, and Mrs. William Harrington. Many of them were close friends of my parents, and most are now deceased. I had my mom back, for another forty-six years.

Mother eventually died of heart failure on September 9, 1998, and my children still talk about their grandmother's gentleness and compassion. They were able to talk with her about anything, feeling that she never judged.

Four months before she passed she told me that it was time for her to go to a nursing home. She had been in failing health for about a year, and never regretted having heart surgery in 1996 to replace a leaky valve. Mom spent four months in a nursing home just a block from her house, which made her feel that she was still a part of the neighborhood. The first two months in the nursing home weren't bad, but her last sixty days of life were a struggle, as she fought to breathe and began experiencing dementia.

Three days a week, sometimes more often, I would drive to Virginia after the ten o'clock news, spend the night in Mom's house, then go to the nursing home first thing in the morning. I'd have lunch at her side in the dining room, then drive back to Duluth in time for the six o'clock news. On her better days, I would take Mom to one of her favorite restaurants for dinner, then we'd go back to her house on Tenth Street and sit for a couple of hours. How she loved going home again, even for short spurts. Who says you can't go home again?

Chapter 7

MINNESOTA SUMMERS

The lake at which we have our family cabin hosts a boat parade each Fourth of July, a flotilla of decorated pontoons that make the forty-five minute trip decked out in red, white, and blue. It's a labor of love for those who spend a couple of hours applying flags, bunting, and paper streamers to their boats, trying to get into the spirit of the nation's birthday.

In 1999, we pushed free of the dock under threatening skies, not knowing if we'd be able to actually get the parade underway at the appointed hour. By the time the boats got to the starting point, the clouds were rolling and turning green as the wind picked up. More ominous was the wall of rain heading our way, so rather than start the parade, we kicked our pontoons into high gear, making a bee line back to our docks, hoping to get there before the storm hit. We just made it.

The rain came down by the buckets seconds after getting the boat secured, and the wind blew through and over the trees as if a giant fan had suddenly been plugged in. From the safety of the cabin, it was nearly impossible to see the end of the dock, and we feared the boats would break loose of their moorings. There was no way to tell how extensive this storm was, or what it was doing in terms of damage. At this point we had no idea that the Boundary Waters was taking the brunt.

Other than a few tree branches on the ground and a power outage, our property was unscathed, but word began to trickle in that the BWCA was particularly hard hit, and by nightfall we knew a lot more. Experts told us that such a storm hits only once every five hundred years.

Video taken from a helicopter showed just how severe the storm had been, knocking an estimated one million trees absolutely flat over a span of many miles. The chopper video showed demolished campsites where fallen trees landed just inches from tents in which campers sought refuge. They were lucky—not one death, not even a serious injury.

Again the newsroom hit the pavement running, with reporters and photographers sent to Ely, hoping to get as close to the damage as possible. Over the next several days we broadcast live reports from Ely, talking with storm survivors, fire officials, and forestry personnel.

And now years later, the threat of forest fires remains in the area, which so far has avoided the flames.

∞

I was still working at KTHI in Fargo when one of the deadliest tornadoes in Minnesota history struck the Northland. It was August 1969 when a twister dropped on Outing, a small rural community one hundred miles west of Duluth, killing twelve people. That storm system spawned another tornado at Island Lake, twenty miles north of Duluth, where two others were killed.

The United Press news teletype machine in the KTHI newsroom had been providing information on a powerful storm system that was moving across north central Minnesota. The wire service indicated this was a dangerous storm with high winds, large hail, and a potential to spawn tornadoes. Keep in mind that the National Weather Service didn't have Doppler radar yet, so tornado predicting wasn't as accurate as it is today.

Eventually, a United Press weather bulletin crossed the wire alerting the media that Outing had been struck by a funnel and damage was severe. Later reports told of fatalities, but it would be late in the day before they had an accurate tally. UPI also reported that two people were killed in their summer cabin at Island Lake, which meant the storm had moved fast across the state.

One of the benefits of working at KTHI was our standing policy to use a leased airplane whenever it was needed. Fargo television stations cover a wide area geographically, which forced us to travel long distances to cover the news, and it was often more advantageous to fly.

That evening before the ten o'clock news, I alerted our flying service that we would need the aircraft first thing in the morning for a trip east. The day dawned sunny and extremely windy, so the plane made good time thanks to a strong tail wind. It was not unusual to travel as a "one-man band" in those days. In TV news parlance, that describes a journalist who is also his own photographer and sound man, which was the case that day. Our photo department had packed me a 16 mm Bolex silent film camera and a CineVoice sound camera with tripod, the latter being the workhorse camera of the 1960s. We had packed plenty of film, enough for several stories, each taking a different approach.

As luck would have it, several media organizations arrived at the Remer airport around the same time, and a small flatbed truck was provided by some kind soul who drove us to the tornado sight.

This was the first time I had seen such utter devastation. A once beautifully forested area was literally wiped away, with hundreds of trees thrown around like broken match sticks, and rubble from buildings scattered through the area. Clothing hung in downed branches. Two bodies were recovered while I was in Outing, and two others would still be missing when I left early that afternoon.

A nearby store, not far from a lake, had managed to survive the swirling wind, and that building became a gathering spot for reporters. How it survived is beyond me, given the fact that nearly every tree around it was either snapped or toppled at the roots.

Word got out that Governor Harold LeVander would be flying in to see the damage, so our newfound friend with the truck drove us back to the Remer airport to film the Governor's arrival.

He flew in aboard a National Guard plane known as a Beaver, a type of aircraft that is popular with seaplane pilots, especially flying services in Canada and Alaska. A Beaver is not fast, but it has power to spare, and it's capable of carrying considerable cargo, sort of a truck with wings.

When a Beaver is not on floats, it's a tail-dragger. For you non-flyers, that's a plane with a small wheel under the tail, as opposed to a plane with a nose wheel, which, for good reason, is called tricycle gear.

Tail-draggers are trickier to land, especially in crosswind conditions, which was the case on this particular day. Some tail-dragger flyers feel they are the "real" pilots, calling those who push tricycle planes through the air *drivers*. This guy showed us how skillful a flyer he was, but I wouldn't be surprised if that skill was accompanied by some nervous sweat.

He brought the Beaver to a point just a few feet off the runway in a crabbed position, its nose pointing into the wind. Then at the last moment he applied right rudder and dipped the plane's left wing to keep it from drifting off the runway at touchdown.

This wasn't a three-pointer. First the left wheel touched followed by a bounce, then a second bounce. The third time it hugged the ground and stayed, while the right wheel made contact. Still fighting the crosswind, the pilot pulled the stick back to his lap, the tail dropped, the left wheel rose a few inches again, then settled back down, uncertain if it would stay on the straight and narrow. We all thought the pilot was going to lose it with an old-fashioned ground loop. It wasn't pretty, but they were down. Pilots call that kind of landing "a confidence builder."

Governor LeVander got out of the plane with a broad smile on his face, no doubt a little shaken from the ride. As the old saying goes, "Any landing you walk away from is a good landing."

∞

In terms of severity, Minnesota's worst tornado month is May; 755 Minnesotans were injured by tornadoes in May between 1950 and 1995. In terms of numbers, most tornadoes come in June, which is the heart of the tornado season. The record year for tornadoes in Minnesota was 2001; seventy-two touched down that year, shattering the previous record of fifty-seven set just three years earlier in 1998.

People who live along Lake Superior have long believed that the lake keeps tornadoes away, which is not the case. Meteorologists in the Duluth weather bureau told reporter Julie Moravchik that the old myth "doesn't hold water."

One of them, Carol Christenson, said on television, "it just hasn't happened yet. We've come close, real close to having tornadoes in downtown Duluth. Take for instance Two Harbors. They had a tornado go right through downtown, right along the shores of Lake Superior."

I once stood at Eleventh Avenue West and Skyline Drive filming a funnel cloud that came out of Carlton County, traveled over Morgan Park, West Duluth, the West End, and eventually right over the Blatnik Bridge and into Northwest Wisconsin, where it eventually touched down. The funnel wasn't large, but it was enough to activate the city's warning system.

Some of our storms are much smaller and don't appear that they could pack a punch. In reality, all it takes is a single lightning bolt to do damage, as folks in Mt. Iron well know. On July 15, 1998, lightning struck the steeple of Messiah Lutheran Church in that town, setting a fire that destroyed the eighty-one-year-old building.

∞

In August of 1972, Duluth was hit by a series of three major storms and two back-to-back floods.

One came on August 16, when a powerful thunderstorm produced a funnel cloud in the Grand Lake area near Twig. It then moved to the Midway and Morris Thomas Roads, never touching the ground but accompanied by torrential rains which inundated Duluth. Basements all over town were flooded including ours, when we lived above Skyline Drive on Seventh Avenue East. Fast-moving water ripped apart several streets, but nothing like the flooding that would occur four days later in a second and more powerful storm.

This time an absolute cloudburst hit Duluth, which ripped up trees and flooded more basements as water rolled down steep city hills in such volume that streets were turned into canyons. Old-timers said it was the most severe rain in their memory, and there was plenty of damage to prove it, with millions of dollars in losses.

Cascade Park was nearly wiped out, an appropriate name for a place almost destroyed by cascading water. Our news department sent photo crews and reporters out to each section of the city that had been hit. Sixth Avenue East was particularly clobbered, as water poured down the main thoroughfare into downtown, ripping away the street and slicing a trench six feet deep or more extending for several blocks down the hill.

Homes and businesses along Sixth Avenue East were gouged off their foundations as the street turned into a raging river. A relentless torrent of water fell, with the town's antiquated storm sewers unable to handled the onslaught. One of the creeks that flows underground from the Miller Mall area to Lake Superior literally popped free of its culvert system, knocking down basement foundations and moving other homes several inches off center. A few Superior Street businesses had heavy losses in their basements, and mounds of debris, including earth and rock, piled up wherever the water ran.

Here again, the story of the storms and floods kept us busy for days on end, with another heavy thunderstorm a few days later, but, luckily, with less flooding.

∞

I have a passion for stories that have to do with boating on Lake Superior, from pleasure sailing and yachting to commercial shipping. The lake has its own life and personality, which draws people to its shores—especially in the summer. One look at that colossal pond has you hooked, never again to be a total land lubber.

One of my favorite vessels to ever ply its waters was the *Incan Superior*, which was the subject of numerous stories that I personally wrote and broadcast. This was a unique vessel, the most visible ship to ever call on the Twin Ports, and we may never see another like it here again—a ferry boat that hauled twenty-six train cars at a time filled with newsprint and wood pulp. The *Incan Superior* was launched in 1974, and for eighteen years it was the first ship into Duluth-Superior every spring, and the last out every winter. It sailed between the cities of Superior and Thunder Bay every forty hours.

Intense competition resulted in a decline of forest-product traffic, and in November 1992, the ship left town never to return. It sailed down through the Panama Canal and up to Vancouver, British Columbia, to begin a new life there.

Lake Superior used to draw a considerable amount of passenger ship traffic, something we now see only once in a blue moon. Since 1997, a German cruise ship, the *Columbus*, has been making occasional visits to the Twin Ports. It was the first international passenger vessel to call here in twenty-two years, and it's still coming. We can't lose putting great pictures of ship traffic in a newscast.

∞

The lake produces another weather phenomenon the city of Duluth experiences with some degree of regularity—fog. Our town has been fogged in tight for days on end, the result of a relentless cold wind off the lake meeting up with warmer air off the land. During the summer, the temperature at the Duluth airport can be twenty-five degrees warmer than it is lakeside.

Since Duluth is a port city, the Coast Guard has to maintain a fog horn to warn ships of low visibility. A diaphone fog horn blasted away for many years, sounding like a wounded moose in heat. We took for granted the deep "bee-oh" sound, and many folks didn't like it when the Coast Guard replaced the thing with what became known as the peanut whistle. It was a high-pitched tone, and some complained that it robbed Duluth of its seaport character.

One night on the news, I casually mentioned my disdain for the shrill-sounding whistle and you would have thought that I just insulted mom, apple pie, and America. It turned out that a lot more folks than I thought preferred the peanut whistle over the diaphone. Phone calls and letters came in telling me to mind my own business. So much for a casual ad lib.

The town became divided, making for many news reports on the foghorn issue and reflecting just how much rancor existed. In June 1995, after a twenty-seven-year absence, the old foghorn came back, once again treating Duluthians to the deep "bee-oh" sound that was long missed by some and detested by others. And with the return of the diaphone horn came a standing joke: "Which makes more noise, the foghorn or the people complaining about it?"

While some Duluthians were laughing, the city council took to a compromise. Even the mayor jumped into the fray. Gary Doty ordered the diaphone shut off at midnight. In the end, the Coast Guard reactivated its back-up horn. City folks are sleeping again, Mayor Doty is out of office, I haven't uttered additional feelings about the foghorn on television, and tourists are pouring into town. Ah, life is good.

Chapter 8

FLYING

For years I harbored dreams of becoming a pilot, not a commercial flyer but a guy with an airplane and the freedom to fly someplace to fish or hunt. That dream started at a young age while living in the flight path of the Virginia airport.

The land where Virginia's Thunderbird Mall now stands was once a general aviation airport with grass runways, a windsock, and three or four hangers located in the city's Ridgewood neighborhood. This was a place for small private airplanes, not airline service. The airport was built on a peat bog surrounded on the east and west by scrub brush, tall grass, and water-filled ditches. It was a great place to build shacks and campfires. Occasionally the peat would ignite and smolder for the next month or more, bringing a call for firefighters to dig out the burning earth.

Those of us who lived in the airport's flight path got a free air show each time a plane took off to the north or landed to the south, facing into the wind. We were just three blocks from the airfield, and those planes flew right over the house. I would sit for hours on a wooden box watching those planes and waving to the pilots, wondering where they were going and when they'd get back.

Grandfather Frank Lind got his only plane ride out of that field, costing him a penny a pound. Grandpa didn't weigh 145 pounds soaking wet, so that was a cheap trip in the skies over the Range.

A twin-engine World War II bomber landed there once—and got stuck in the mud. Plus, there was a crash or two that made newspaper headlines. One happened as I was washing my bicycle in the back yard. Dad and a neighbor were giving me tips on cleaning the bike when we heard a plane's engine quit as it was taking off. The four-seat Navion aircraft dropped into the Lavine home on Twelfth Street, tearing open a corner of the home's basement. There was no fire, but there was plenty of excitement. We, and most of the neighborhood, ran to the scene and waited for the ambulance and fire trucks. Even though the plane was heavily damaged, it stayed pretty much intact, and no one died.

Dad would take us kids to the airport to see the dead wolves and bobcats hanging from the hanger's eves. Many a pilot had flown north to hunt, with a shooter in the back seat firing from the plane as it flew just a few feet above frozen lakes and fields. Things were done a lot differently in those days, legally and otherwise.

∞

Regrettably, I never got a flight out of that airport. Instead, my first flight came after that place closed and the airport was moved south of Eveleth.

Dad's Massachusetts cousins Louise and Babe spent a week with us, and when the subject of flying came up, Babe suggested we go for a plane ride. You would have thought they gave me a million dollars.

Dad's brother Luther got in the car with us and off we sped. The memory of that day will never pass, not even the smells inside the small airport office or the black-and-white aerial photos on the walls. It was a lasting imprint for this twelve-year-old kid.

Babe and my father had flown before, so Luther got in the plane with my brother Jim and me, us kids in the back seat and Luther in the front with the pilot. The plane was a new Piper Tri-Pacer, its fabric-covered fuselage and wings painted tan with red-and-black trim.

Pilot Ray Glumack shouted, "Clear," part of the pilot's ritual to assure that everyone is clear of the propeller before it's cranked over. That first flight didn't last long, maybe twenty minutes. It looked like a miniature city sliding below us, and when Glumack put the plane into a steep left bank the view of an open pit mine was unforgettable.

This had to be the most exciting day of my life, and after we got home I took the time to put those memories in an essay titled, what else, "My First Plane Ride." Babe picked up the tab, $2.50 each. My second plane ride was just as exciting, and it was free after helping the pilot wash his yellow J3 Cub. I was hooked—and trouble wasn't far behind.

Several of us kids were making a tree fort in a wooded area a few blocks from home. Mom knew that I would be there most of the day, so she packed me a lunch and shouted for me to be careful as I rode off on my bike.

At some point during the day, tree fort building got boring, and a ride to the Eveleth airport seemed in order. That's a long bike ride for a kid, a good share of it uphill.

By now it was late in the afternoon. Mom and Dad hadn't seen me for hours, and had no idea where their son could have gone—they had no reason to think about the airport. Had I been kidnapped? Had I fallen and hurt myself? Parents think the worst and it was well-past supper time. Most twelve-year-old boys don't miss a meal, and my parents were worried sick.

The downhill ride home from Eveleth and the airport was much faster, allowing a tardy kid to peddle at a good clip. All of a sudden there was the sharp wail of a police siren, and a light brown Hudson Hornet police car pulled up alongside as I raced toward home. My first thought was, "Uh-oh, speeding."

One of the officers leaned out his window and asked if I was Dennis Anderson. How did he know that? Then he bellowed, "Pull over." There I was, stopped alongside the highway with two cops demanding to know where I'd been, and why my parents weren't informed. To make matters worse, one of the officers lived directly across the street from us. He was so intimidating that we never spoke again, in all the years he lived there. Was I going to jail? No, they took me home, but not without a good lecture. That brush with the law never shook my fascination of flying.

∞

Fast forward to 1973. I'm at the Duluth Air National Guard base doing a story with Colonel Wayne Gatlin about a pending open house. Wayne is a Duluth man, now a retired Major General, and a joy to know. He invited me for a ride in a fighter jet "someday," as he put it, so you can imagine the thrill when he called the very next day.

The local air guard was flying F-101 Voodoos at the time, a two-place jet with plenty of get-up-and-go, at least from this novice's perspective. They briefed me for about an hour before the flight, giving a quick lesson on the plane's oxygen and ejection systems, just in case we needed to bail out. They had me seated in a cockpit mockup on the floor of a hangar, nothing sophisticated but a good teaching tool.

Major Al Amatuzio of Amsoil fame was the officer chosen to fly me. He explained that the jet's canopy would be jettisoned if there was an emergency, and suggested I pull a certain lever to blast myself from the cockpit before he did the same. The good major said the F-101 had a gliding ability similar to a grand piano falling from the sky, so "don't delay any ejection."

The ride was beyond expectation and I still have the 16mm movie film from a news camera I brought along. Other cameras captured the takeoff from the ground, for use on television that night.

An hour into the flight, a full-burner climb pushed me back into the seat with such force that I got a case of tunnel vision for a few moments. Just when it seemed like the plane could go no faster, Amatuzio really kicked it in the pants; I let out a half-paralyzed scream before temporarily losing my ability to breathe. He later said we pulled five G's during that flight. At five G's, we were five times our actual body weight. My lips would have been pulled back over my nose and halfway back to my ears if I hadn't had an oxygen mask strapped on. The flight lasted about ninety minutes and included a practice strafing run on an eight-engine B-52 bomber lumbering through the sky between Duluth and Park Rapids at 37,000 feet.

The very next day I drove over to the less-congested Superior airport, plunked $800 on the counter, and asked the manager to teach me to fly. That was my introduction to Bill and Kathy Amorde, who have been managing the Bong Airport for four decades. Bill is a magnificent instructor, as thorough as he is friendly. He made learning to fly a joy and we became friends. Within six months a private pilot's license was in my wallet. Finally, I had become one of those pilots once watched with envy by a twelve-year-old boy in Virginia.

Cloquet airport manager Arne Odegaard, who has more than 32,000 hours flying airplanes, was my flight examiner. A candidate for a pilot's license must pass a lengthy written test, an oral exam, and a check ride with a federal examiner watching every move, similar to a driver's license examiner.

Even before my check ride, the Cloquet *Pine Knot* newspaper was at the airport to get a picture of Arne congratulating me on being licensed. Now the pressure was really on. Well, I passed, and the picture was published the following week. Since that day I have found that one of the joys of flying is taking others for their first trip aloft, hoping that they will get as big a kick out of it as I do—or as big a kick as I got from my first ride.

∞

One of my most memorable plane rides was a trip to Alaska with the North Dakota National Guard in 1969, a few years before I got my license. We flew aboard a restored C-54, the military version of the DC-4 civilian passenger plane. The Fargo unit was known as the Happy Hooligans, and the Alaska trip was part of their training.

North Dakota Governor Bill Guy, along with other politicians and members of the media (including myself), flew to Anchorage, where the Fargo unit was making maneuvers. It was a long ride in that four-engine propeller-driven plane—twelve hours, including a stop in Montana to take on more gas and oil.

Flying over the Yukon Territory and southern Alaska proved to be the most beautiful part of the trip, and for a couple of hours I got to ride in the right seat, the copilot's chair. Since the C-54 was not pressurized, we had to stay below twelve thousand feet, where we got quite a bit of ice buildup on the leading edges of the wings and engine nacelles. Air-inflated boots knocked the ice clear of the wings, so it didn't appear that we were in any danger.

That plane made another trip to Alaska, after getting us safely back to Fargo. But that trip didn't go well. The plane crashed on a mountain and burned, its wreckage not found for several years. No one survived, including the pilot who had flown us north just a few days earlier.

∞

Despite this near miss, I still believe flying is a safe way to travel and provides the freedom to go almost anywhere. We are safer flying than in the car on the way to the airport. Thrust and lift keep us in the sky for a view unlike that from any place on the ground. Eventually I convinced Judy that we needed an airplane. That wasn't easy to do. An old friend by the name of Art Edelstein was selling his 1968 Cessna 150 for $3,000. Its engine already had a top overhaul and I was familiar with the plane, having previously rented it several times. Plus, it was reasonably well-equipped with instrumentation and radios. An instrument panel packed with the latest hardware can cost nearly as much as the plane itself.

The plane's N number (the aircraft's call-sign when talking with air traffic controllers, displayed on the outside of the aircraft) was N50617. Its color wasn't ideal, a pea green with a greenish-yellow trim that Judy said looked like baby poop. She was more convinced about ownership after learning that I could make money on the plane with a lease-back arrangement with Bill Amorde. He would rent the plane to other pilots, then he took a portion of the rent and gave me the rest. It made the payments and paid for my gas, so it was a great way to own an airplane.

Cessna Aircraft had great success with the model 150 and, later, the upgraded 152, most of them purchased new by flight schools for use as trainers. The plane became known in flying circles as "The Little Wonder." Cessna's best years with the 150, in terms of numbers sold, were between 1965 and 1969. Mine was one of 2,007 Cessna 150s made by the company at its plant in Wichita, Kansas, in 1968. Its ten-thousandth plane came off the production line that year, a good indication of how popular a plane it's been. The 150's cabin is a little tight for a couple of big guys, but it burned no more than six gallons of fuel an hour, making it an affordable, fun machine. It wasn't speedy—about 110 miles per hour—and was a lot slower with a head wind.

N50617 served me well for the next few years, taking us on short jaunts around the Northland, nothing further than Fargo to the west, International Falls and Ely to the north, Eau Claire to the south, Houghton, Michigan, to the east, and a lot of places in between. Half the time there was no one in the plane but me, a chance to escape from the pressures of the news business.

There was a need for a larger airplane as our family grew. The Cessna 150 is a two-place side-by-side aircraft, and a bit cramped. It also had a child seat in the rear that could hold two small kids, if within weight and balance limitations.

With the plane now too small, I found myself renting the larger Cessna 172, a true four-place aircraft capable of carrying four adults, if you left some fuel at home. Pilots must keep an eye on what they put into an airplane, since its useful load with full fuel is limited.

Those of you who have spent time piloting your own plane know what a thrill ownership can be. It's the freedom to get away, even for an hour or two. "Isn't flying expensive?" you ask. "Expensive" is a relative term, depending how you want to spend your money. If you want a new car every two or three years, maybe you can't afford an airplane too. Paychecks only go so far. But if you're content keeping the old buggy rattling for awhile longer, if you stop smoking, make fewer trips to the restaurant, and quit the annual junket to Cancun, you may be able to afford an airplane. Most of us can't do it all. How I miss N50617. Whenever I bring up the subject of buying another plane, Judy says, "We don't need another airplane." Wanna bet?

Neither my mother nor my father were big on flying, but they did make a few trips in airliners. It took some convincing to get Dad to fly with me, something he did just once. I'd tell him, "But dad, I'm a good pilot." He'd answer, "Dennis, there are better pilots than you in the cemetery." Mom went up with me a couple of times, just to say she did it.

Chapter 9

CRIME STORIES

Debbie Race's body drifted ashore along Duluth's posh London Road on the morning of May 12, 1982, the day after she was reported missing. Debbie and her husband Larry had been to Lakeview Castle, just up Highway 61 from Duluth, the previous night to celebrate their fourteenth wedding anniversary. They would not celebrate another.

Larry Race isn't a man in the realm of celebrity or a player on the national stage, but he got plenty of ink and airtime in the news. Over twenty years later, people are still asking, "Did Race kill his wife, or didn't he?" The state of Minnesota says he did, while Larry says he didn't.

Whom do I believe? After all, I've written countless stories about Debbie's death and Larry's efforts to free himself from prison. Plus, we've corresponded by letter and by telephone, and I've been to Stillwater State Prison to interview him about his wife's death and his subsequent conviction for first-degree murder.

So, did he kill his wife by leaving her unprotected in the icy waters of Lake Superior? Or, was it as Larry claims, a terrible accident that took place out of his control when their pleasure boat took on water, making them believe the boat was sinking?

Sooner or later into every newsroom comes an assertion of innocence, and many a journalist has tried to prove that someone was wrongly convicted and sent to prison. We've all heard horror stories of the innocent going to jail, which does happen, and much too frequently. But as a prison chaplain once told me, "Everyone here claims he's innocent."

Sometimes overwhelming evidence, even an eyewitness account, puts the wrong people behind bars. Eyewitnesses are not always good witnesses, and honest investigative errors have resulted in convictions. Every time an innocent person is sent away, it was done by people who truly believed in the bottom of their hearts that the individual was guilty beyond a reasonable doubt. That includes police, judges, prosecutors, and juries.

Thanks to DNA testing, many who were wrongly imprisoned have been set free, while others were finally convicted and got their due. DNA is wonderful thing. But for Larry Race, this was not a case of mistaken identity where DNA would free the innocent or convict the guilty. This was a case in which the State said Race staged an accident, or took advantage of an incident, and murdered his wife.

I got to know Race a few years before Debbie died. He called me one day at the television station mentioning that he had 16mm film of underwater shipwrecks, and wanted to know if WDIO would be interested in using that film on the air. Larry had been scuba diving since 1976, and he took some great pictures from the bottom of the Lake Superior.

We arranged to meet a few days later to look at his films, which were unlike anything we'd broadcast before. He had enough to make several television documentaries, so we gave it a shot. I wrote and edited a thirty-minute story, which went on the air to good reviews and received several pieces of mail asking for more.

Early one evening, Larry and Debbie came to the television station to show me the twenty-two-foot boat they had bought and named the *Jenny Lee*—the vessel that would play a crucial role in Debbie's death. It was a homemade boat built in 1949, and Larry was as excited as a kid with a new toy. I don't remember Debbie's reaction, which incidentally was the only time we met.

After their anniversary dinner at the Lakeview Castle, Larry and Debbie took the *Jenny Lee* out for a ride. Larry contends the boat started taking on water through the engine, so, fearing the boat was sinking, he put on a diving suit and helped his wife into a life raft. The State of

Minnesota says Race then dove under the raft and cut it with a knife, leaving his wife to float away in a life jacket in water temperature that was just thirty-five to thirty-seven degrees. Pathologist Dr. Volker Goldschmidt testified at trial, stating that Debbie died of immersion hypothermia under stressful circumstances.

Race was found guilty of killing Debbie, and repeated efforts to secure a new trial failed. At least two new lawyers came to his aid, truly believing that Race got a bad call from the jury, but neither attorney was able to convince Judge Jack Litman or an appeals court that another trial should be granted. My stories rekindled interest in the case each time Race played another legal move, each within his rights.

His family never doubted Larry's story that Debbie died in a tragic accident and that his conviction was yet another tragedy. The prosecution, the jury, and investigators all believe that Race is guilty as charged.

So let's get back to the question I posed a few paragraphs ago: Do I believe that Larry Race killed his wife? To be honest, I'm not sure. And in the end, it really doesn't matter what I believe. But I will say that I have attended murder trials in which the accused were found innocent with even more solid evidence against them than was introduced in the Race case. And that's not a criticism of the jury or the courts, just an observation.

When push comes to shove it matters instead what Larry Race knows, what his children, his grandchildren, and his in-laws believe, and what the State thinks. Race contends he was found guilty for a murder he didn't commit because of his extra-marital affairs. I personally know one member of the trial jury that convicted him, and that gentleman is convinced well beyond any reasonable doubt that Race got what he deserved.

∞

I think too of the Katie Poirier family, who learned on the first day of July 2004 that Donald Blom had been denied a new trial by the Minnesota Supreme Court. Five years had passed since Blom kidnapped and killed Katie, a dastardly act that will continue to violate the young lady's family for the rest of their lives, even as they work to regain a sense of balance and peace.

Katie's abduction from a Moose Lake convenience store rattled the Northland, with the attitude that "if it can happen to her, it can happen to anyone." Her disappearance headlined every newscast for weeks, and it didn't take long to arrest Blom, a Twin Cities man who, with his family, had a mobile home on land in Carlton County. That's where they spent weekends to get away from the bustle of the metro area, and where he burned Katie's body in a fire pit, which gave up a few bone fragments. Blom confessed in a news interview from jail, but he later took back that confession, claiming it was made under pressure. He said his mind had been clouded by prescription drugs.

The stress of the case found Sixth Judicial District Judge Dale Wolf calling for the ouster of chief public defender Fred Friedman after earlier dismissing public defenders Joanne Piper-Maurer and Rodney Brodin. Judge Wolf's public assertion was that the public defender's office delayed entering a guilty plea while they awaited DNA results from a tooth and bone fragments. Before that squabble ended, it was Judge Wolf who was pulled from the case by the district's chief judge John Oswald. Blom's trial was moved to Judge Gary Pagliacetti's courtroom in Virginia, again attracting the attention of throngs of media, not just from Duluth and the Iron Range, but from Minneapolis-St. Paul. Our Dana Larson covered the case with surprising access to all sides. She brought prosecutors, defense attorneys, and Katie's family on the air in one of the state's highest-profile cases in recent memory. Lloyd Simich, Katie's grandfather, told Range reporter Colleen Mahoney, "It's hard to picture a nut like this. And he's got to be a nut. Why would you take something that precious and stamp it out, for no reason?" Blom will serve out his prison sentence with no chance for parole. His own lawyer called the State Supreme Court's July 2004 decision, "the end of the road for Donald Blom."

∞

Unlike Katie Poirier's parents, the parents of Jacob Wetterling never saw their child's abductor brought to justice. The first word of Jacob's disappearance crossed the Associated Press wire on the night of October 22, 1989. The story had not originally been included in the ten o'clock news lineup, but after studying the information, I finally told the producer that this could turn out to be something big, and it should be in the broadcast. It was inserted, and my hunch was right.

Jacob had been biking near his St. Joseph, Minnesota, home with his younger brother and a friend when a masked gunman took the eleven-year-old. Thousands of clues were eventually examined and leads followed, but the investigation went nowhere. The last word was a raid on the workplace of a Bloomington man where police found thousands of images of boys and girls in sex acts. Police allegedly found references to kidnappings during that raid, but, like so many other clues, this lead ran cold too.

Jacob's mother Patty Wetterling, has been at the Channel 10 studios on a couple of occasions for interviews. I believe from her off-air comments that she knows in her heart that Jacob is dead. Patty and Jacob's father, Jerry, helped form the Jacob Wetterling Foundation that focuses on safety education for children and families. They have tirelessly appeared on national television programs, including "America's Most Wanted," educating others about this menacing crime that has invaded so many families right here in the Northland.

∞

One of the earliest crime-victim families I met as a journalist was that of Mr. and Mrs. Fabian Paciotti, the parents of Barbara Paciotti of Hibbing. Twenty-year-old Barbara was last seen at a Hibbing pizza shop on the night of June 14, 1969.

Barbara was working in a stock broker's office in Minneapolis, and had returned home for Father's Day. She was a tiny young lady who stood just four feet eleven inches tall, weighed ninety-eight pounds, and had brown eyes and black hair. She left the pizza place with a young man and was never seen again. Her purse was found in his father's 1964 Oldsmobile.

Barbara became the subject of an intense search in an area south of Hibbing. Police suspected the young man all along, but with weak evidence, no confession, and no body, there has never been an arrest in Barbara's disappearance.

News departments don't normally get emotionally involved in crimes, but WDIO and the Hibbing Athletic Association played a benefit softball game to help raise money for a reward fund that had been started. The reward, which grew to about $2,700 in 1969 money (roughly $14,000 today), failed to shake loose any substantial leads.

Barbara's parents had their hopes raised each time skeletal remains would be found in the area. One of those skeletons was discovered near Central Lakes, south of Eveleth, along highway 53, a few years after Barbara went missing. The weather-bleached bones were just fifty feet from the south-bound lane of the busy highway, lying in a thicket of small Norway Pine, and had never been buried. It turned out not to be Barbara, but another woman who had gone missing. To this day, no remains of Barbara have been found, and her parents lived out their lives hoping that someday the case would break open. Her disappearance remains a cold case that has not shown a hint of heat for a long time.

∞

At 12:30 on the afternoon of August 29, 1996, a body was found in the trunk of a car which had been driven into a water-filled ditch on the Fond du Lac Reservation, west of Cloquet. A game warden first spotted the submerged car, still with its parking lights on. Carlton County Sheriff David Seboe confirmed the following day what everyone had suspected, that the body was that of Paul Martin Antonich. Paul was a Two Harbors boy who attended school in Duluth, where his parents were teachers. His abduction and murder shook the region to its core.

The longer a person is in the news business, the more he begins to think he has seen it all, that nothing more bizarre could top what he has already reported. Sadly, that's not the case. By the next day, more details of Paul's last hours of life were beginning to surface, and it was bothersome to say the least. His very last evening was at a church event in Hermantown.

Paul was a well-liked Duluth Central High School student, and the discovery of his body in the car trunk was the latest in a list of problems that we had been reporting on the reservation. Previously there were bomb threats, arson, and a drive-by shooting, and the media rightly wanted to know if there was a tie-in. The very next day, Sheriff Seboe said there was not.

What we learned next was enough to disgust even long-seasoned reporters like myself. Five men were in a car stopped at a red light at the intersection of Sixth Avenue East and Ninth Street in Duluth. Paul was on his way home from that church meeting when he accidentally bumped their car with his 1987 Toyota Tercel. It was a minor bump, but a fatal mistake.

Those men jumped from their car, and one of them beat on Paul through his open window. If that wasn't enough, another man jumped behind the steering wheel of Paul's car and drove him to a more secluded area on West Skyline Drive, where they pulled him out and beat him again. From there Paul was driven to the Ditch Bank Road nine miles west of Cloquet, where he was shot dead with a .22-caliber pistol, then put in the trunk of his car, which one of the killers drove into a ditch filled with four feet of water. The public was outraged, and the newsroom got calls and letters from viewers who told us they were sickened by what happened. That's the kind of reaction that flowed through the community for days, both in and out of the media.

Eventually, the five suspects were arrested after some good citizen got the license number of their car at the scene of the abduction. It took a seventeen-hour manhunt to bring one suspect into custody, twenty-four-year-old John Steven Martin. Fifty police officers, some with tracking dogs, searched a wooded area north of Duluth along Highway 61, where they made the arrest.

It was John Martin who shot Paul. The others arrested were twenty-six-year old Lester Dale Greenleaf, twenty-year-old Jamie Lee Aubid, thirty-four-year-old John Alexander "Mike" Martin, and twenty-one-year-old Andy Leo DeVerney. All five were from Duluth.

News of Paul's death numbed his friends and even those who had never heard of this young man. Flowers, teddy bears, letters, and other items began piling up on the sidewalk at Sixth Avenue East and Ninth Street, where it all began. For several nights, groups of teenagers gathered there to light candles, to pray, sing, and remember Paul. Others stood or sat in silence.

There was an outpouring of public sentiment and pain, the likes of which I haven't often seen in all my years as a reporter. By September 10, the community was like a pressure cooker. It needed someplace to gather collectively to express its hurt. That evening hundreds of folks met at First United Methodist Church, the "Coppertop," for a service of healing and to make a promise to work for peace.

In her story broadcast from the church that night, Dana Larson said, "Much of this service focused on anger. But not so much anger over recent violence, but anger from the Native American Community, over long-term injustices."

All five men arrested for Paul's killing were Native Americans. Toward the close of the service came a pledge for peace. Dana concluded, "People were vowing to bring peace into their families, their neighborhoods, and their community."

Eventually all five suspects were tried and convicted for killing Paul, but not before much legal wrangling. Three of the five had their cases considered by the Minnesota Supreme Court. Mr. Greenleaf's case went there simply because it's automatic that the high court consider the appeal of anyone convicted in Minnesota of first-degree murder.

The attorney for gunman John Steven Martin took the case to the high court, to appeal testimony that would be used against him at trial. He also appealed what defense he could use.

Before John Martin's trial began, Larry Antonich told Channel 10 reporter Sophia Vahamaki, "We think about Paul all the time and it gives us a greater degree of comfort to hear our son's name, to hear a story about what he and his friends did, and acknowledge that Paul was part of their life and is still part of ours, and always will be. I'm always gonna be Paul's dad."

The jury in Hastings, Minnesota, where the trial was moved in a change-of-venue, let the Antonich family know after Martin's guilty verdict, that, "we'll never forget your son."

Lester Greenleaf's attorney claimed his client's trial in Hastings wasn't fair, saying testimony wasn't truthful, and he (Lester) had improper jury selection. Prosecutors said that was nonsense, saying the jury's verdict was "not a rush to judgment, revenge, emotion, racial bias," or anything else.

The state supreme court was called up in Jamie Aubid's case to consider what evidence the prosecutor could use, specifically which of the other suspects' testimony could be used against him. As part of a plea agreement, Mike Martin had to testify against Aubid, but the other suspects refused.

Aubid was charged with aiding-and-abetting first-degree murder, which is a life sentence in this state. Plus, it was Aubid's .22 pistol that was used to shoot Paul.

Aubid was found guilty and sentenced to thirty years behind bars. He said at his sentencing, "I deeply and will continually regret the death of Paul Antonich." Paul's sister Karen sat in the courtroom wearing her brother's jacket. She tearfully told the judge how painful life is without Paul. "It's so wrong," she said, adding, "I don't know how this guy [Aubid] can even understand what remorse is, because of what he has done."

By the time the dust settled following one legal delay after another, all five convicted killers were sent to prison. The last defendant was John Alexander "Mike" Martin, who got the most lenient of the sentences, eighteen years. The media called it a reward for cooperating with prosecutors.

At his sentencing Martin told the court, "I wanted nothing to do with the beating, abduction, and murder of Paul." He went on to say, "I am deeply ashamed of myself for not having the courage to put a stop to what happened, and that is what I will forever regret." Paul's mother Mary spoke directly to Martin in the courtroom, telling him that he showed strength for standing up and cooperating with authorities. For his own safety, Martin is not in a Minnesota prison.

Paul's parents, Larry and Mary, and his sister, Karen, are slowly moving forward with their lives. Larry stopped to see me one day at my lake cabin, where we talked freely about Paul and the long road to healing.

For the first and only time in my professional career, I found myself stepping out of my role as journalist to connect with the Antonich family. I was so moved by the death of this young man that I wrote Paul's family a letter expressing my sympathy and telling of all the wonderful things I had heard about Paul. The letter was private, so I don't want to disclose the details of its contents, but I did write, "Even in death, Paul is touching lives."

I have reported on thousands of heinous crimes over the past forty-plus years, and none touched me like the death of Paul Antonich, a seventeen-year-old boy who looked to the future and dreamed. Sadly, Paul's dreams won't be realized. As Carlton County Sheriff Dave Seboe told me, "It's so senseless."

Chapter 10

FROM FUNERALS TO RADIO

If I had gotten the first job I applied for at the little A&W Root Beer stand on Hoover Road in Virginia, I might not have become a broadcast journalist, but an entrepreneur instead. Washing root beer mugs for fifty-five cents an hour sounded appealing at the time, but in the end the job went to someone else. It was my first and only taste of corporate rejection, and it hurt.

So much for the job market in 1958. Lady Luck wasn't with me that day, but she gave me a sweet kiss a few days later when I landed a part-time job helping my grandma Ida clean the old Rural Electrification Association building in Virginia. It was only a summer job, filling in for a woman who was my grandma's regular cleaning partner. The REA business was located in what is now the *Mesabi Daily News* building, so my first job was slopping floors in what eventually would be a newspaper office. The pay was $30 a month, enough to buy a typewriter before school started in the fall.

A year later I landed a real job in a funeral home cleaning the place and washing cars, forever washing cars. You have no idea how often those big black cars get washed. Funeral limos and hearses are kept sparkling clean, and I had the hands to show it.

I had walked over to the Tamte Funeral Home in Virginia, just a block from the high school, to get information for a term paper on funeral service. And wouldn't you know, I walked out of there an hour later with a job that paid a dollar an hour. Who needed sticky root beer mugs? This was nearly double the salary, and every once in a while I got to wear a suit to help out at funeral services. I actually learned how to tie a necktie by dressing the dead.

∞

You could call me a daydreamer. I used to sit in a seventh grade geography class bored to death staring out the window making plans for after school. Many teens have a bit of adventure in their system, and some even leave home early to pursue a dream. One of my boyhood pals actually left town with a circus the summer he turned eighteen. Poor John, he didn't last more than three months shoveling elephant dung and bathing horses. Whew, not my kind of work. By the time I was in the twelfth grade, it was a choice between a Lutheran minister, a funeral director, or a radio broadcaster.

As I mentioned, radio fascinated me. It got right to the heart. To this day it's impossible for me to understand how a speaker's voice can be thrown through the air and into a receiver many miles from the microphone. Our critics would say, "Now if they could only invent a device that could throw the speaker that far." If radio boggles the mind, imagine me trying to understand television. Grandpa Frank Lind used to say, "Someday there will be pictures on the radio." Little did he know.

As of this writing, radio as we know it today is eighty-four years old. KDKA-Radio in Pittsburgh is considered the nation's first radio station, and there probably isn't anyone around who remembers its maiden broadcast, the presidential election between Warren Harding and James Cox. The broadcast wasn't exactly nationwide; it was only heard in four states on a thousand radios, but a new industry was born—mine.

Mom would tell stories of how I, as a boy, would use a wooden stick as a microphone and pretend to be on the radio. It turned out to be preparation for what lay ahead.

Eventually, someone came to my assistance. Her name was Jean Healy, the speech and debate teacher at Virginia's Roosevelt High

School. While my friends were walking the halls with football, basket
ball, golf, and hockey insignias on their lettermen's jackets, I lettered in
speech. A pair of lips instead of a basketball. Well, not really a pair of lips,
but yes, I got my letter in speech and I'm proud of it.

Miss Healy insisted that my ducktail haircut had to go, but I was
equally insistent on keeping it as long as possible, since my hair was
already beginning to thin. God gave athletes good legs to run, big hands
to hold basketballs, strong arms to throw footballs, and what do I get?
Thin hair and good lips. Well, perhaps it's the voice. Have you noticed
how we hear ourselves differently from how others hear us? Remember
the first time you heard yourself on tape and you couldn't believe that's
what you sounded like? The same for me. To be truthful, I still don't like
the sound of my voice, and I've been listening to myself on tape for years.
I'm my best critic, and for me that's a healthy attitude. It's time to call it
quits when the hat can no longer fit on the head. I've often said, "I have
a face and a voice for radio, but decided to try television anyway."

Miss Healy gave me encouragement during my junior and senior
years. My senior year was a busy time. I "starred" in a production of *Stage
Door*, in which I had a lead role as David Kingsley. I was also an active
member of the Pep Club, the Ro-Hi Thespians, and the choir, singing
bass—to this day, I'm a johnny one-note, and that one is flat. (My grandchildren think their grandma married a geek, but one of my daughters
told them it's best to marry geeks, that they end up making more money
than high school sports stars.) But it was Miss Healy's speech class, one
of my favorites, that provided the chance to become a member of the
debate team and the high school radio club—and it was the radio club
that got me into broadcasting.

∽

WHLB had been on the air since 1936 (flagshipped in those early days
out of WEBC in Duluth as a member of the Arrowhead Radio
Network). When I was in school, WHLB provided fifteen minutes a

week to several Range schools to broadcast their school news, and I, along with our leader, Bunny Zulsdorf, and thirteen others comprised the radio club. David Twa, who years later became St. Louis County Administrator, came on board. So did Leslie Alar, Elaine Boitz, Georgene Koskela, Judy Harvey, Nancy Norri, Judy Merilla, Judy Hunsinger, Colin Kelley, Ann Crandall, Bruce Branigan, Jim Sersha, Lee Alto, and Gary Rankila. It was up to us to find whatever school news we could scrounge and put it on the air at 4:30 each Friday afternoon. Leslie Alar teamed up with me for our first broadcast in the fall of 1961, and it was the start of a career.

Talk about stage fright. This was my first time on the radio since appearing with the Sunshine Club to sing religious songs a dozen years earlier. Butterflies were working overtime that afternoon. The theme song opened the show, and for the first time ever I said hello to the Northland.

Conrad Gabrielson was the radio station's engineer on duty, operating the controls. Midway through the broadcast, Gabrielson held up a hastily scribbled note indicating that he wanted to see me when the show was done. The thought of committing some terrible wrong flashed through my mind, but that wasn't the case.

It turned out that WHLB's general manager, Jim Parise, was listening to the broadcast in his car. He phoned the station, telling Gabrielson to keep me there for a few minutes after the program because he wanted to talk to me. Parise was a good-looking curly-haired man who dressed sharply and had a professional demeanor, just what a boy of seventeen would expect to see in a business manager.

Jim got right to the point, saying he enjoyed my delivery on the broadcast and wanted to know if he could talk me into accepting a part-time job. What, me on the radio? He had to be kidding! Demanding that he repeat the offer, it came back the same way. It would be one night a week, Sundays from 2:30 in the afternoon until station sign-off at eleven o'clock. The job paid $1.15 an hour. Parise said, "Mr. Gabrielson will break you in."

Connie Gabrielson didn't remember it at the time, but we had actually met before, the day he tossed me out of the radio station a few years earlier. Connie was the host of the *Teen Time* show at night, and Iron Range teenagers tuned in by the thousands to hear their favorite rock-and-roll hits. Plus, the radio station took requests. I used to listen to Connie spin the records on a transistor radio hanging from my bicycle handlebars.

One evening while dancing to Sonny James' "Young Love" at a James Madison School dance, a friend told me that we could actually go into the radio station and watch the disc jockey work his show. So we hopped on our bikes and peddled the few blocks to WHLB.

Connie was working the control booth spinning records while sitting in front of a complicated-looking control board and a microphone. He was on the other side of a large window trying not to pay attention to these two young waifs who had invaded his territory. Conrad wasn't exactly thrilled to have a live audience, and he later told me that he wasn't all that excited about doing *Teen Time*. He was the station's chief engineer and did announcing begrudgingly.

No more than five minutes after parking ourselves in front of that radio booth window, Conrad lifted his big frame from the chair and walked out of the control room to where we were standing. He looked at us and barked about a half dozen words, "All right, you've been here long enough." The radio announcer gave us the boot. We turned on our heels, stormed out, and mumbled something about never listening to him again.

Now, a few years later, Connie was given the assignment to break me in as a radio man. We became great friends, and each year on the anniversary date of my being hired at WHLB, he would call to wish me well. Connie would laugh and laugh each time I told him the story of how he kicked me out of the place. Sadly, he is no longer with us. At his funeral, I shared the story of the beginning of my professional career and the role Conrad played.

∞

Working at a small town radio station gives a broadcaster a chance to pull many duties, ranging from news casting to spinning records. After being hired full-time, I worked the morning shift, from 6 A.M. sign-on until two in the afternoon, sometimes putting all eight hours on the air. Usually I was off by 9 A.M. to allow me to gather news, do commercial production, handle remote broadcasts that were sponsored, and host a daily show called "Tourist Time," interviewing visitors to the area. I also hosted a program that I started on WHLB, called "Open Mike," an early radio talk show, a forerunner to talk radio. I've always said, "Radio was fun, television is work." In his book *Gracie, A Love Story*, George Burns said, "We never knew when the radio fad was going to end." It ended too soon.

I was gifted with a strong voice and had a working knowledge of the region and a pretty good handle on the local sports scene. So when chief announcer and sportscaster Ken Mertes left WHLB, management suggested I give it a try, and wouldn't you know, it worked. That took care of my Friday and Saturday nights, calling play-by-play for high school and college basketball, hockey, and football. There was lots to do, but I was young and ambitious.

Much of my play-by-play was patterned after WHLB sportscaster Mundo DeYonnes, whose incredible voice had quite the following. The station had another talented sports announcer in the form of city treasurer Hank Tillman, who spent most of his life in a wheel chair after an attack of polio. Hank became a friend after first meeting him as a Sunday school teacher at First Lutheran Church. He could call a game with the best of them.

The 1951 Region 7 semi-finals pitted Gilbert against defending state champion Duluth Central, a series that became legendary basketball on the Range. My childhood neighbors Katheryn Dasseos and her husband, Steve, owned and operated a popular little hamburger stand in Virginia, simply called "Steve's." Kathcryn's younger brother was Big Bill "Boots" Simanovich, a six foot nine senior standout on the Gilbert team along with junior guard Andy Snyder. Snyder was an artist with a basketball.

The game was tied at forty-two all, with just two seconds left. The crowd was insane with excitement and Mundo DeYonnes was almost swallowing the microphone while the engineer back at the radio station kept his hands on the dials trying to keep the transmitter's tubes from popping.

Snyder was at the free throw line with the game depending on his next toss. Andy, who was the only junior in the starting lineup, took aim and swish, the ball went in. The crowd went nuts and DeYonnes railed into his microphone.

WHLB used to have a recorded transcription of the last quarter of that ballgame which I listened to many times while working there. It was in the form of an oversized record that could be played only on the station's extra large turntables and was played from the inside out. That means the needle arm was placed in the middle of the record near the label, and as the record spun the needle eventually ended at the record's lip—the exact opposite of a traditional LP. Many radio commercials and programs were cut on records in that format before the advent of audiotape.

The Gilbert Buccaneers went on to win the state tournament that year, thanks again in large part to Snyder. He tossed the ball an incredible sixty-four feet at the buzzer to end the third quarter in the championship game, the longest shot ever made in Minnesota high school basketball.

That was radio sports in the 1950s, and in the next decade it was my turn to bring that kind of excitement to our audience. And we did—with me at play-by-play, Bill Wade on the color commentary microphone, and Gordy Dahl handling the field engineering.

Calling the action came relatively easy because I knew the games and the terminology inside out. And I tried to develop a style from listening to the old DeYonnes-Tillman team. The faster the game, the easier it was to call. Hockey and basketball were my favorites, with football third.

We traveled all over the Northland broadcasting sports, and in seven years we missed only one game because of bad weather. A blizzard was howling by the time we got to Duluth for a game at UMD, and we got into a fender bender, never making the broadcast.

And who could forget the coaches of that era—Tom Reagan of Aurora, Guvy Olson of Cook, his brother Richie Olson of Virginia, Bill King of Orr, Virginia's John Beste, and Bob McDonald of Chisholm with his seven-hundred-plus wins.

WHLB radio had just a thousand watts of power—it reached barely sixty miles on a good day—but I didn't care. My seven years at WHLB radio were some of the finest in my long career. Sadly, it no longer exists. Someone bought it in the late 1990s, changed its call letters, and turned the place into a religious station. It folded, and now years later it's still off the air. What a shame. The city of Virginia once had a voice called radio.

∞

The loss of WHLB means even more to me than a nostalgic symbol of my early days in broadcasting, for the radio station changed my life in more ways than the start of a career. You see, WHLB put Judy and me together.

One night while listening to me on the radio, she called for a request, asking to hear Bobby Helm's hit record, "My Special Angel." She was at a pajama party where a few of her girlfriends were dancing to the music of my radio show. She called again the next night and the next, and before long we learned that her neighbor was dating one of my good friends.

And so we met, but it wasn't love at first sight. She thought I was arrogant. I thought she was pretty. She thought I was too old. I didn't care.

Over time, I became something of a big brother to Judy, after all she's four years younger, and that can be a lot during those trying teen years. She started bringing her boyfriend troubles to my shoulders, which meant we began seeing each other a little more often. I came to her house on the night of her junior prom and shot movies of the happy couple. She was a knockout, dressed in a blue-and-white knee-length formal with spaghetti straps. My jealousy doesn't show on the film.

Judy eventually had another boyfriend who neither her mom nor dad appreciated, so the first time I called to ask her for a date, Judy's mom said if she didn't go out with me, she couldn't go out, period. Guess who had a date that night.

Eventually, her parents, Warren and Gloria Huot, gave us a beautiful wedding reception after our marriage on January 15, 1966. They are two fabulous in-laws, who still live in Virginia and are in relatively good health. I had an opportunity to return the wedding favor by conducting a ceremony when they renewed their vows on their fiftieth wedding anniversary. It's still hard to believe that beautiful Judy became my bride.

Without much money, our honeymoon was a simple affair, a one-night stay in room six of the Star Motel in Hibbing, an $18 deal which included a bucket of Henny Penny Chicken. A towing company's $5 charge to get our car started the next day was extra. Temperatures were deep below zero, and our 1959 Chevy didn't have much oomph.

I was only making $5,100 a year, so we used to buy a lot of fish, which was relatively inexpensive in those days. Judy made salmon three times a week. Let's see now, there was salmon salad, salmon croquettes, salmon steak, poached salmon, grilled salmon, salmon bits, and stuffed salmon. When spring came, I had to resist the urge to go north and spawn.

After another honeymoon trip to the Twin Cities, we came back with twins. A later trip took us to Three Rivers, Ontario, and, wouldn't you know, we came back with triplets. Now she's afraid to go with me to the Thousand Islands. After raising teenagers, I think we should have gone to the Virgin Islands. That's a joke folks—it's been one of my main-stays in speeches, and it brings down the house every time. In reality, we have four children—three daughters and a son—and thirteen terrific grandchildren.

Chapter 11

COVERING PRESIDENTS

While driving back to the radio station one morning after a live report from a house fire, I turned on the car radio to learn that Marilyn Monroe had died. That was 1962, and the news of her death dominated radio and television for the next several days. I loved the immediacy of radio news, of being a part of the machine that reported stories to a waiting audience. It's an appetite that has never been satisfied, with the zeal to tell a story as strong today as it was in those early years.

Chances to do significant reporting were not as available at WHLB as they were later in television because of my multiple duties at the radio station. I was its news director, newscaster, morning announcer, sportscaster, public affairs director, and program director. That didn't keep me from ignoring my nose for news, however. We were quick on the air with breaking news stories, and there were plenty of them.

I was sitting at the control board of WHLB when I answered a phone call from a woman who asked if we knew anything about the president being shot. "What president?" I asked, not knowing if she was referring to the president of the local college, the community club, chamber of commerce, or *the* president. After getting that straightened out, I walked over to a small closet off the radio station lobby where we kept our United Press teletype machine, which clacked out stories twenty-four hours a day. I no sooner opened the door than the machine's alarm bells sounded, alerting subscribers that a bulletin was coming in. Then those first words of the national nightmare came rolling off the UPI machine.

BULLETIN:

(DALLAS)——President Kennedy and Governor John Connally of Texas have been cut down by assassins' bullets in downtown Dallas. They were riding in an open automobile when the shots were fired. The President, his limp body cradled in the arms of his wife, Jacqueline, has been rushed to Parkland Hospital.

"My God, this can't be," I thought, with nothing more than a blank stare at the words coming across the teletype. For a few moments it wouldn't register. President Kennedy had been in Duluth for an overnight stay just two months earlier. This was like hearing of a death in the family—a numbing sensation, the kind of emotions you never want to experience.

After a few seconds of trying to absorb the insanity of it all, I made a mad dash to the microphone and, using the most somber voice a nineteen-year-old man can muster, told my listeners that President Kennedy had been shot. Minutes later he was dead.

FLASH:

(DALLAS)—Kennedy dead.

BULLETIN:

(DALLAS)—President Kennedy is dead. He was killed by an assassin in Dallas. John Fitzgerald Kennedy was 45 years old...in his first term of office. He was shot as he rode in a motorcade through downtown Dallas.

At this point, and with the permission of KDAL radio, we plugged into their broadcast to carry CBS news. We stayed with them for the next three days, interrupting only for legally required station breaks on the half hour. All commercials were pulled from the air, something that wouldn't happen again until the terrorist attacks of September 11, 2001.

This was history in the making and we were living it. I saved all the news bulletins and stories that crossed the United Press wire service from November 22, 1963, plus the stories of Lee Harvey Oswald's killing a couple days later. I've seen similar collections sell for $5,000 in auction catalogs, but mine is safely tucked away to become the possession of my grandchildren. I also had the presence of mind to save a couple of newspapers from that day.

Kennedy's death was the beginning of an unforgettable decade in American history, a time wracked with assassinations, war, civil disobedience, race riots, free love, and mass murders. I had a front-row seat sitting behind the microphone.

∞

While Kennedy was the first president I covered as a journalist, he wasn't the first president I saw. That was Harry Truman, who made an appearance in Hibbing during his famous Whistle Stop Campaign of 1948, the one the media said he could never win. Well, "Give 'em Hell Harry" came through with flying colors, winning the White House in his own right. There is little memory of that day for me, but it must have been a thrill for the thousands who flocked to Hibbing to see him. I was just four years old.

Not knowing where my career would take me at the time, I rarely took a still camera on interviews and saved just one radio interview on tape, that with Vice President Hubert Humphrey in Eveleth during Lyndon Johnson's Administration. I also interviewed Richard Nixon after he served as Dwight Eisenhower's vice president but before he became president. I believe the interview took place either at Denfeld High School or at the airport. I remember thinking how boyish-looking Nixon appeared, but then this was long before Watergate aged him into an old man, defeated by his own power.

Gerald Ford, the man who replaced Nixon after his resignation, was the most unpresidential former president I've met. His presidency lasted just three years, and two or three years after he left the White House in 1977, he made a visit to the Twin Cities. The "accidental president" had published his memoirs, calling the book *A Time to Heal*, a reference to his attempt at restoring confidence in government after the resignation of Richard Nixon. It wasn't a one-on-one interview, but Ford told the gathered media that his pardon of Nixon is what cost him the Oval Office. Even so, he felt it was the right thing to do. It was obvious he didn't expect the outrage that echoed from across the country, with his approval rating dropping overnight from a high of seventy-one percent to fifty percent. Mr. Ford was taller than I expected and exceedingly friendly. His pipe-tobacco-stained teeth and broad grin made me feel that I was in the presence of a regular guy.

I was introduced to former-Vice President Walter Mondale through his friend and WDIO's founding father, Frank Befera, and over the years I have gotten to know Mondale on a little more personal level. Frank and Fritz, as Mondale is called by his friends, had been fishing buddies dating back to Walter's days as Minnesota's attorney general. The former vice president and I both served as pallbearers at Frank's funeral in November of 2004. I have a particularly nice picture of Mondale in my home library, signed, "To Dennis, Fritz."

Vice President Mondale would make occasional appearances in Duluth, and whenever he was in town he would stop by the Channel 10 studios to see Frank. Secret Service officers would canvass the place hours earlier, and the fact that Mondale's chief of staff was a Duluth native helped tie the country's number-two man to the Twin Ports. Mondale used the Channel 10 building as a place to relax, and it usually gave me a chance to talk with him at some length before another interview.

Weeks after his defeat to Ronald Reagan, Mondale was back at the TV station, this time by himself. Former vice presidents don't get lifelong Secret Service protection or any of the other perks afforded former presidents, such as a secretary and office space. Smoking a delicious-smelling cigar, Mondale told me how embarrassing the defeat had been, talking openly about the shellacking he got from Reagan.

It was Mondale who twice got me into day-long briefings at Jimmy Carter's White House and got me a third Washington briefing at the

State Department. Mondale had two offices, one in the West Wing just down the hall from the Oval Office and another next door in the Old Executive Office Building. I've been in both, but clearly the site adjacent to the White House was the more relaxing and less formal of the two. I, along with a few other Minnesota journalists, had breakfast there with the vice president. Next, after a Cabinet Room meeting with President Carter, we (including Judy) gathered at the Admiral's House, the vice president's official residence, for a reception. One of my favorite pictures of Judy is of her standing in front of the fireplace in the vice president's dining room.

My first trip to the White House was made possible only through the generosity of my wife. You see, Judy and her doctor agreed to have our son Chris induced two days earlier than her due date, to allow me to fly to Washington. That's right, Chris was born on October 12, 1977, because I had an appointment to meet President Carter on the fourteenth. And twenty-seven years later she still reminds me, "That was selfish!"

The obligatory pictures presidents take inside the White House with visiting guests are fun, if not for the presidents, at least for us. I have a small collection taken during the Carter years, snapped by White House photographers in the Cabinet Room next to the Oval Office. Carter made a visitor feel comfortable in a place that leaves most visitors in awe. He was cordial and fielded questions with ease.

The first time I met President Carter was also my first time in the Executive Mansion, and where media types got more than the normal guided tour. We were walked in through a front door of the West Wing, and right into the Roosevelt Room named for President Theodore Roosevelt, and just across the hall from the Cabinet Room. His cousin, President Franklin Roosevelt called it the Fish Room, since this is where he kept his fishing trophies. It was quite a thrill for a boy from the Iron Range to see the seat of power from the inside.

On a second trip to the White House, I found Mr. Carter more pre-occupied. Steelworkers had been on a long strike and the president refused to intervene. Gasoline was in short supply, creating long lines at the gas pumps. In fact, more of the economy was in the tank than gasoline. Interest rates had topped twenty percent and the Iran hostage crisis kept the president a hostage in his own White House for 444 days. Carter had a sign on his Oval Office desk: "The Buck Stops Here." He had experienced the sign's true meaning.

In one conversation around the big Cabinet Room table, I asked Mr. Carter if he would intervene in the steelworker's strike, to which he replied, "no." He thought it best that they work out their differences without intervention, which the two sides eventually did. Looking back, I asked him what now sounds like a trite question, "How do you like being president?" He had been in office just nine months and—I'm paraphrasing here—he said he was enjoying himself, that he found a lot of challenges and that he was looking forward to serving the American people. Carter also told us that he was concentrating on the chance voters gave him to help his fellow man. Unfortunately, he didn't live up to their expectations, and they voted him out four years later after Ronald Reagan asked, "Are you better off now than you were four years ago?"

I would see President Carter one more time when he and Vice President Mondale campaigned together in Duluth. The TV station had me cover their arrivals live from the airport, first Mondale, followed a couple hours later by Carter.

Working out the logistics to cover this event was interesting in its own right. In those days, local television stations didn't have the sophisticated equipment we use today, so channels 10 and 6 decided to pool some of our coverage. WDIO provided the live video from the airport and KBJR provided the live pictures from the arena auditorium where Carter and Mondale would hold their campaign rally. I narrated the events for us, while a Channel 6 anchor narrated for their audience. This shared video project worked well, but by the time the next president came to town both stations had enough equipment to handle their own broadcasts without pooling resources.

There is one thing I could never understand, and that's why members of the media need Secret Service clearance to cover a president or vice president when they come to town. You see, we are kept several feet back from the president's podium, while the public stands between us and him, pressed up against the presidential stage. The public is just a few feet away from the nation's highest officer holder, and none of them have credentials.

A sitting president has come to Duluth four times in my career—Kennedy, Carter, Clinton, and, most recently, George W. Bush running for re-election in the summer of 2004. (Dubya's father was here before becoming president, and John F. Kennedy visited at least once as a senator.) Presidential visits are always an interesting affair, and each is attended by many who have never seen a president. Some folks are brought to tears when a president walks into a room greeted by a thunderous roar of approval. It's a moving experience, not unlike a performance by a famous rock star, and usually just as well choreographed.

President Bill Clinton's 1994 visit to Duluth was a moving experience for those who flocked to UMD to see and hear him. Yet this rousing event failed to ignite the electorate during the midterm elections. Clinton was in Duluth to stump for senate candidate Ann Wynia, who lost easily, and today she's a footnote in Minnesota political history.

Mr. Clinton arrived in Duluth the day before his UMD appearance, staying at the downtown Holiday Inn. The next morning he went jogging with Mayor Doty and a few other invited locals, along with his ever-present Secret Service body guards. As he jogged along scenic Skyline Drive, no doubt getting a guided tour as he ran, our cameras caught up with him at Eleventh Avenue West. Several neighbors were allowed to talk with him, but we reporters were kept at bay.

The six thousand or so who filled the DECC for George W. Bush's 2004 campaign appearance couldn't have been more enthusiastic. Who says you can't find Republicans living in Northern Minnesota? They are here by the thousands, and they were a raucous group that day. President Bush's Duluth appearance came eleven days after John Kerry drew a sizeable crowd of Democrats to Cloquet, but, let's face it, a sitting president gets more press attention.

Tucked safely inside the DECC, the president was kept a distance from protestors, whom he never saw—or if he did, he more than likely ignored. Protesting a president is nothing new. The most serious form of protest comes from those who have either tried or succeeded in assassinating a chief executive. And because of that, the Secret Service takes no chances, keeping protestors at a distance, just to make sure. One of our greatest freedoms is our right to speak our mind, even to the president of the United States. That's what a protest is, a verbal and visual communication (albeit one way) to the man who holds the highest office in the land. Most of us get to see a president so infrequently that any chance to say something to him is impossible, so it's done with crowds and placards. Even individuals get into the act. While the president was speaking, a Duluth man stood in the aisle and shouted "Shame on You." It was loud enough to be heard by Mr. Bush, who looked in that general direction but failed to make a response. The man was escorted out and ticketed for his actions. The *Duluth News-Tribune* reported that it took forty-five seconds for security to remove him. Several others were arrested on disorderly conduct charges near the Radisson Hotel, where the president spent some down-time resting. Protestors are generally left alone by police if they are not breaking the law.

∞

My most memorable presidential visit was that of John F. Kennedy, and for a couple of reasons. He was the first president I had covered as a journalist, and at that age, and with little experience, it didn't take much for me to be impressed. When he was assassinated a scant two months later, it seemed to give even more importance and excitement to the fact that I had spent time with him in Duluth, even if from a distance.

The Bay of Pigs fiasco, the Cuban Missile Crisis, the building of the Berlin Wall, and the worsening racial strife during that hot summer of

'63 forced Kennedy to become more presidential. There was doubt in certain circles that he could win a second term, after all he had barely squeaked past Richard Nixon.

The president's sexual escapades hadn't yet been reported, and wherever he went, he was drawing huge crowds. His flashy smile and his quick wit had captured the hearts of younger Americans who saw him as a family man with a beautiful wife and young children. Despite the fact he came from great money, segments of the American public could relate to this first TV president. Eisenhower had used television, but Kennedy perfected it.

At the time of Kennedy's death, his biggest challenge was coming from African-Americans, who were demanding equality and getting little. Kennedy knew that to get re-elected he needed to win the South, and Dallas would be the perfect place to test his political might, if he still had any. If he was well-liked there, perhaps he had a chance after all.

But first he had Duluth, a safe trip to the North, where as a Democrat he could do no wrong. Grandma Ida and family friend Pamela Carlson of Cook also wanted to see the president, so the three of us drove down. I was armed with a tape recorder to capture what the president might say and sample crowd reaction.

The weather was dark and overcast with more than occasional showers. The waiting crowd was lined five and six deep at the airport fence, and television and newsreel cameras were poised on a platform. In addition to my tape recorder, I carried an 8mm home movie camera, getting some great pictures that years later have been seen on television.

What a day. Even the lousy weather couldn't put a damper on this jovial crowd. Never before had Air Force One landed in Duluth. The sight of Air Force One gets the blood stirring; after all, it's a presidential perk that symbolizes the free world, which the chief executive can use to his advantage wherever he goes. The silver-and-blue plane, now a Boeing 747, boldly announces that the president of the United States is arriving.

First a press plane touched down, followed minutes later, at 2:46 P.M., by the president's aircraft, SAM 26000, the number on the tail of the Boeing 707 in use at the time. His limo, the one in which he would later be murdered, was parked at the fence, its convertible top in place to ward off the rain. It had arrived the previous day.

The president wasted no time getting off the plane to the delight of a screaming and waving crowd. After shaking hands with local dignitaries, he turned and walked straight for the fence and his adoring fans. He was hatless and wore no overcoat to fight the chilly air. It seemed as if everything clicked into slow motion. Here was President Kennedy, the most powerful man in the world, walking just a few feet from where I was standing, reaching out his hand to an eager audience, that famous face grinning broadly.

He worked the fence for fifteen minutes, then moved quickly to a waiting helicopter for a flight to Ashland, where about ten thousand people waited to hear him speak at the airport which eventually took his name. After Kennedy's chopper lifted off, I brought my grandma and Pam Carlson back to Virginia, dropped my audio tapes at the radio station, then drove back to Duluth for his 7:30 speech at UMD's Romano Gym. The president made an overnight stay at the Hotel Duluth (now Greysolon Plaza), in a room redecorated just for the occasion. By the time the two days ended, I had enough taped material to use in future radio newscasts, with several of those sound bites getting another play after his fateful ride in front of the Dallas Book Depository building.

Duluth felt a special closeness the day President Kennedy was killed. Those events in the autumn of 1963, will forever occupy a corner of my memory.

Chapter 12

RADIO TURNS TO TELEVISION

Covering local elections was always a treat at the radio station. Maybe headache would be a better word. You see, one year I thought someone was going to call the police on me.

There used to be a place on Virginia's Second Avenue South called Andy's Motel, where they would clear out a rental unit and use it as a voting site. One particular stormy election night, I walked into the room backwards to keep the door from slamming shut. We checked on election results at several precincts and brought them back to the radio station for airing. Wouldn't you know, when I turned around there was a plus-sized woman standing in the middle of the room wearing nothing but a bra and the largest pair of panties I'd ever seen. I'd walked into the wrong suite, she let out a scream, and I bolted into the safety of the room next door where the election judge asked what all the yelling was about.

Back at the radio station one of our WHLB salesman came into the announcer's booth with a handful of updated numbers. Jim Roderigo got caught up in the moment while bending just inches from the microphone listening to results of a particular contest. Forgetting for a moment where he was, Jim bellowed, "Hell, he doesn't have a chance." It went out over the air as loud as could be.

My mother used to pack a thermos of warm spaghetti, chili, or soup for my lunch at the radio station, and office manager Ellen Lund used to laugh at the grocery bag I'd carry in every morning. One day I had the flu, but gobbled down a thermos of spaghetti just the same. That was a mistake. Two minutes into a sportscast—read from an announcer's booth, whose microphone was controlled by an engineer in another room—I puked. That's right, I threw up live on the air with Chef Boyardee noodles and tomato sauce flying in all directions, no doubt assisted by the bottle of Coke that had washed it down. It's a good thing it was radio and not television.

It was that episode on the radio that encouraged my director and me to work out a signal if I were ever to get sick on television. Remember how Carol Burnett used to grab her ear to greet her mother? If you see me grab my ear, you and the director know that I'm about to toss my cookies, so hopefully he fades to black, and fast. The Northland will watch me vomit if he isn't quick enough.

Those radio days were made even more fun with a news car decked out with microphones, a tape recorder, record player, loud speakers, and a red police light on the roof. We used that car on remote broadcasts, flipping on the rooftop light each time we'd hit the air waves. It helped draw a crowd and kept other cars from hitting us.

One particular night I decided to have a little fun with that car, albeit not exactly lawful. A freeway was being built around the south end of Virginia in the 1960s, and the stretch that passed by the radio station became a favorite place for teenagers to park their cars and make out. After signing off the air at 11 P.M., I drove the mobile unit to this impromptu lovers' lane and flipped on the red light and the loudspeakers, shouting into the microphone, "Hey, get the hell out of here." Heads bobbed up, clothing was readjusted, and cars shot off in all directions.

For a while it appeared that my radio career would be short-lived—the world nearly sampled Hell itself in the fall of 1962, after American spy planes discovered Soviet missile pads under construction in Cuba. There I was on the radio, broadcasting in stark detail President Kennedy's blockade of ships loaded with nuclear missiles, bound for that tiny island nation, ninety miles off America's shore. It looked like the Cold War was about to burst into the hottest war the world had seen, and we were scared.

Every newscast I read for thirteen days lead with stories of the stand-off between President Kennedy and Soviet Premier Nikita Khrushchev. It was still a war of words, and the world hoped it would stay that way. We were on the brink of a nuclear holocaust and the U.S. military was put on high alert, a status just beneath a state of war.

More than two dozen ships were steaming to Castro's Cuba with missiles and whatever else it took to get them set up and deployed. Kennedy sent out an armada of war ships extending some five-hundred miles off America's coast, hoping to block the Soviets.

People who couldn't watch television during the day pressed small transistor radios to their ears, not wanting to miss a single word. The situation was as tense as it could get, something to which we in America were not accustomed. We were teetering on the brink of war and finally Khrushchev blinked. Kennedy had threatened to immediately invade Cuba, and the big Soviet bear backed down. Khrushchev got his missiles out of Cuba, and the threat of nuclear war ended, for a while.

Many of you can relate to those frightful days in October and November of 1962. We were out of the Fabulous Fifties, and the world was changing. Now that I was in the news business, each headline had more meaning and each broadcast suddenly became important. The journalism bug bit deeply during the Cuban Missile Crisis, and I knew it was a life calling.

∞

A year after WDIO went on the air, I was asked to anchor the Saturday night news, which meant a drive to Duluth every weekend. WHLB manager Jim Parise wasn't happy about it, since he now had to find another sportscaster for Saturday night games. But professionally this was a good move.

The summer of 1968 found Judy and me vacationing in Fargo, North Dakota, to show Judy's aunt our first child, Sally, who was three months old. We happened to drive by the Channel 11 television station on the south end of Fargo, so I suggested we stop in and check out the place. It was KTHI's news director who persuaded me to cut an audition tape as long as I was in the building, and just in case they someday needed another newscaster.

Well, that someday came quicker than anybody thought. Three months after that unexpected audition, Channel 11 management offered me a job as both news anchor and news director.

So the switch was made to full-time television, and a whole new career. We had a small news department in Fargo, which ran us ragged chasing down enough stories to fill two major newscasts a day. KTHI was mired in third place in the ratings, with WDAY and its long-time anchor Marv Bossart leading the pack. Like me, Marv started in radio, and he became the longest-running TV journalist in the Red River Valley. (In 1994, Fargo's CBS affiliate, KXJB Channel 4, offered me a job, giving me a second chance to go head-to-head with Bossart.) In March 2000, Marv signed off for the last time after forty-two years on the air. The *Fargo Forum* printed a full page ad to honor Marv and wish him well in what they called, "A well deserved retirement."

Nine months after we got to Fargo, John Boller offered me a job at his station in Pierre, South Dakota, because he liked my style on KTHI. Boller had several television properties, all of them beginning with the letters KX (KXJB had been one of his). Throughout the Dakotas, Boller's stations were known as the KX Network.

Judy and I packed our year-old daughter into a chartered airplane at Fargo's Hector Field for a flight to Pierre to check out the place. As God is my witness, the television station was nothing more than a couple of double-wide mobile homes, with a small studio attached. We didn't move to Pierre.

KTHI gave me the chance to hone my television skills, which helped tremendously when I was hired back to Channel 10 in Duluth as a full-time employee. Fargo-Moorhead is a great metro area, and if WDIO hadn't come calling, Judy and I may have stayed there for the rest of our lives. We liked it a lot, and by the time we left twelve months later, our ratings were making headway.

☙

Years after joining the WDIO news team, other offers came from both in and out of the Duluth market. Such was the case in 1976, when WEBC radio's general manager Bob A. Grann came to the station one night asking if I'd be interested in doing a three-hour stint on the radio, Monday through Friday, reading the morning news. Dick Gottschald, Channel 10's first news director, had been WEBC's news director before switching to WDIO and had built the radio station's news reputation into something of pride, winning numerous awards. For years, WEBC was a rock-and-roll station with a good signal, a strong reach with five-thousand watts of power, and a sweet spot on the dial at 560 AM. Now the popular radio station wanted to draw some audience away from longtime powerhouse KDAL.

Knowing it would mean a short night in bed, I set my price high, not sure he would bite. But Bob did. So a week later, I was getting up at 4:30 in the morning to be at the WEBC studios by 5:15, with my first newscast of the day at 6 A.M. By 9:05, I was heading back home for a rest, then off to Channel 10 for the remainder of the day. It was a grueling schedule, and even though the money was good, I couldn't keep it going for more than eighteen months. The wear and tear was beyond expectation. Keep in mind, I was also the news director at WDIO, so the hours were long and the pressure was high.

By June of 1980, the dual role of news director and anchorman became too much. Each week was filled with seventy-two hours on the job with huge responsibility. I found myself no longer willing to give up that much personal life, and made the decision to resign.

A year earlier I had befriended Bernie Kalkbrenner, who had purchased the Johnson Mortuary from Maynard and Warren Johnson. Bernie knew that I had worked in a funeral home in my high school years, and that I was actually searching the market for a small funeral home to buy. The board of directors of an Iron Range funeral home had authorized the sale of their place to me, but the bank kept upping the ante when it came to a down payment.

So Bernie offered me a position at Johnson's, but for considerably less money than I was making as a journalist. However, not long after joining the firm, he offered me and two other staffers a chance to become part-owners of the funeral home, which provided higher salaries, a car, and certain tax breaks. Plus, this happened at the same time WDSE-TV called, asking if I would be interested in doing some work for public television.

This became a perfect setup, allowing me to keep my hand in broadcast journalism while working as family service director at the funeral home—for me, the best of both worlds. WDSE put me on as moderator of their *Legislative Report* series, a weekly question-and-answer session with Northland lawmakers. I was also given the opportunity to work on special reports, including an hour-long documentary on the history of Minnesota iron mining called "A Century of Red Earth and Iron Men." Plus, I hosted their spelling bee and later became rotating host of what is now *Almanac North*. In addition, my friend Ken Engstrom, who was managing WHLB radio in Virginia, where I had cut my broadcasting teeth, asked me to do some on-air things for him.

By early 1985, I was visited by WDIO news director Joel Anderson at the funeral home. He said the TV station wanted me back, but I turned him down. He returned a month later with another offer, and again I said no. Then a few weeks later Joel said, "General Manager Frank Befera wants you back, you name the price." Now I was interested.

Joel and I had a spaghetti dinner at Frank's apartment where we agreed on a price. That fall, I came back on the air anchoring the news.

Chapter 13

TURBULENT TIMES

One day I was talking to an intimate gathering of parents about troubled children and the media's role in social behavior. One parent said she didn't like all the television coverage given to school shootings, believing that TV news could inspire copycat crimes. Before I could even respond, a young parent stood up and took issue with her. He was probably in his mid- to late twenties and admitted being a troublemaker when he was younger.

He said, somewhat paraphrased, "S---, folks, let's not flatter ourselves. Do you think for one minute troublemakers are watching TV? It's all about drugs and booze. It's all about young people being put down. It's all the crap we had to put up with in our families. Who gives a s--- about television? I was in trouble because my old man and ma are druggies. What the hell chance did I have? It ain't about TV, folks. You got to get your head out of your a--."

Some folks are convinced that it's not money, but television that's the root of all evil. And there are a lot of TV shows that I don't waste my time with, especially all the reality shows that have cropped up. I also don't like game shows, cop shows, soap operas, award presentations, beauty pageants, and I'm sick and tired of sitcoms. Yet there are good programs. Peter Jennings is far and away my favorite network news anchor, and nobody can beat Ted Koppel of ABC's *Nightline*, television's best interviewer.

So why do vast numbers of people blame television for this country's social ills? Because TV is an easy target. Blame TV, then society doesn't have to look at itself. We should be smart enough to realize that this country was fraught with problems long before television, long before the first radio show, or the first newspaper. Crime, booze, and illegal drugs were running rampant in the 1920s, all without television. There's nothing new under the sun.

What causes society's ills? We do. There has always been mental depression. We are constantly bouncing in and out of economic unrest; unemployment breeds crime, alcoholism and other drug addictions are as commonplace today as they were years ago. We need to take responsibility for who we are. Plus we need to monitor what kids watch on TV. That too is the responsibility of adults, no matter what.

∞

A major issue in the 2004 election was the ongoing war in Iraq. Some critics are calling it "Dubya's Vietnam." To this day, the Vietnam War is a divider. In his book, *A Reporter's Life*, Walter Cronkite called the Vietnam War "its own worst enemy."

President Lyndon Johnson, who took office after the assassination of President Kennedy, made the decision to bomb North Vietnam in 1965, and the war escalated. It was never a declared war, rather a conflict like the Korean War. It dragged on, becoming more unpopular, eventually crushing LBJ's administration as television brought the war into America's living rooms.

Most U.S. presidents don't have a great deal of time for the morning papers or the evening news, but LBJ had three television sets and a United Press news wire installed in large cabinets in the Oval Office. With the sound usually turned down, all three screens were constantly illuminated, and if something of interest happened, LBJ wasted no time tuning in. One night after watching Walter Cronkite in a broadcast unfavorable to the war, Johnson said, "If I've lost Cronkite, I've lost America."

The president believed he could not win another term, and to the shock of some and the delight of others, he announced that he would not seek nor accept his party's nomination for another four years in the White House.

This was America's longest war, and we lost. Night after night, year after year, first on radio and then on television, I reported on American casualties and the politics of this war that critics believed prevented the military from taking command. In the end, the communist North Vietnamese drove the United States out, achieving a military victory.

The Vietnam war took 57,939 American lives. One of them, Sergeant Herbert R. "Andy" Anderson of Virginia, was a childhood friend of mine. He was a member of the U.S. Army's Special Forces Group, authorized to wear what became their outstanding symbol, the Green Beret. My friend died believing that what he was doing for the United States and for Vietnam was right. I guess this is the first time I've said it: "Thank you, Herb, and know that you are not forgotten."

Andy was killed in January 1968, with confirmation of his death coming a couple of days after he was reporting missing in action. A few weeks later, with Andy's body back home in Virginia, Judy and I attended his funeral, an Episcopalian service filled with scripture readings that told of God's love for his people and salvation for the dead. Andy was buried later that day in Greenwood Cemetery, forever twenty-four years old. He should be in his sixties now.

Andy and I spent a great deal of time together in elementary school; we lived just a block apart and were almost inseparable. We went to each other's birthday parties, we became members of the school patrol together, we traded comic books, slept at each others homes, went to the movies, and in high school we skied at Lookout Mountain. We thought we would know each other for a lifetime. It was too short a lifetime for him.

As a newscaster reporting on the war every night, I honestly believed this country was turning against itself. As far back as 1963, Buddhist monks were burning themselves to death on the streets of Saigon. Later,

Charles Manson and his "children" were murdering movie stars and business owners out in California. While protesting the Vietnam War at Kent State, innocent students were shot to death by National Guard troops. The My Lai Massacre was big news along with Lieutenant William Calley, whom many believed was the Pentagon's scapegoat. There was a popular slogan of the day: "Don't trust anyone over thirty." It was as if something had grabbled hold of us, and kept shaking and shaking, never to let go.

I was telling stories that included names like General William Westmoreland, President Diem, Ho Chi Minh, Pham Van Dong, General Nguyen Cao Ky, President Charles de Gaulle, General Maxwell Taylor, Secretary of State Henry Kissinger, and Defense Secretary Robert McNamara. You heard of places like the Mekong Delta, Ben Tre Province, Cambodia, Laos, Thailand, Gulf of Tonkin, Hanoi, Saigon, Checkpoint Charlie, Hue, Phnom Penh. And words like guerrilla warfare, covert war, and sorties crept into our language. Reporters were teaching a new vocabulary and daily geography lessons.

On April 23, 1975, President Ford said the war was finished. From the time I had first broadcast a story of the war early in my radio days to the fall of Saigon, I longed for the day I could say, "The Vietnam War is over." I never got a chance to say those words on the air; I was on vacation when the war came to a close, watching it on television in Red Lake Falls, Minnesota. It would have been nice to deliver the good news for a change.

∞

Another national tragedy made headlines while Judy and I were on the way to a movie. The announcer on the car radio interrupted the broadcast to report the shooting of Martin Luther King, Jr. Early reports gave no indication if King was seriously wounded, so we didn't know that he was dead until after the movie. Once again, the nation was outraged.

By then I was seven years into journalism, and the hot summer of 1968 would get hotter. Two months later to the day, Robert Kennedy was assassinated, which I learned at 4:30 on the morning of June 4 while driving to the radio station. After these two killings, many people across the country wondered if this nation could be saved.

Kennedy was as liberal as Arizona's Barry Goldwater was conservative. Kennedy appealed to large masses of the young and was almost assured the Democratic Party's nomination in the race for the nation's highest office.

Los Angeles radio newsman Andrew West was beginning to tape an exclusive interview with Kennedy as they walked through the Ambassador Hotel's kitchen when shots rang out from a .22-caliber pistol fired by Sirhan B. Sirhan.

Four days after Kennedy's murder, the killer of Martin Luther King, Jr. was arrested at Heathrow Airport in London. James Earl Ray died thirty years later in prison. Sirhan Sirhan is still behind bars.

∞

Growing up on the Iron Range, it was rare to see a black person, and when we did, admittedly, we stared. We had not mingled with blacks simply because there weren't any living in Virginia, and as a result they got our attention. Children from my era were not blind to what was written and said about blacks, and the horrible names they were called. Growing up in a white America was all I knew, and, looking back, I was cheated.

My first black friend was Ira Kemp from Washington D.C. Kemp, Harry Hawkinson of Ortonville, Minnesota, and I became inseparable during army basic training. Ira made it clear that after he left his all-black neighborhood most whites had treated him with disdain and suspicion. He also felt cheated.

I envy my children and now my grandchildren who were and are being educated in a multiracial atmosphere. They don't think of their nonwhite friends as being different. It took another forty years after brave Rosa Parks defied the racist laws of the South to get where we are, but it is still far from perfect. As the late Reverend Arthur Foy told me, "Racism is alive and well in Duluth."

∞

Those of us born in the early to mid-1940s were in our late teens when the fight against segregation captured the attention of the country. It was a quiet but powerful act of defiance when Rosa Parks refused to give up her bus seat in Montgomery, Alabama. Her courageous decision got her arrested and fingerprinted, and it opened the door to the civil rights movement. Court rulings started to knock apart this nation's long and often deadly tradition of keeping whites and blacks separate, a principle that was ringing hollow with a growing number of people.

I was lying on my bed listening to the radio that fall day in 1962 when James Meredith tried to get into the University of Mississippi in Oxford. Meredith was blocked for no other reason than the color of his skin. The live broadcast from Oxford was interrupted by the sound of a fire truck siren just a block from my house, enticing me to chase the firefighters in case of a news story. I was ten months into my career as a budding journalist and many sirens were chased in those early years. There were sirens in Oxford too, as riots claimed two lives that night.

Alabama Governor George Wallace, a notorious segregationist, vowed in 1962, "Segregation now, segregation tomorrow, segregation forever." A few years later I covered a Wallace speech at UMD, an appearance that brought booing and catcalls from his audience. Even so, he packed the house. My insides churned as he spewed his ideology. During his third presidential campaign, in 1972, he was shot and permanently paralyzed. His wounds stopped the campaign dead in its tracks. In the late 1970s, he recanted his segregationist views and became a born-again Christian.

∞

But it isn't just the South that has an ugly history of racism. On June 15, 1920, three black men—Elmer Jackson, Elias Clayton, and Isaac McGhie—were dragged from Duluth's old city jail to a waiting lamp post. The lynching was attended by a mob of between five- and ten thousand people screaming for justice. A few days earlier, a nineteen-year-old white woman claimed she had been raped by the three circus workers, based on flimsy evidence that was proven wrong after the men were hanged. The next day, Duluth's Catholic Bishop told his flock that all who were present at the hangings had better get to confession, for they were all guilty of murder.

By the time I arrived in Duluth in 1969, any talk of the lynchings was rare. This dastardly deed had been put in a closet and folks in this town were trying to forget—just think how many people in Duluth have ancestors who attended the triple lynching. I opened up that old wound on a couple of occasions with stories of the crime, and both times viewers called and wrote telling me to "let it be." It was an ugly wound that Duluthians tried to cover with a band-aid, but it was festering and still hurt.

A Seattle man's search through his ancestry ended up bringing him to Duluth eighty-two years after the lynchings of the three men, when the city held a special Week of Remembrance in their honor and unveiled a permanent memorial at the site of the old secret. Two years earlier, as Warren Read worked on the internet to unearth his genealogy, he discovered that his great-grandfather had helped rally the crowed that lynched Clayton, Jackson, and McGhie.

Read told *Eyewitness News* reporter Emily Ahs that his reaction "was shock and disbelief." He said his family had no idea that their ancestor was one of three men convicted of inciting the riot that lead to the lynchings, adding, "I knew that if there was anything I could do to help support and put a human face on another person involved, then I had to do that." It was as if Read needed to be in Duluth to atone for the sins of his grandfather.

Now when I tell stories of the triple lynching, people listen and no longer tell me, "Let it go." It isn't a dirty little secret anymore.

∞

The priest sex-abuse scandal that rocked the Catholic church got plenty of media attention, and it was heard worldwide. Father John Forliti, who wrote a commentary in the *Catholic Spirit*, the St. Paul-Minneapolis Diocese newspaper, said it well. He wrote, "We can criticize the media for ganging up on the church, but we should really thank them for the pressure they have created to force the Catholic community to begin to respond more responsibly to the problem." Father Forliti, who is the pastor of St. Olaf in Minneapolis, concluded, "If it is humiliating to be Catholic these days, so be it. Some of our number [in the clergy] have failed us, and we have failed them. Let us not conceal our outrage nor be timid in our determination to pursue justice."

Most clergy, Catholic and otherwise, are trustworthy—yet thousands of children were injured and much of it was swept under the rug. This did not occur only in the Catholic Church, but it was Catholic victims who came forward in numbers, hundreds from individual dioceses in some cases. Safeguards are in motion that should reduce the problem in the future, and trust is returning. In the meantime, the church must continue to help those who were victimized.

Chapter 14

CELEBRITIES

I got tipsy with comedian George Gobel once. Maybe "in the presence of," rather than "with," would be more accurate. Lonesome George was a low-key comedian who became a TV star in the 1950s; his show went off the air in 1960. For thirty years Gobel talked about his wife "spooky ol' Alice" while a guest on *Hollywood Squares,* the *Tonight Show* with Johnny Carson, and just about every variety program seen on television through the 1980s. George was a big-name television entertainer, a movie actor, a funny man, and one of the nicest stars you'd want to meet.

Another reporter had brought a flask of libation with him to a news conference, offering me a sip. Then another. And another. By the time George was through entertaining us with his gossip about "spooky ol' Alice" and his famous one-liner "I'll be a dirty bird," I was the dirty bird feeling no pain.

We finally walked over to a coffee shop with George looking like the Pied Piper leading his troop of giggling rats. I was sitting on a stool to the right of George when, during the middle of a joke, he reached over the counter to emphasize his story and jabbed the laughing waitress in the ribs with both index fingers. She was standing on a small step stool reaching into a shelf, and, wouldn't you know, she squeaked out a little flatus. The more she laughed the more I laughed, and the more I laughed the more George looked deadpan. That in itself was funny.

I hope this little anecdote doesn't make you think I'm a drunk, and I have to be fair to George—I don't know if he took a drink or not. And please don't think for one minute that I'm one of those guys who tosses names around to give you the impression that you're talking to a big shot. As my dad used to say, "Most big shots are people who forgot to dot the *i*." But if you don't mind, I'll throw a few more names around for you.

∞

Many of the celebrities I've interviewed made their fame performing in movies or radio and television shows geared toward children. One of the thrills of my life was meeting Spanky McFarland. To the rest of the world he will forever be known simply as "Spanky," the chubby little kid immortalized on celluloid as the star of the Our Gang / Little Rascals films. Spanky appeared live one day on Channel 10's *Peggy Chisholm Show*, and I thought my oldest daughter Sally would get a kick out of meeting him. He spent the better part of two hours at the Channel 10 studios, signing autographs, posing for pictures, and being interviewed on the air. He told me about a restaurant chain he and a financier were establishing and how he hoped it would succeed. Spanky was at that time fifty years older than his movie character, so there had been many physical changes, but it was the same old Spanky. And as nice as ever. He truly was a joy to talk with, and he made me feel as if we were old friends. He spoke easily to strangers and had a glint in his eye when discussing his Little Rascal days—and the shooting death of Carl Switzer, who played Alfalfa, which was ruled a justifiable homicide. Spanky gave my daughter an autographed card with his picture on it.

Those of you old enough to remember the *Chase and Sanborn Hour* on radio can't forget the stars of the show, Edgar Bergen and his dummy Charlie McCarthy. For those who don't remember Edgar, he was a ventriloquist who found fame on the vaudeville stage before shifting to radio, as did many other vaudevillians with great talent. Edgar was also the voice of other dummies, including Mortimer Snerd. I had the great pleasure of doing a short interview with Bergen back in the very early 1970s. It amused me how much his mouth moved when he slipped into the voice of his wooden-headed pals. Perhaps that's why his greatest fame came on radio and not television. It's not good for a ventriloquist when much of your audience says, "Hey, you can see his mouth move." Years later, Edgar's daughter Candice, of course, made fame in her own right as a model and actress, most famously for her role as Murphy Brown.

I got a chance to meet and interview both Bob "Captain Kangaroo" Keeshan and Buffalo Bob. The Captain spent several hours at the Channel 8 studios where I dragged my son Chris to meet him. Chris wasn't nearly as thrilled as I, and I'm not sure how Mr. Keeshan felt, but he was cordial and almost seemed disappointed when we left.

Some time in the late 1980s or early 1990s, I got to interview Buffalo Bob Smith at UMD, where he was reliving stories and memories to a generation who heard their parents speak of him. I remember talking with students who said they never saw the *Howdy Doody* show, but remember their parents talking about Buffalo Bob. (I also remember teasing my friends in junior high school that they had to "run home and watch *Howdy Doody*," never letting on that I never missed an episode myself.) Mr. Smith was a television pioneer in children's programs who hailed from Flat Rock, North Carolina. His program ran thirteen years, ending in 1960. Buffalo Bob was the cowboy-suited favorite of baby boomers in the early years of television, starting each show by blaring, "Say, kids, what time is it?" Then his peanut gallery—the kiddy studio audience—would shout back, "It's Howdy Doody time!" His show was pure magic, with puppets as the real stars— the freckle-faced Howdy Doody, dressed in cowboy jeans and a plaid shirt, Mayor Phineas T. Bluster, Flub-a-Dub, and Princess Summerfall Winterspring.

Puppeteers may have pulled the strings, but the show's producers knew how to pull kids to the television set as soon as we got home from school. Along with Buffalo Bob, Clarabell the Clown was the only real person on the show, and it was none other than Bob Keeshan who originally played that role, the speechless, horn-honking clown who drove me nuts. Bob had far more influence as Captain Kangaroo.

∞

Charlton Heston, Moses himself, has been to Duluth on two or three occasions on behalf of the National Rifle Association, which he chaired for many years. I met him just once, during a news conference in town, and again it was like meeting an old friend. He almost too willingly posed for pictures and worked the crowd as a suave, sophisticated movie star, grandfatherly in his approach and with eyes that smiled as gleefully as his mouth.

Entertainers Sonny and Cher made it to Duluth for a concert, in the early 1970s, flying into town on the Playboy Bunny Jet, a black DC-9 decked out with a private bedroom for Hugh Hefner and his favorite bunny. Cher refused to talk, but Sonny was cordial to us reporters as he tossed a few one-liners he had mastered on their weekly TV variety show. Cher stood by his side, just shaking her head whenever a question was put her way. A strikingly beautiful woman at her side, Cher's sister, eventually took Cher by the arm and walked her to their waiting limo.

I also interviewed Caesar Romero and Agnes Moorhead when the pair was in town for Denfeld's all-class reunion in the early 1980s. Many of you might remember Romero as the original "Joker" from the *Batman* television show and Moorhead as Samantha's mother on TV's *Bewitched*, but to me they are two giants of the silver screen. They remind me of the old studio system of movie making. They were actors who often took their performances over the top, unlike so many of today's method-acting stars who put more realism into their delivery.

Rick Jason, star of the television show *Combat*, did more than just answer questions. The first time I met him was at the WHLB radio station in Virginia, where he told my audience how to cook a turkey in a paper bag. The second time was a couple of years later when he replaced Dick Wallack at the WDIO anchor desk for one night's six o'clock broadcast.

I interviewed Little Jimmy Dickens, master of the country novelty song, when he was in Duluth in the mid 1990s making an appearance at the DECC's annual Boat, Sport and Travel Show. Because the interview wasn't in a news conference format, we were able to spend several minutes of quality time just getting to know each other with small talk. That's a great way to loosen up an interviewee. Once the camera started rolling, our natural conversation continued, and it became a good piece for playback on the air. Dickens was one of those stars who didn't have to have his ego stroked. I've interviewed a few like him; *Your Hit Parade's* Gisselle McKenzie, Sony Bono, Bobby Vee, and Johnny Cash.

Two cartoonists are on my list of interesting fellows I've queried for the nightly news: Chester Gould of *Dick Tracy* fame, and Al Capp, the creator of *Li'l Abner*. I was given a few minutes of time by famed movie wardrobe designer Edith Head, comedian Dick Gregory, and General Jimmy Doolittle. Oh, and I met actress Eva Gabor once when she was starring in the hit TV series *Green Acres*. She was sexy. But so was her costar, Arnold the Pig.

∞

Some larger-than-life individuals carry their fame well, trying to stay grounded even while much of the world stares. Others walk with their noses in the air, seemingly preferring not to be bothered even when they are out on publicity appearances.

I'm a huge fan of the old Martin-Lewis buddy pictures—that's Dean Martin and Jerry Lewis, for you younger folks. So it was a treat to watch Deano entertain in Las Vegas and to actually meet Jerry Lewis when he flew to Duluth in a private jet to promote his annual Labor Day telethon. Yet, I was disappointed with Lewis.

I'll be the first to admit that anyone can have an off day, when he or she simply wants to be left alone. But those who have chosen public lives have also chosen to be approached by that same public. It comes with the territory. Lewis's news conference at the airport drew a number of media people and we dutifully put what he had to say on the air without commentary. Yet he wasn't the man I expected him to be. I felt we were bothering him, like he was a million miles away even though he stood just six feet from me.

I also met Elizabeth Taylor on what may have been one of her off days. She had come to northern Wisconsin back in the 1970s to promote a hospital. She too was larger than life, her physical appearance had greatly changed from her *National Velvet* days. But the one thing that stood out about covering her appearance was her voice. It was overly sweet, Jackie Kennedy-like. She seemed to talk as if she had just inherited a false accent. What she said may have been important, but how she said it, the tone of her voice, was phony, like that of a bad take in a movie.

Some celebrities are finicky, such as TV star Dennis Weaver, who first made it big on *Gunsmoke* playing the stiff-legged partner to Marshall Matt Dillon. And he played a cop on another successful show, usually dressed in cowboy boots and a brown western suit. Weaver was in Duluth in the mid 1980s, and I had him on the six o'clock news for a live interview. He had to leave his hotel room early to get to our remote location. The interview lasted about two-and-a-half minutes, and when it ended he turned to our field producer and asked, "that's it?" He apparently thought the interview should have lasted longer. The interview itself was less than memorable, but his comment made me realize that stars have egos, and apparently a short interview wasn't worth his time.

My interview with singing star Roger Miller was just the opposite. He had come to the WDIO studios to appear on the *Peggy Chisholm Show*, which was running hot in the 1970s. Miller had a number of hits including, "Dang Me (Gonna Take a Rope and Hang Me)," "Tie Me Kangaroo Down Sport," and of course "King of the Road" as well as several others. After Peggy's live interview with Miller, and before my taped interview with him, nearly the entire staff of the television station sat around the studio with him, singing his hits. It was a grand afternoon.

∞

Some celebrity encounters have happened quite by accident. Country singer Johnny Cash caught us media types off guard when he accidentally walked into a news conference in downtown Duluth in the early 1970s. Cash was not performing in the city, simply passing through and hitting Superior Street stores for a little afternoon shopping. Every camera in the place swung over to The Man in Black. His craggy face and baritone voice immediately took control, and he got more air time that night than the original subject of the news conference.

Seeing Johnny Cash walk unexpectedly smack dab into the middle of that news conference couldn't have been more exciting if the president walked in. Cash was as big as they get, in my book—the absolute tops, with a gritty singing voice almost as much off-key as my own. He was a man's man, and he couldn't have been more cordial that day, almost shy. I've long forgotten what I asked Cash, but that doesn't matter. At that time he was riding as high as they come in the world of country music. He spent about fifteen minutes with us, then went about his business walking Superior street and shopping.

I was also lucky enough to cross paths with Muhammad Ali. The champ was traveling by car through Fargo-Moorhead in early 1969, on his way to the west coast, when he got bogged down in a snowstorm near Dilworth. From there he hitched a ride into Fargo where I took the opportunity to interview him (if memory serves me right, he took a passenger train the rest of the way). Sadly, I've searched boxes of notes and records with no luck finding remnants of that interview. But I do remember that he floated like a butterfly and stung like a bee, to paraphrase his favorite catch phrase at the time.

You never know who you're going to bump into. I got a chance to meet the world's tallest man at the Piggly Wiggly supermarket in Virginia in 1965. Henry Hite was touring the Northland for a meat-processing company, and at eight feet two inches he was an imposing fellow. Henry joked that he arrived in Virginia by Volkswagen—two of them, one on each foot. He was so tall that he found it hard to walk, carrying a great deal of weight on that leggy frame. Every fifteen minutes or so, Henry had to sit down to rest. There have been taller people than Mr. Hite (obviously a professional name), but at the time he was the tallest anywhere.

∞

One of my more interesting interviews was with the country's most infamous yippie, Abbie Hoffman. Hoffman was a strange dude. Our first interview was in Fargo, where he told me about his plans to stage a demonstration at the Pentagon. He and thousands of his fellow yippies were going to grab onto the five-sided building and lift it a few inches off the ground to protest American war action in Vietnam. When I heard that, I actually turned off my camera and walked out of the news conference, not wanting to give Hoffman a second of air time. I didn't. Hoffman did not offend me politically, but I found him to be such a goofball that I couldn't understand why the national media had given this guy so much time—so I chose not to give him any myself.

Our second meeting was in Duluth, where he appeared in front of our cameras with a more closely cropped beard and his wild hair somewhat tamed, but Hoffman himself hadn't changed much. That interview was given coverage, but it wasn't my idea. News director Dick Gottschald assigned me the story, and my protest fell on deaf ears. Again, it had nothing to do with his politics or mine. I simply found Hoffman to be so uninteresting, I remember nothing about the story we aired that night.

∞

As you've read, my list of interviews includes the famous, the infamous, and the ordinary—but none of them was more real than Elie Weisel. Here's a man who survived the holocaust and has spent much of his life memorializing the victims of Adolf Hitler. In 1985, Mr. Weisel was honored with the Congressional Gold Medal, Congress's highest award for civilians.

Weisel spoke at the College of St. Scholastica, but not before spending time with the media. My notes include a description of Weisel: "a thin face, a worn look, and eyes that have seen more than any eyes were meant to see." I found him to be a quiet man still hurting emotionally from years of Nazi abuse. He was willing to relive his painful memories for anyone who would listen, telling of the cruelties that were dealt to himself and millions of other European Jews. With our cameras rolling, he talked of his mother and sister, who were murdered the very day the Weisel family arrived at Buchenwald concentration camp. His father was spared, since the Nazi war machine needed able-bodied men to work hard labor, but died three months before Elie's liberation in 1945. He, more than any other person I have interviewed, held me spellbound. It was an honor to have shaken Elie Weisel's hand, not once but twice.

∞

Of course there were people I wanted to interview but never got the chance. Gus Hall was born on the Iron Range, in the city of Virginia, and try as I might, he and I never connected. This man lead the American Communist Party for forty-one years and ran repeatedly for the presidency of the United States. His four attempts didn't ignite the interest of too many people, but his efforts kept his name alive and his beliefs in the press. Hall died in 2000, living long enough to see President Reagan play a roll in the collapse of the Soviet Union. Even with the collapse of Soviet communism, he told an interviewer in 1992 that he still believed "socialism is inevitable."

He was born Arvo Gus Halberg, the son of Finnish immigrants, and in his early years he lived in Cherry. By 1926, after two years studying political ideology at the Lenin Institute in Moscow, Hall had become a communist activist.

In 1949, just as the American free enterprise system was gaining steam following World War II, Hall was convicted of advocating the overthrow of the American government, a violent overthrow no less. He hid in Mexico for a while, but was captured and extradited back to America where he spent eight years in prison. He was released in the early 1960s, about the time I was graduating from high school.

Since Hall was a product of northeastern Minnesota, I had heard a lot about him. He had somewhat of a cult following up here, with rumors of other communists living across the Range. Undeterred by his prison sentence, Hall was revered by his fellow American Communists, and hung on to his position as National Secretary of the American Communist Party until the day he died. By then his party had lost most, if not all, of its clout.

Chapter 15

ON BEING A DEACON

Many of you may not realize it, but in addition to being a journalist I am also an ordained minister—the Reverend Mr. Dennis Anderson. Deacon John Pistone, the Executive Director of the Bishop's Committee on the Deaconate Secretariat, says I am the only deacon in the country who is also a television anchorman.

I went back to the classroom for four years in the late 1970s and was ordained at the College of St. Scholastica by Bishop Paul Anderson on June 26, 1982. My first parish was St. Anthony's in Duluth, which closed its doors two years later. Bishop Robert Brom then assigned me to St. Benedict's Parish, where I've been a permanent deacon since 1984.

I gave serious consideration to two vocations while in junior and senior high school, neither of which had anything to do with journalism. For quite some time there were serious thoughts of going into the ministry or becoming a funeral director.

Growing up Lutheran, my family attended First Lutheran Church in Virginia, pastored by the Reverend Nels Edward Vickburg. He was not only our minister, but his wife and kids were friends, and Grandma Ida cleaned the parsonage a couple of times a week. So it was only natural for us to attend Pastor Vickburg's funeral when he died in 1957. That's when I got my first glimpse of morticians from the Cron and Son Funeral Home at work. Call me odd, but what they did looked intriguing to this thirteen-year-old.

A few years later, I got a job at the Tamte Funeral Home, as I mentioned earlier. There I met with owner Ken Tamte, who also operated the Sand Lake Resort a dozen miles north of Virginia and later, after his funeral home closed its doors, became the pastor of the Sand Lake Chapel. Ken and I hit it off, and we are still friends. He and his wife attended my ordination into the ministry and a post-ordination get-together at our home, and he eventually invited me to preach at all three of the churches he served in Sand Lake, Cook, and Loon Lake in Palo. So it was a toss up—do I become a mortician or a Lutheran pastor? The career in journalism had not yet called to me, but years passed and marriage and children entered the picture—along with my broadcasting profession. I was now a Catholic and becoming a Lutheran pastor was not in the plans.

The transition from Lutheran to Catholic came easily; that is, my Christian faith didn't change. The Catholic Church focuses not only on Holy Scripture but also on tradition more heavily than other Christian denominations, and for that I am grateful. You can't ignore tradition in the church any more than you can ignore your family history. The Second Vatican Council made the transition easier for me, since the church was now making changes that seemed to make sense to a non-Catholic. Vatican II allowed Mass to be said in English or in any native tongue, the altar had been turned so the priest was now facing the congregation, and the people were now singing along with the choir. While many long-time Catholics—many of them Catholic from the cradle—found the changes difficult, to me they made sense. Actually, I became a Catholic a full year before Judy and I married, and for me it was a good move.

Eventually, the Diocese of Duluth began looking for men to ordain into the permanent deaconate. Unlike deacons in Protestant churches, a Catholic deacon is an ordained minister, one of three clergy offices in the church, the other two being priest and bishop.

The deaconate is as old as the church itself, but the office of deacon died away after the first millennium. It was restored by Pope Paul VI, after the idea resurfaced during the Second Vatican Council. It would mean a married clergy in the Roman Catholic Church for the first time in a thousand years, and there were all sorts of questions and fears coming from nearly every corner of the church.

A number of parish priests feared the ordained deacon. Some still do, but their numbers have dwindled. Other priests didn't think a deacon was needed, and some still don't. It was new and threatening, and they were afraid. Some priests were angry that a married deacon would have what they called "the best of both worlds," meaning marriage and Holy Orders. Priests also voiced concern that deacons would usurp their ministries. They appeared more concerned about what we do than who we are. The real concern of all clergy should be about who am I as a minister. Bringing the presence of God to His people is not something reserved for clergy.

Deacon candidates are chosen by a screening team composed of priests, deacons, and active members of the laity. The same was true in the 1970s, but there were no deacons yet to be screeners. Father Stanley Dolsina was instrumental in helping discern my decision to seek a religious vocation. A greater priest you will not find. Father Stan is kind, gentle, and truly loves the Lord. This great priest has lived out his ministry in honorable fashion, forever telling others that "we are in this together." He was always secure in his calling and in himself, never fearing that someone would take his responsibilities away.

Father Stan was my pastor at St. Anthony's Church in Duluth when he suggested I look into becoming a deacon and told me to pray about it. He believed then and still believes in the power of prayer, and he understood that I had entertained thoughts of becoming a Lutheran pastor many years earlier. I was already active in the church and he said if it was God's will, it would be done. So I applied.

Judy and I were both interviewed by the screening committee, and within a week or two they had turned me down. "Too spiritual," they said.

Too spiritual? Me? They must have been talking about another Dennis Anderson. All sorts of things went through my mind. What had I said to the committee? How could I be overly spiritual? What does that mean? I was hurt, angry and frustrated, and I remembered that one priest on the committee had asked, "Would you leave the church if you were turned down for ordained ministry?"

"Of course not," I answered, "I don't *need* ordination." All Christians, I told them, are, by virtue of their baptism, supposed to serve Christ—it's just that I felt a "call" to the deaconate, and in fairness, I needed to exhaust all avenues of discernment, which the church helps accomplish.

Did the screening committee really know me? Oh, they knew I was on television and all that, but did they really know me? Oddly, on the very day I was rejected by my own church, I was scheduled to speak at a non-Catholic church in Cloquet.

A couple of days passed and I felt comfortable enough to call Bishop Paul Anderson. Judy and I got to know him through our involvement in the church, and he suggested that we meet for lunch, during which he encouraged me to try again the following year. The Bishop was surprised by the committee's decision and thought I should give it another chance, keeping the discernment process alive. It was good advice, for the screening committee gave its blessing nine months later.

A candidate must be at least thirty-five years old at ordination to become a Roman Catholic deacon, and also meet all educational and other requirements. The Duluth Diocese had a four-year program of study when my formation began. If the candidate is married, as most are, his wife is expected to walk with her husband through the formation process. Our wives took the same courses in fundamental theology, Christology, ecclesiology and sacraments, pastoral theology, canon law, theological anthropology, social ethics, church history, liturgy, mystery of God and salvation, moral theology, spirituality, homiletics (preaching), and Old and New Testament studies. The wives didn't have to preach, however.

Nearly a year was given to the development of individual spirituality which included such topics as discernment, reconciliation, ordained ministry and marriage, married clergy and the Catholic Church, faith, personal prayer, spiritual direction, the deacon in relationship to bishop, priest, and lay persons, the Holy Eucharist, and more.

Because the deaconate is a vocation of ordained ministry, the church has the right and the need to help the candidate discern God's call, with a solid basis for this in both scripture and tradition. In the Bible, the Apostle Paul advises Timothy to exercise his pastoral responsibilities carefully in selecting deacons for the church at Ephesus: "Deacons must be serious, straightforward, and truthful. They may not over-indulge in drink or give in to greed. They must hold fast to the divinely revealed faith with a clear conscience. They should be put on probation first; then, if there is nothing against them, they may serve as deacons. Deacons may be married but once and must be good managers of their children and their household."

So deacons in the Catholic Church are members of the clergy, called to Holy Orders. Deacons in non-Catholic churches serve more like members of the church board, a vast difference between the two.

Unlike Roman Catholic priests and bishops, members of the permanent deaconate are allowed to be married. However, nonmarried men who are ordained as deacons must remain celibate after ordination, just as a priest. If my wife were to pass away before me, I would have to remain celibate for the rest of my life. We are called "permanent" deacons, because we remain in that office. There is another deacon in our church called the transitional deacon, a position he holds for about a year before ordination into the priesthood.

The ministry of deacons has flourished in the United States, with nearly eleven thousand of us, and another twenty thousand worldwide. As of now, there are no deaconesses in the Roman Catholic Church, although that possibility is being explored. Exploration in the church takes time, a lot of time, so the issue of ordaining women as deacons will not be settled quickly.

For a number of years, efforts have been made to get Rome interested in talking about the possibility of women priests. Only men are ordained deacons and priests in the Roman Catholic Church, following the tradition that Jesus chose only males as his apostles. While there was a married priesthood for the first one thousand years of the church, there was never an indication that women were ordained, although there were deaconesses. However, there is some debate about whether they were actually ordained or commissioned to serve, so we do not have deaconesses in today's church. The lack of female clergy in the Catholic Church has angered some women who have argued that there is not equality in the Church. Would women make good pastors? Certainly! I have known several female clerics—including Jewish, Lutheran, and Methodist—but that is not the direction the Catholic Church has chosen to take. Since I am a firm believer in tradition, and a married priesthood is a tradition of the early church (as are deacons), I am comfortable with the church's current stand on a male-only clergy. That had been the church's tradition from the very beginning. Churches are not a democracy, and there are some aspects of our faith that will remain constant. That isn't to say the church believes women are second-class citizens. I certainly don't and neither do my fellow clergy. Neither does Rome.

And while I doubt the Church will allow women priests in my lifetime, I most assuredly await the day priests are allowed to marry. I believe we are missing out on much talent, faith, and example from a marriage commitment and experience that only husbands, wives, and parents can give. I'm convinced that someday marriage will be an option.

"How," I am asked, "as an ordained clergy can you not compromise yourself as a journalist?" That's a valid question that can't be answered in a couple of words, but let me try. Most deacons in the Roman Catholic Church have a secular profession in addition to their ministry, and it seems to work well. It is imperative that we find truth in both our

Christian and secular work; those of us who profess a faith are expected by God to take Him into all aspects of life. My set of ethics, my interpretation of God and faith—and we each have our own interpretation—can't be put on a shelf for a few hours each day while at work. My private life and my profession are shaped by what is inside me. That is true for all of us, even if we have no faith. Millions of faithless people still live by a set of ethical standards.

That means I don't compromise myself in my on-air reporting of the news. Can that be successfully accomplished? Absolutely, no question about it. I have found a proper respect for both callings, and there is a balance between compassion and hard news. That's part of my credibility.

We covered well the stories of sex abuse in the Catholic Church and the so-called "Holy Wars" involving Jimmy Swaggart and Jim and Tammy Faye Baker. But those were easy stories—as *Los Angeles Times* media critic David Shaw once wrote, "It's easy to cover the scandalous side of anything."

We shouldn't, however, be talking religion only when there is a critical bend to the story. There should be positive stories about people and how they are affected by their faith, whether they be Jewish, Christian, Muslim, or Buddhist. And there should be stories about the variety of churches found in the Northland, and what's happening behind those walls, and in the lives of their membership. As of this writing, the Religion Newswriters Association has 265 members. That's not a large number by any stretch, yet it is twice that of a few years earlier. The media is starting to pay more attention to a subject that we have largely ignored out of fear, ignorance, or lack of desire. David Shaw says, "There are two things American reporters know how to cover well; politics and sports, so we try to reduce everything to that."

That's especially true for television. But the *Duluth News-Tribune* has long had a religious editor, coming up with stories that carry a great deal of interest. It's clear that we TV journalists need to connect with our viewers about subjects other than war, politics, money, car chases, and city issues. For millions of people, religion and spiritual issues are what life is all about, and we are missing their stories.

It would be great if we in TV news took more time for thoughtful stories of religious experiences, not to promote one religion over the other, but to show how those experiences affect those who have them. Ignoring how religion fits into American life makes little sense and shuns a subject that interests vast numbers of our audience.

∞

While my day at the television station begins at four in the afternoon, my day in ministry never technically ends. I'm usually in my church office a little after nine each morning, and before crawling into bed at night I may have been called to a hospital to visit a sick parishioner, to a nursing home to pray with a dying resident, or to visit with a frustrated parent whose teen is testing his or her wings.

Other time is spent in marriage preparation with couples soon to tie the knot. There are monthly grief support sessions, baptism preparation classes, and communion services at nursing homes as well as witnessing marriages, officiating at wakes and funerals, baptizing and preaching at weekend masses, and attending to many other needs that surface. It's a busy life, but those to whom I minister give a lot in return.

At one time a jail ministry was sandwiched in there too, but it was put on hold after a prisoner threatened me. He was in the county jail awaiting trial for attempted murder, and after a church service he told me he didn't like the way I reported his story. He went on to explain his plan to shoot me once he got out of prison.

Fortunately, the jail service that day turned out to be a blessing. You see, we ended up praying together and embracing, delighted that we had had the time together in a religious setting.

This incident opened my eyes to a potential problem with my dual role of clergy and journalist. I made certain to wear a clerical collar when at the county jail so prisoners and staff could differentiate between

Dennis Anderson the journalist and the Reverend Mr. Anderson. But after all, I was telling their crime stories on the nightly news, then attempting to minister to their spiritual needs behind bars. So jail ministry was put on hold until after retirement.

*

As a public person known primarily for being a television newscaster, I often surprise people when they see me dressed as a cleric conducting a wedding, performing a baptism, or preaching a funeral. Life is full. It's exciting, and I embrace my ministry and faith with the same gusto with which I cherish my career as a newscaster.

Ministry is a position of trust, and sadly we have moved into a dark time in the church, frustrating clergy and the laity. The church now knows that today's parishioner is different from those of earlier times, demanding answers and accountability from the clergy. Pews are occupied by folks who may be better educated than their Father, something that wasn't the case a couple of generations ago when the pastor, lawyer, doctor, and teacher were the best educated people in town.

Writing in *Ministry and Liturgy* magazine, Duluth priest William C. Graham—who now holds an endowed chair at the College of St. Scholastica where he is designing a Catholic Studies program—says, "The active role of the laity is not to be overshadowed, forgotten, relegated to insignificance, or confused with spectatorship." He calls our worship a "communal call to holiness," pointing out that the church's new General Instruction of the Roman Missal makes clear that the faithful "give thanks to the Father [God] and offer the victim [Jesus] not only through the hands of the priest, but also together with him and learn to offer themselves."

Some folks in the church either don't like change or are totally unaware that the church is always in a state of change. It has changed greatly since Vatican II, and it's certainly far different from what it was a thousand years ago, just like the church of a thousand years from now will look nothing like it does today. That doesn't mean the church is adrift in a sea of radicalism, but it will continue to address life and societal issues like women clergy, homosexuality, priestly marriage, euthanasia, abortion, and a litany of issues we haven't begun to imagine—and it will always ask, "What would Jesus do?"

With the guidance of the Holy Spirit, the Eucharist will, and must, remain central to the life of the Catholic Church. Even so, there will be many changes to come, long after the sod has been packed down on you and me.

The late Father Emeric Lawrence, my dear old friend and a monk from Collegeville, wrote, "The greatest suffering and the greatest joy can co-exist in one and the same life; they can be intimately connected to one another." As he grew old and frail, Father Emeric, like the rest of us, had to come to terms with change, with suffering, pain, and dying, calling salvation the greatest vocation of all.

Chapter 16

PLANE CRASHES

My interest in all things flying kept me focused when reporting on Minnesota's worst plane crash, which happened on December 1, 1993. That morning found me looking out the window at overcast skies, and despite the outdoor gloom, I was upbeat, for this was the thirty-second anniversary of my broadcasting career and my brother's forty-eighth birthday.

That day must have dawned full of promise for those who got up expecting to fly safely back to Hibbing or International Falls later that night. It was impossible to know what fate awaited Northwest Airlink Flight 5719.

Some journalists say that network TV journalism came into its maturity during those awful four days in November 1963, when President John Kennedy was murdered in Dallas. Locally, the deadly Hibbing commuter plane crash did much to demonstrate the ability of Duluth television stations, whose news departments were just beginning to use the latest live satellite technology.

In my opinion, WDIO did as good a job covering the crash as any station could have, given the distance involved, the time of night, the location of the crash, the expertise of our reporters, and the state of local TV technology.

The newsroom received a phone call at around 9:20 that night from a person in Hibbing, asking if we knew anything about a plane that had gone down. The caller had no idea what type of plane it was and said simply, "I think it's down someplace in the Hibbing area, by a dump." I personally took that call and told him that we'd check out his tip, and if it turned out to be anything, we'd have it on the ten o'clock news.

I had no reason to believe the plane was anything but a small private aircraft, the type that commonly fly in an out of local airports. There are occasional plane crashes around here, and never did it cross my mind that this would be a passenger plane.

So I got right to work on the tip, calling the FAA control tower at Duluth International Airport, and I hit pay dirt. The person who answered the phone said that a plane was "missing and presumed down," and to their knowledge it had not yet been found. He also said that a large-scale search was being organized.

"What kind of plane is it?" I asked. "Do you know where it was going?"

"It's a Northwest Airlink on a flight from Minneapolis," said the voice on the line.

"A commuter plane?" I asked.

"Yes, a commuter, inbound to Hibbing."

I could feel the adrenaline kick in, knowing that this was big, and we needed more information for the newscast now just thirty minutes away. I swung my chair around to look directly into my producer's eyes and bellowed something like, "It's a Northwest commuter plane that has apparently crashed. We need everyone on it, now!"

Generally, a small staff of reporters and photographers work the night shift in our newsroom; however we had an extra reporter and an additional photographer on duty that night.

News director Steve Goodspeed was called at home to apprise him of the developing story, while the rest of the staff went to the phones, making calls to law enforcement agencies, airports, the FAA, Northwest Airlines, and anyone else we felt could provide information. There was not much time to get what we needed, so you can imagine the flurry of activity.

We got three people rolling immediately for the trip to Hibbing, now that we had confirmation of a crash. We sent reporters Colleen Mahoney and Julie Hill, along with a photographer who would operate both the live camera and shoot video tape. Julie had been working with us for a while, but Colleen had only recently joined the staff, and this was her biggest story right out of the gate.

Our ten o'clock news ratings are strong, meaning we would have a huge audience, and I suspected then and there that some of those viewers would have family on that plane. Flight 5719 was to terminate in International Falls, after a brief scheduled stop in Hibbing. There was no doubt in my mind that our fast approaching newscast would inform some people that their loved ones were presumed dead. I don't like that, yet tragedies of this nature cannot be kept off the news. Our graphics department went to work on their computers to electronically build a map of Minnesota, pinpointing the search site and the city of Hibbing, labeled with the words "Northwest Commuter Crash," or something to that effect. Since there was no other visual for this story, it was important to get a locator on the screen; the known details of the crash would be read over the graphic. After being told that it was a passenger plane, Steve Goodspeed rushed in from home, and with other reporters feeding information, I wrote and rewrote the lead story using what we knew, with details changing by the minute.

Fifteen minutes before air time, I learned that the plane had crashed on an old mine dump, and a sheriff's deputy had looked into the crash, finding no survivors. The state patrol called, asking what I knew, and I talked with a couple of police officers at the scene, who told me what they saw.

Three minutes before air time, I ran from my newsroom desk over to the studio on the far end of the building, grabbing my suit coat and an unfinished cup of coffee on the way. My collar button was fastened, the necktie knot adjusted, a duel set of microphones were clipped to my left lapel, talcum powder was dusted on my face to reduce shine from the bright overhead lights, and with seconds to spare, I took a deep breath.

Bill Hackbarth was directing the newscast that night. "Ready to spin open," Bill barked into his headset to the rest of the crew. These were people on the technical end of the broadcast, including three studio camera operators, a studio floor director, a teleprompter operator, two engineers, a sound operator, a technical director, a producer, and a graphics operator. "Spin open," Bill commanded. That was his order to play the tape that announces, "This is *Eyewitness News* with Dennis Anderson."

Three seconds later Bill again directed, "Stand by. Cue him." The floor director in the studio repeated the stand by to me, then brought his arm down and pointed his right index finger, giving me the cue that I was on the air. I could see myself on the TV monitor embedded in the desk and on the monitor positioned alongside the big television cameras. I was now on live, and looking straight into the camera I began telling the Northland what we knew. It went something like this:

> Good evening, everyone. Topping tonight's news: a deadly plane crash in Hibbing. *Eyewitness News* has learned that a Northwest Airlines commuter plane has crashed into a mine dump near a city park, just east of downtown Hibbing tonight, and authorities on the scene say there don't appear to be any survivors. It's believed there were twenty people aboard the plane, which was apparently attempting a landing in Hibbing, on a flight from Minneapolis. First reports from the scene indicate search crews have looked inside the wreckage and found no one alive. The plane was Northwest Airlines flight 5719. Northwest spokesman John Austin confirmed that 5719 is a Hibbing flight, but could not confirm that the plane has crashed. However, the Duluth FAA tower and Hibbing police tell us that the plane is down, and again, it appears that no one has survived. Northwest Airlines says the plane is capable of carrying nineteen people and a crew of two, including the pilot and co-pilot. There is fog and freezing drizzle around the Northland tonight, including the Hibbing area, but at this point we don't know if bad weather played a role. To repeat: a Northwest Airlines commuter plane bound for Hibbing has crashed into a Hibbing mine dump while attempting a landing at

the Chisholm-Hibbing airport. There were about twenty people
aboard the plane, and we have been told that there are no survivors. We'll provide additional information throughout the rest of
this broadcast and the rest of the evening, as it becomes available.

There, I had done my job. I had just informed the Northland of the
worst plane crash in Minnesota history.

Several times during the half-hour newscast, we updated our information, and then stayed on for a special report at 10:35. It was somewhere
around 1:30 or 2:00 in the morning before we got off the air, and not
before we went live to Hibbing for several reports from Colleen and Julie.

After a quick trip home for a shower and a change of clothes, I was
back at the television station by four A.M., and at five o'clock we were
once again on the air with another special, including additional live
reports from Hibbing and video from the crash area. Eighteen people
died in the accident.

The Associated Press reported that this type of aircraft was "at the
center of a debate between the FAA and the National Transportation
Safety Board since a 1989 plane crash in Washington state, in which
icing played a role. Six people died in that crash."

Other officials said fog and freezing rain in northern Minnesota that
night posed problems for aircraft, including icing. NTSB spokesman
Brent Bahler was quoted by us as saying it was "too early to tell if icing
was the case here." Of course a long and detailed investigation followed,
and we covered it every step of the way. Local families who lost loved
ones in the crash wanted as much information as we could deliver, not
only at the time of the accident but over a period of many months.

In time, the politicians started voicing their beliefs. Congressman
Jim Oberstar blamed the fatal crash on the Bush administration (George
H. W. Bush), which he said delayed regulations for the airline industry.
Oberstar was the subject of a letter-to-the-editor published in Virginia's
Mesabi Daily News after that statement. A man from Hackensack,
Minnesota, wrote:

Rep. James Oberstar using the tragic plane crash in Hibbing to slam [President] Bush is opportunism at its height. It is totally irresponsible of Oberstar to comment as such when initial reports indicate the investigation is focusing on crew performance. Shame on you Jim Oberstar.

Oberstar said the crash could have been prevented if the plane had the correct equipment. The plane was lacking a device that would have warned pilots that they were flying too close to the ground.

After the NTSB began focusing its investigation on the crew of the doomed airplane, it didn't take long before headlines concentrated on them. The plane's captain, forty-two-year-old Marvin Falitz, took the brunt of the probe. A report written by the Associated Press's Philip Brasher indicated that Falitz had failed three proficiency tests and was the subject of complaints of sloppy work and poor relations with fellow crew members.

The plane came down far short of the Hibbing Airport, and the accident became somewhat of a catalyst for changes in the commuter airline industry. The crew didn't know they were about to strike the mine dump, according to the cockpit voice recorder. Everything appeared normal, and then it was all over in a second. Here are their final words:

> 7:28:28 P.M. First Officer Chad Erickson—"Ladies and gentlemen, we've begun our final descent in for landing at Hibbing, and, ah, just like to make sure you have your seatbelt on and check around your seat to make sure that any carry-on baggage is stowed at this time. Looks like overcast skies in, ah, Hibbing, at this time. For those passengers continuing on to International Falls, it'll be a few minutes on the ground and we'll be off shortly. Thanks for, ah."

> 7:38:45 Erickson (performing check list) talking to Captain Falitz in cockpit—"Passenger briefing's complete, seat belt sign's on, utility...landing lights are on...fuel cross feed is normal. Briefing and V speeds is complete. In-range check list is complete."

7:44:32 Falitz talking to Erickson—"Okay, put one down there to show we're cleared for the approach and since we're established, what altitude can we go down to?"

7:44:43 Erickson—"Thirty-five hundred."

7:44:44 Falitz—"Okay, put that in there."

7:44:55 Erickson—"Just...you just stay up here as long as you can?"

7:45:00 Falitz—"Yes."

7:49:39 Erickson—"Landing gear down, three green hydraulic pressure brakes two thousand tested."

7:49:43 Falitz—"Two thousand tested left."

7:49:44 Erickson—"Prop sync's off...prop sync's off, speed levers high a hundred percent. Boost pumps on...before landing checklist to the box."

7:50:10 Erickson—"One to go."

7:50:14 Falitz—"To what alt; to what forty...okay?"

7:50:15 Erickson— "Twenty four...to, ah, ten point oh."

7:50:27 Falitz—"Did you ah, click the, ah, airport lights...make sure co-common traffic advisory frequency is set."

7:50:40 Falitz—"Click it seven times?"

7:50:42 Erickson—"Yup, yeah I got it now."

7:50:42.5 (sound of scrape lasting for 0.1 seconds)

7:50.42.9 (sound of raspy grind lasting for .7 seconds)

7:50.43 (sound similar to increase in propeller rpm frequency)

7:50.43.8 (momentary sound of raspy grind lasting for .2 seconds)

7:50.45.5 (recording ends)

With the end of the recording came the end of eighteen lives. Radio and television stations from around the country began calling us for details.

An all-news station from Australia, of all places, called and interviewed one of our producers on a live talk show. The Hibbing tragedy was getting exposure, putting us in the middle of a national story. There were allegations of tension between the two pilots, but the cockpit voice recorder showed none. A permanent memorial now marks the site of the crash.

In the end, the Air Line Pilots Association released a statement indicating its disappointment with federal investigators for singling out the captain as the "probable cause" of this accident. In part, their statement said, and I reported, "The captain was placed in the impossible position of having to fly the airplane, deal with poor visibility and icing conditions, operate without crucial safety equipment that is mandated for larger commercial aircraft, and compensate for the low experience level of the First Officer [co-pilot]."

Among those killed in the crash were Craig Sterle, Robert Tiburzi, William Valeri, and Bernice and George Angelo, all of Hibbing, and David Halteman and Everett Moore, both of Pickle Lake, Ontario. The youngest victim was eleven-year-old Tony Trujillo of Palmdale California, who was the only child on board and was flying to the Range to visit family.

Lorilei Valeri, the daughter of crash victim William Valeri, became consumed with a mission to make commuter airline travel safer. She started a non-profit organization to help promote airline safety and help families of others who have died in commuter airline crashes deal with their grief. She wanted families told in advance that they would be flying on commuter planes, which at the time of the Hibbing crash flew under a completely different and less stringent set of federal guidelines.

∞

Call it habit if you will, but I have a constant eye on the news wire services which now come into newsrooms by computer. The day of those loud clacking United Press and Associated Press machines is long gone, as is UPI itself. Today's younger journalists have no idea what a newsroom used to sound like, with those wire machines typing out stories twenty-four hours a day, seven days a week.

Printed news copy was torn from those machines and spiked along the walls under labels marked LOCAL, MINNESOTA, WISCONSIN, FEATURES, NATIONAL, INTERNATIONAL, and BULLETIN. You had a mess on your hands if you got behind on that job.

One evening in August 1987, I watched a story come across the wire about two Minnesota natives killed in a plane crash the day before. Northwest Airlines flight 255 crashed on takeoff from Detroit Metropolitan Airport, killing 157 people, up to that point the second-worst plane crash in United States aviation.

The wire mentioned that one of the victims was forty-three-year-old Mary Henry, a native of Virginia, Minnesota. As you can imagine, that got my attention. I also noticed that Mary was my age, yet the last name of Henry wasn't familiar. Reading further, I picked up on the victim's father's name, Cyril Wennen of Virginia. That's when it hit me—the victim was Mary Wennen, the girl I took to the high school prom in the eleventh grade.

The immediate phone call I placed to Cy was difficult, with both of us reminiscing about Mary. He told me that he began worrying about his daughter on Sunday night after hearing that a plane had gone down in Detroit on a flight to Phoenix. He was aware that Mary and her husband were stopping in Detroit that very day, and would be flying into Phoenix's Sky Harbor Airport, but he didn't know the flight number. We chatted about Mary's ready smile and her positive manner and outlook on life.

The next day, Cy told *Duluth News-Tribune* reporter Candace Renalls that Mary and I dated in our junior year, and Candace called me for a few quotes. I told her how the two of us got little work done in our art class, giggling all the time. Mary and her husband died on their nineteenth wedding anniversary, returning from a trip to Europe. Their plane was brought down by a powerful wind sheer.

∞

It was December 21, 1972, when I went on the air with a report that a North Central Airlines flight, bound for Duluth and International Falls, had crashed on takeoff in Chicago. Nine people were killed when the DC-9 jet struck a Delta Airlines Convair 880 from Florida that was taxiing to the terminal after landing. Three Duluthians and a Superiorite were on the North Central plane—and all of them escaped, barely.

The fact that TV station manager Frank Befera was also on the Duluth Airport Authority helped us get some of the facts through airport officials. The airport manager went as far as to set up a television set in the terminal lobby, allowing passengers to get information directly from us off the air.

Befera had contacts in high places, so we got details a lot quicker than Channels 3 and 6, and later in the evening we had the names of those on the plane. One of them was Raymond Higgins of Duluth, (no relation to WDIO's Ray Higgins), who helped get others off the burning aircraft. He said the DC-9 jet had just lifted off, when it struck the smaller Convair, a propeller-driven plane, then came "slamming back down [on the runway], on its belly."

∞

All stories about aircraft are not and should not be bad news stories, taking into account an airplane success story called Cirrus Design. The Duluth-based airplane maker has become a major player in the building of a four-place, high-performance aircraft, which in 2004, topped Cessna in terms of sales.

Cirrus began its operations in a Baraboo, Wisconsin, barn, with brothers Alan and Dale Klapmeier at the wheel. In 1994, they moved to Duluth, to launch the SR20 and SR22. Within ten years they overtook Cessna, which for a long, long time was the number one manufacturer of small planes.

An infusion of $100 million from an Atlanta-based venture capital company took Cirrus to a new level, out of the hands of private ownership but with more money than it ever had, to pay down debt and to cash out early stockholders. The rest was used to increase their production technology and get some key people on board.

Like all companies involved in flight, they've had some tragedies, including the deaths of two test pilots and crashes involving their production planes. Colonel Bob Overmyer died flying the company's VK-30 aircraft—which the NTSB found "had inadequate handling and performance design capabilities"—crashing the plane nose first into the ground not far from the airport. And Major Scott Anderson, the company's chief test pilot in 1999, died when the SR-20 he was testing crashed into a building at the federal prison adjacent to the airport. And there have been a rash of crashes with consumers piloting the planes as well, with eleven people dying in Cirrus plane accidents in just three and a half years.

CEO Alan Klapmeier went to work focusing on improving pilot performance as they transition to these high-performance planes. Cirrus has survived these tragedies and solved the problems that caused them. They have earned a great deal of global attention from national publications, which have touted Cirrus planes as the first certified civil airplanes that come equipped with a parachute—which have been successfully deployed in emergencies, saving lives. Cirrus is enjoying a great run, and if general aviation continues to grow as fast as it has after the dreaded terrorist attacks of 9/11, the company should have a fabulous future.

Chapter 17

STRANGE STORIES

As important as journalism is in my life, it doesn't encompass my entire thought process twenty-four hours a day. I have many interests, not the least of which includes reading, fishing, and even home improvement. Some of that is done to save a dollar or two.

Take for example my refusal to call the plumber when our sewer became plugged. After hours of trying to snake the manhole clear, I went out and got a sump pump to get rid of the standing water. With the pump in place, I asked Judy to plug it in. That was a mistake. The hose came loose from the pump, and human feces went flying in three directions, much of it across my face and teeth. Judy collapsed to her knees in laughter, while I stood in one spot shouting, "AAAHHHHH! AAAHH-HHHH! AAAHHHHHH!"

Fearing that I might have been poisoned, I insisted Judy call my doctor to see if I should come in. After a slight chuckle, he told her I should be fine, "just have him brush his teeth and rinse his mouth with Listerine." That's why I'm a journalist, not a plumber.

∞

My attention has been drawn to a good many stories, some of which lasted for a year or more. The end of 1999, and the beginning of 2000, was not just the changing of a year, but was thought of as the end of a decade, a century, and a millennium.

For a solid year or better, we had been reporting on the much-feared Y2K bug—which in reality turned out to be the joke of the millennium—and a lot of people fell for it hook, line, and sinker. While companies, agencies, and industries all over the world had to make certain their computers would change over at 2000, there were certain other people who had money to make.

They wrote books warning that the nation, if not the world, was in peril, that banks and utilities would fail at the strike of midnight. Stock up on food, they warned. Buy an electric generator. Get your bottled water while you still had time. Don't get on an airplane on New Year's Eve. Install a gas fireplace or a wood burner. The sky is falling, the sky is falling. Look out, Chicken Little.

They had an agenda: write books, sell books, make millions. People all over the country were scared into buying these books and their writers smiled all the way to the bank, the very banks they were warning us to be leery of.

We in the newsroom measured our stories on Y2K, but we did report on how the public was reacting to these doomsday prophets who warned that there would be a worldwide computer breakdown at midnight, putting the globe in turmoil.

I was live on the air hosting the St. Mary's/Duluth Clinic New Year's Eve Party from the DECC when the millennium changed. The lights did not go out, the TV cameras didn't shut down, there was no panic in the crowd, and no airplanes fell from the sky.

I'm old enough to know that many of the world's inhabitants need to believe in legends and folklore—for what reason is unexplainable. Tens of millions believe that planet earth gets regular visits from life outside our solar system, that UFOs regularly zoom into our skies to check us out.

Is there intelligent life on other planets? Personally, I don't think so, and I think flying saucers are a lot of hoopla. "Why," I ask myself, "would other life forms come this far to check us out and not make contact?" Just because there seems to be no explanation for strange lights in the sky—or some story that Uncle Charlie swears is true—doesn't mean they came from Planet X. Much of life can't be explained.

And what about those, you ask, who say they were taken aboard spaceships by aliens, then released after some mysterious flight into the unknown? Garbage.

If flying spooks aren't enough, then we need Bigfoot, the two-legged ape-like creatures spotted all over the world, but never really proven. They've been "seen" from America's Pacific Northwest to the Himalayas. I call it vivid imagination, another pipe dream perpetrated by that forty-year-old piece of 8 mm movie film where the ape-man is seen walking through a wooded area swinging his arms at his side. You know the one I mean—the hairy giant pauses for a moment, looks at the camera from a distance, and strides off. Recently an investigator tracked down the guy who made the Bigfoot suit and the guy who wore it.

Is there a monster swimming in the cold waters of Loch Ness? I call it a tourist trap, promulgated by more bogus pictures. The most famous photo of the Loch Ness Monster, taken years ago, proved to be a model neck stuck onto a toy submarine, as confessed late in life by one of those involved in the hoax.

Was more than one person involved in the assassination of President Kennedy? Was President Lyndon Johnson involved in Kennedy's death? Did he order the killing? Did Lee Harvey Oswald act alone? People love a conspiracy, and despite computer enhancements of the assassination, and in particular, the single-bullet theory recently put to the test on ABC, some folks will never be convinced that Oswald acted alone.

It was that same need for mystery and conspiracy that fueled Y2K. I have an acquaintance who was not only convinced that the lights would go out, he was certain January 1, 2000, would mark the end of the world. So he stocked a small room in his basement with enough provisions to last a month, never telling me why he thought he would survive if everyone else died. He even bought a recliner to wait out Armageddon in comfort. No matter what anyone said, you could not convince him that he was wrong. Frank, I'm the first to say, "I told you so." Y2K turned out to be a fart in the wind.

∞

All sorts of telephone calls come into the newsroom night and day. Some are from people offering news tips to our staff, while others come from viewers complaining about something they saw or heard on the news. Still other calls come from folks who are lonely and need to talk. I've had a couple calls over the years from people who are convinced that I am spying on them, that I can actually see them through the TV camera. Another caller said he just wanted to let me know that I was an ass.

Once a viewer called and said he had found thousands of dollars in cash and endorsed checks inside a bank bag, and that he felt safer calling me than anyone else. I went to his house to verify his story, where we called the police.

It turned out that the money bag had been put on the roof of a car while the driver was preparing to take his company's daily receipts to the bank. He forgot about the money while loading other items into the car and drove off, causing the bag to fall to the ground. The caller got a reward, and I got my story.

∞

One night a call came for me during the middle of the ten o'clock news, and obviously it's impossible to walk off the air to answer the phone. Most of the time I don't answer newsroom calls anyway, simply because so many people want to talk with me even though someone else could easily help them. This particular caller was agitated and insisted that he absolutely "had to talk with Dennis Anderson." He said he was being held hostage.

That got my attention, so during the sports segment I dashed back into the newsroom to check on this guy. The voice on the other end of the line told me that he and three others were being held hostage at gunpoint inside the main guardhouse at the Mt. Iron Minntac Plant. He said something about hundreds of people coming there to blow up Minntac, and other taconite plants across the Range.

I scribbled a note telling another newsroom staffer to call the sheriff's department to get them to trace the line, or at least alert them to what was happening. Remember, we didn't know if this was a kook or a legitimate call.

Seconds later, another voice came on the line, this one a man who identified himself by name as someone who had gone to high school with me. He told me in no uncertain terms that if I came to the scene, our news cameras would have to be kept "two hundred yards from the guardhouse, or I'll shoot." He also expressed anger for my alleged snub of him at one of our high school reunions. Then he hung up.

While Ken Chapin was on the weather segment, I placed a call to the St. Louis County Sheriff's office. The night dispatcher admitted they were aware of the situation. Once the broadcast ended, I called C. W. Niemi, the superintendent of Minntac operations, who said he also got a call and that the incident "is apparently real."

The perpetrator told authorities that a number of things were bothering him at work and that several media outlets needed to be notified, including me at WDIO. The *Mesabi Daily News* in Virginia was also called, as were radio stations on the Range and in Minneapolis.

A half hour after talking with me, he released one of his hostages after mentioning that it was time for him to take his high blood pressure pills.

About a dozen sheriff's deputies spent the better part of the night on the scene working to defuse the situation. We sent a news crew there which came back with the story very early in the morning. One of the men held hostage told the *Duluth News-Tribune* the next day that, "I never felt threatened. He [the gunman] kept asking, 'Are you comfortable?'"

The gunman did fire a couple of shots at a floodlight, but no one was hurt. It was almost five o'clock in the morning when the ordeal came to an end, and the thirty-five-year-old man was taken into custody.

∞

Police and firefighters are regularly called under unusual circumstances, as they were on the Fourth of July, 1988. That was the year the city's famous pyrotechnic show lasted all of ten minutes, setting off a grand finale the likes of which we had not seen before—or since.

Channel 10 has three remote television cameras permanently mounted outside the TV station. One is about three quarters of the way up our broadcast tower on Observation Road, another is on the roof of the DECC, and the third is on Channel 13's tower in rural Hibbing. We use the Duluth tower and DECC cameras each Fourth of July to show a live segment of the city's fireworks display—this time something went wrong.

A dud didn't get far off the ground, falling on other fireworks that were being set up for the show's grand finale. The resulting explosion sent dozens of rockets blasting off in all directions, many of them running horizontally just a few feet off the ground, raining sparks on the thousands of people who were at the waterfront to watch.

I had taken my family there, and for a few moments we thought this was part of the show. Then it became clear that it wasn't, and people ran screaming, leaving behind lawn chairs, blankets, and beverage coolers. Others fell flat to the ground to keep from getting hit by flying rockets and sparks.

Those watching the event live on Channel 10 weren't sure what they were seeing. That's because our anchor that evening didn't realize that this unusual but colorful display wasn't part of the how, until someone from the newsroom ran into the studio and told him that this was an accidental explosion.

Seconds after the explosions stopped, and with a heavy pall of sulfur smoke hanging above the bayfront, the sound of police and fire sirens pierced the air, seemingly coming from all directions, including the main fire hall just a few blocks away. Within minutes there were eleven fire trucks on the scene, along with thirty firefighters.

The explosions had ignited a nearby construction site located near liquid propane tanks, quickly getting a great deal of attention. The tanks never blew. City fire crews were helped by two Coast Guard boats using water cannons to spray down the area, putting out several small fires. Local paramedics set up a triage area, tending to people who had minor burns, but no one was seriously hurt.

Fortunately we also had news cameras at the scene taping the event, so we had extraordinary pictures on the air the next day. A spokesman for the fireworks company said that $33,000 worth of fireworks went up in one gigantic explosion, including shells that were up to twenty-four and thirty-six inches long. The thirty-six-inch shells had the explosive power of several sticks of dynamite. Our video was given to ABC News, which in turn sent the story to their affiliates through a closed circuit system, for use in local newscasts across the country.

∞

Some of the stories that we report are truly bizarre. Take, for example, the ocean ship leaving the Twin Ports for its journey overseas when its crew got a gruesome surprise. As the ship's anchor was lifted from the muddy harbor bottom, it caught on, and pulled to the surface, a sunken automobile. Inside the car were two bodies, a man and a woman. The two had been reported missing exactly five years earlier to the day. It was widely believed they accidentally drove the car off a pier and into the water, but what they were doing on the pier in the first place is anyone's guess.

Then there was the story of the woman found mummified in her Duluth home. She hadn't been seen in years, yet her lawn was regularly mowed, the postman delivered the mail, and the bills got paid by a family member. She had died of natural causes.

And in August 2004, there was another mummified body found, this one in Winnipeg. All his condominium bills had been paid after he died in bed two years earlier. One friend asked, "How can that happen, for God's sake?"

Chapter 18

MINNESOTA GOVERNORS

Only once did I meet Minnesota's one-time boy governor, Harold Stassen, who became the state's perennial presidential candidate, running more often than Gus Hall. Stassen and I met in 1988 for a rare interview in the ornate lobby of the former Hotel Duluth, and the first thing that caught my attention was Stassen's ill-fitting toupee.

The second thing was the need to pull every answer out of him. On that day, he out-silenced "Silent Cal," President Calvin Coolidge, of whom Will Rogers said, "Coolidge didn't say much, and when he did he didn't say much." I was more impressed with meeting Stassen than getting the interview, which was dull and flat and barely usable on the air.

Stassen, who died in 2001 at the age of ninety-three, ran for the presidency no less than nine times, the last in 1992. His best shot at getting the Republican nomination was in 1948, which he lost to Thomas Dewey, who in turn lost the election to Harry Truman.

Just thirty-one years old when he became governor, Stassen was the youngest ever in the history of the state. He was a liberal Republican and considered to be progressive when it came to social issues. Stassen resigned from office while in his third term, even though still popular, to join the Navy.

∞

A lot of governors have occupied the mansion on St. Paul's fashionable Summit Avenue, and far and away the two most interesting in the past fifty years have been Rudy Perpich and Jesse Ventura. One was a dentist turned governor and the other a professional wrestler turned governor. Both thought about running for the White House (neither had a snowball's chance), and neither cared about conventional politics. They both were opinionated and boisterous, and let you know when they felt you crossed the line—which was fairly often.

Rudy was Minnesota's longest-serving chief executive, and as I said in an editorial when he died, "He was many people wrapped into one." He could be arrogant, stubborn to a fault, warm, unselfish, and a champion for the middle-class no matter what it cost the taxpayer. His biggest national claim to fame was when a national news magazine branded him "Governor Goofy," a name that stuck for the rest of his time in office.

Perpich had called the media together at the very headwaters of the Mississippi River, with reporters believing that he was going to make a major announcement. It was nothing more than something laconic, like, "I'm running for re-election." He dragged the media that far out of the way for that simple announcement. Rudy may have thought it was unique, but the media was not impressed, thinking he had lost it.

Perpich once got into a war of words during an on-air feud with WDIO's *Capitol Corridors* pundit Carl D'Aquila, which forced me and Chisholm newspaper publisher Veda Ponikvar into the fray.

The three of us appeared on the weekly TV show, taking a candid look at the issues facing the governor, the legislature, and the people of Minnesota. We had many distinguished guests on *Capitol Corridors*, which we often taped on Thursdays in the WDIO studios or at KSTP in Minneapolis. We'd fly down in the morning, then catch a late-afternoon flight north after the taping session. Those guests included a variety of politicians the likes of Vice President Walter Mondale, Minnesota Governor and U.S. Senator Wendell Anderson, many Minnesota lawmakers from both parties, and even Alabama Governor George Wallace.

The feud with Perpich started when the governor got into a heated debate with D'Aquila—who had served as a Republican legislator years earlier—on Hibbing's WMFG radio, over the taconite-production tax, Perpich complained that D'Aquila had wrongly accused him of supporting a bill that would have sharply increased the tax. The governor, on the air, called Carl "the worst possible liar in this state."

That was just the opening volley. Perpich's brother George, who was then a state senator, wrote a letter to the editor asking to see some of the five- to six hundred letters that D'Aquila said he got each week in support of his political positions.

Then the feud moved over to our *Capitol Corridors*, program when the governor appeared as an invited guest. By now this very public skirmish was getting press from one end of the state to the other, and two Minneapolis television stations set up their news cameras in our studios to catch the fur flying. Newspaper reporters from the Range, Duluth, and the Twin Cities sat behind the cameras, with pencils and notebooks at the ready.

After introducing Governor Perpich, I gave D'Aquila the first shot in this on-air rematch, and Perpich didn't like it. He quickly interrupted me saying, "I've been on a lot of programs and this is the first time they didn't even ask the governor to say hello." From that moment on, the gloves were off, and Perpich vehemently denied running for Congress as D'Aquila had often intimated.

The governor looked directly into one of the TV cameras and said, "I want to let the public know that if you ever see my name on the ballot for United States Senator, you vote against me. I have no intention of running for the Senate and wouldn't take it as an appointment." Then looking right at D'Aquila and raising his finger, Perpich said, "I'll tell you what I'll do right after this program is over. I'll sign a statement saying that if I ever run for the United States Senate or if I ever accept an appointment, all my worldly possessions will go to you. And I expect you to do the same with all your worldly possessions if I don't file or show an interest in the Senate." Such a declaration was never signed, but his comments did make for good television, and it silenced the debate over any run for Congress.

Brother George wrote another letter to the editor in which he said, "I have maintained that the sole purpose of the television program *Capitol Corridors* is to take political punches at the Perpiches."

Then I got letters, many of them. They accused me of being Republican, anti-Perpich, and rude. One viewer wrote: "Anderson, you owe the governor an apology, and I'll never watch you again until you do." Another was put this way: "Dennis, you are way off base, shame on you. Veda and Carl, stay home and practice your tennis."

When the long-running show came to an end, we got letters asking us to continue, but the program was pulled after running its course.

Richard Berrier, the manager of the Hibbing Chamber of Commerce, paid me a wonderful compliment in a letter to the *Hibbing Tribune's* "Open Forum": "Denny Anderson of WDIO should be commended for doing an outstanding job as moderator. His fairness, honesty and dedication has added much to the program."

It should be mentioned that Governor Perpich and I never again brought up the feud to each other. Many interviews followed his *Capitol Corridors,* appearance, and he and his wife Lola once invited me to join them for a lunch after a funeral service.

∞

Even the decision about which of Perpich's pictures should hang in the capitol became a public battle royal. The original picture was installed in the capitol after his first term, which was three years. Four years out of office, he ran again and won, and because he served two nonconsecutive terms, he thought he should have two separate portraits. His critics thought he had a lot of gall. Eventually a second portrait, depicting his wife Lola at his side, was allowed, but this one had to be paid for by private monies. At that time, the first portrait came down, and just one hangs in the capitol.

In the end, Governor Perpich wore out his welcome with the voters. He served ten years as governor, once without getting his own party's endorsement. It was the longest tenure in state history, but he was defeated for re-election in 1990. Even so, and right up to the end of his life, he talked about making a comeback in 1994.

In the meantime, he served as a trade consultant to the government of Croatia and lived in Zagreb, the capitol of the Yugoslav Republic. He said if he ran again, he planned to ignore his party's endorsing convention and run as an independent.

By mid-1994, and just five hours before the filing deadline, Rudy told WCCO-Radio that he was not financially ready to seek re-election that year, but would in 1998. Rudy Perpich died of colon cancer in September 1995, with only a few people aware that he was gravely ill.

He was, for the most part, revered on the Iron Range, where Ironworld stands as a memorial—albeit a costly one that consistently loses money. Rudy was the son of immigrant parents, and he felt that the Range needed an interpretative center where the story of the great melting pot could be told. He was a product of that melting pot, a first-generation son born in America, a heritage of which he was fiercely proud. And he sounded like an Iron Ranger, a dialect that is detectable in those of us who came from there, although more pronounced in some.

A website (at www.geocities.com/Heartland/1302/perpich.html at the time of writing) is filled with accolades for the late governor. The president of the Minneapolis NAACP said, "[Perpich] broke down barriers for people of color." Bill Davis said the governor "came across as a person who understood poverty." A woman from Keewatin spoke of his great respect for Lola, calling it "one of the most genuine love matches I have ever seen."

A fellow from Willmar says, "I was putting gas in my car and here comes Rudy. No staff, no security, no troopers. He said, 'I'm tired. I escaped to the country today.' He was just out driving around all by himself, talking to people. That was Rudy."

Marlene Johnson, his Lieutenant Governor, wrote, "I think Rudy made half of his decisions while eating ice cream or carrot cake. He called me once to meet him at The Brothers at Southdale. At the time, I didn't know that the man never ate a vegetable. He said matter-of-factly: 'Do you want to run for Lieutenant Governor?' I was so taken aback...I said something like, 'Why are we doing this in such a public place?' He responded, while eating his triple-scoop chocolate sundae, 'Oh, this is fine. The ice cream is good here.'"

U.S. Representative David Minge of Minnesota's 2nd District wrote, "Before most of us had even heard the phrase 'global economy,' Governor Perpich was advocating for companies on the international level. Without his leadership, the state would have entered this era a step behind, instead of a leap ahead of the pack."

The Range, its Democrats especially, was thrilled to have a governor from their own backyard, feeling they were well-represented in St. Paul. While Rudy Perpich contemplated running again as an independent, he was a DFLer at heart.

∞

To say that Governor Jesse Ventura was the most unusual of governors is an understatement. He came on the scene as a member of the Reform Party, and many people thought his run for office was a joke. Here was a former pro wrestler (often seen decked out in shocking pink tights and a pink boa), a radio talk show host, an actor, a one-time Navy Seal, and a former mayor of Brooklyn Park, Minnesota, all rolled into one. But he showed the establishment just who could get the last laugh.

He embarrassed the major parties by defeating their candidates, Democrat Skip Humphrey and Republican Norm Coleman, both mainline candidates who were humiliated when the voters gave Ventura thirty-seven percent of the vote. He convinced young voters that they had a voice and it should be used, and for that Ventura should be congratulated. When the results came in, he told his supporters, "Mom and Dad, [who are deceased] are looking down and saying, 'I can't believe it, look what he's done now.'" The next day's headline in the *Duluth News-*

Tribune, printed in bold lettering above the fold, read "BODY SLAM." Great headline.

In his inaugural address, Governor Ventura said, "We must put down the partisan party politics and look at the bigger picture. We must look at the picture of these young people who have now come on board, who want to vote and take part in the great thing we have here called the United States of America and the State of Minnesota." He stressed in his campaign, in his inaugural address, and for the next four years that, "The one thing you'll get from Governor Jesse Ventura, you may not always want to hear, but you will get honesty." He concluded his remarks with a boisterous "Hoo-Yah!" His friend Arnold Schwarzenegger, now governor of California, attended the inauguration.

So began the four-year reign of Governor Ventura, which was not an easy ride for him, the state legislature, or the media. From the start he did things his way. He appointed Alan Horner as the state's Natural Resources Commissioner. It didn't matter to the new governor that Horner had been cited three times for game and fish violations. The governor said the violations were minor and technical.

One of the governor's early pet projects was to live up to a campaign promise to cut taxes, cut motor vehicle license tab fees, and pass a sales tax rebate for more than two million eligible taxpayers. The bill approved by the Senate was a modified version of the sales tax rebate proposal, designed to return $1.1 billion to the people.

The House approved an income tax rebate, giving back $1.1 billion to 1.9 million taxpayers. Eventually, legislative negotiators reached a budget deal that included a long-term tax cut of at least a half-point percentage on all three income tax rates, and $100 million in new spending for K-12 education.

Just a month into office, the governor granted me an interview at his Capitol office, the first of several he would give over the years. I said in my report that the governor almost looked out of place behind his big desk, which didn't matter to his constituents. Just a few months into office he had a seventy-five percent approval rating, which months later dropped to fifty-four percent. He said he didn't care.

He once granted me an interview in his hotel room on a visit to Duluth, something not usually done by governors. I found him less intimidating one-on-one, unlike his approach at news conferences where he would sometimes verbally beat up the media, the "jackals," as he liked to call us. Yes, we can be used, and he knew which buttons to push, all the while realizing that it was the media that had propelled him into the national spotlight.

Every once in a while he would engage his mouth before his brain, one time getting heat for what he said on *The Late Show with David Letterman.* He suggested that St. Paul's street system was designed by drunken Irishmen. St. Paul Mayor Norm Coleman, now Senator Coleman, wasn't amused. But then again, Coleman lost the election to Ventura. Another time he was quoted in *Playboy* as saying, "Organized religion is a sham and a crutch for weak-minded people." That went over like a lead balloon. And there was the time when he said he had "no respect for people who commit suicide because they are weak."

His controversial book, *I Ain't Got Time to Bleed,* raised the eyebrows of some lawmakers who said the autobiography sent the wrong message to kids. In it, the governor wrote about losing his virginity at age sixteen, using the services of prostitutes, underage drinking, smoking marijuana, and a few other things that would make most parents of teens cringe.

But young people loved his honesty, and the day after the book hit the stands, the governor got what the Associated Press called "a wildly enthusiastic welcome" from students at Grand Rapids High School, where he spoke the day before the Minnesota fishing opener.

Ventura was often in a budget chopping mood, which included funding to public broadcasters who pleaded with lawmakers not to cut their monies. The governor said it was time they stood on their own, that their funding would have to go.

His first legislative session found the governor feeling his way and lawmakers trying to hold their own against him. They learned to tolerate each other for the next three years, although he pushed the idea of a unicameral legislature, which I favor. Minnesota has one of the largest legislatures in the country when it comes to numbers of lawmakers compared to its population; we don't need two legislative bodies in St. Paul.

Ventura got mad on more than one occasion, and in one of his last gestures against the grain, he decided to move out of the governor's mansion on 1006 Summit Avenue and close the place. The sixteen-thousand-square-foot English Tudor house isn't something you just decide to close up—after all, it belongs to the state.

Some Minnesotans would come to see Ventura as an embarrassment, and in the end he chose not to seek a second term. He seemed to be reinventing himself throughout his term, becoming something of a promotion machine, probably realizing that he would need a job if this governor's gig didn't work out. I believe he chose not to run for a second term because he would have lost. One thing can be said with certainty: he was never boring.

∞

Governor Tim Pawlenty occupies 1006 Summit as I finish this book. Karl Rolvaag, the state's Democratic governor from 1963 to 1967, and his wife Florence were the mansion's first residents. Rolvaag ran for reelection against Republican Harold LeVander, but unfortunately for Rolvaag, his own lieutenant governor, A. M. "Sandy" Keith, decided he wanted the state's top job too. He ran against his boss, splitting the party.

Rolvaag was making a campaign swing from Aurora to Grand Rapids, and after his stop in Virginia, I decided to follow along with the WHLB radio mobile unit to do live reports from each city along the way. As we got ready to leave Hibbing, the governor said he wanted to ride with me and get an idea what people on the Range were saying about him.

So, Rolvaag climbed into the front seat, and a state trooper jumped into the back, for the ride to Grand Rapids. I told him, "Governor, I think your going to lose the election." He got out in Keewatin, just eight miles down the road. Sandy Keith's effort to unseat Rolvaag did nothing but divide party voters and LeVander won.

An older and long-retired Karl Rolvaag eventually moved to Northeastern Minnesota, and he called me on three or four occasions after newscasts, just to chat and pick my brain about Minnesota politics. I actually saw him only twice after he lost in 1967; once in Duluth and once at a party on a lake just north of Virginia. I never reminded him that it was me who told him he would lose in that radio news cruiser so long ago.

Chapter 19

OPINIONS AND PET PEEVES

Many people have asked if I'm tired of reporting nothing but bad news. Well folks, it's not all bad, not by a long shot. Most local newscasts are a good mix of stories. Former network correspondent Connie Chung said, "Viewers want to know that local anchors care. They want to feel the anchors are involved with them. There's a feeling of distance between the viewers and network news and its 'stars.' Local news is about people."

Some news viewers will watch whomever they simply like looking at. It's an impression a viewer gets from the newscaster, and if it's favorable they'll watch. It may be nothing more than the way the anchor delivers the news, the tone of voice. Or it may be as shallow as the way the broadcaster combs his or her hair, a smile, the eyes, clothing worn, mannerisms. The audience is choosy yet fickle.

It should almost go without saying that the greatest element a newscaster must possess is trust. Does he or she have a reputation for being fair? Do they have a history of covering the news without bias? Is the newscaster relaxed, not uptight? Real, or plastic and phony?

I believe people have learned to trust me. Like Rome, trust can't be built in a day but over a long time. You don't sit down in front of a television camera for the first time and say to the audience, "Here I am, you can trust me." Your viewers have every right to say in return, "Prove it;" something I attempt to do every day. It's humbling when someone calls you the "dean of television broadcasting" in this area, as columnist Dick Palmer did in a profile published in July 1996.

Trust means honesty and fair play. Those are key words when it comes to the public and how they perceive a newscaster. Granted, some audience members just don't care, but folks who truly demand something more from their anchor than a pretty smile and a sweet demeanor are probably more serious news watchers.

∞

News organizations must have commitment, and Channel 10 has a commitment that dates back to the early days of manager Frank Befera. He believed in three things: making money, a strong news organization, and making money. Frank would ask, "What's the best program on television?" and like a tired joke he would give the answer: "A sold program." A TV station can't exist without sponsors.

Every good news organization must also have experience, an attribute sometimes lacking in many newsrooms today. Older, more seasoned reporters have left the business frustrated, while others have retired. As our older stable of reporters leaves, younger reporters move in and replace them. The trick is to keep a balance of older, more experienced reporters along with younger, fresher voices who will become the experienced reporters themselves and who bring a different perspective to the news. Unfortunately, seasoned reporters retire or move on to larger pastures or entirely different careers. And the Duluth market is too often just a starting point for promising journalists, and many of our future stars head off seeking opportunities in larger markets, hoping to one day work for the networks.

Upon his retirement, the late WCCO-TV newscaster Dave Moore said, "I think every station ought to have not only somebody who has aged, as I am, but somebody who's working on native soil.... An older person who has worked here and knows something about [local people and issues] can give a news organization something that younger people simply can't." The Minneapolis newscaster hit the nail on the head. I have the advantage of perspective given only to those of us who have lasted awhile.

And accuracy counts. To be less than accurate, or to demand less than accuracy, is to cheat the viewer. Recently I was sitting with a man who was the subject of a story in a local radio newscast. It was a story favorable to this gentleman, but as we listened he counted five factual errors in the report. Balance, accuracy, and fairness walk together as partners in journalism. When you have balance and when you attain accuracy, you have fairness. Trust me.

∞

So if you think that the news media is an infallible institution, allow me to burst your bubble. On the other hand, if you think the media, both broadcast and print, is made up of men and women with their own axes to grind, private causes, pet peeves, and preconceived notions, just like the rest of society, you're right.

For example, allow me to say that I'm a firm believer in the right to bear arms as granted by the United States Constitution. I also believe in Minnesota's conceal-and-carry gun law—and although some feared that there would be gunfights in the streets and vigilante action in our neighborhoods, we have not had a return to the days of the Wild West since its inception. But my belief in conceal-and-carry does not mean that I personally want to carry a gun. There is no need for me to pack a rod under my suit jacket.

Here's another opinion: I'm opposed to the death penalty. Minnesota abolished it in 1906 after the botched hanging of twenty-eight-year-old William Williams. He had been convicted of killing two people, a sixteen-year-old friend and his friend's mother.

His executioners failed to take into account the stretch of the rope; after the trapdoor was sprung Williams fell until his feet touched the floor. They had to hoist him back up a few inches, and it took fourteen minutes to snuff out his life.

He was strangled, not hanged, and critics of the death penalty were mortified. So was Governor Adolph Eberhart, who, after lawmakers battled for a half-dozen years, signed the bill to abolish executions in Minnesota. Five times since, most recently in 1997, attempts have been made to reinstate executions, each time meeting failure.

Citizens and lawmakers are sick of violent and repeat offenders, but the law provides for life in prison without possibility of parole under some circumstances, such as the killing of a police officer. So I am not in favor of a return to capital punishment.

But I also want you to know that most of us journalists are able to lay our personal agenda aside while practicing our craft. However, and this is most important, know that each story you hear, see, or read is that one reporter's interpretation of an event, and nothing more.

Even when I don't agree with a story, I have to remind myself that the fourth estate is a collection of professionals dedicated to the idea that a free press helps keep the rest of us free.

The day the government takes away that freedom is the day America has lost its freedom.

∞

To me, one of the most annoying aspects of modern journalism is the dual anchor format—you could say it's my pet peeve. I don't like it—never have, never will. The anchors not only get in one another's way, they get in the way of good journalism. Putting two anchors on a newscast is show business, and news is not show biz. People often tell me they are glad that I am a solo anchor.

What about the famous twosome of Chet Huntley and David Brinkley, you ask? That seemed to work well when NBC television paired them for the Huntley-Brinkley Report in the 1960s. Indeed it did, but most of us forget that Mr. Huntley was the main anchor and read most of the news. David Brinkley handled just Washington-based news, most of which was political and often seen toward the end of the half-hour. Hence, Brinkley was more an addendum to the newscast than a co-anchor in the sense of what we see today.

For a brief period in the early 1970s I was teamed with Jack McKenna as dual anchors. Jack's popularity as a weatherman was legendary, something Channel 10 wanted to cash in on as a co-host of the six o'clock news. So Jack and I sat together—and it didn't work. We were both uncomfortable and it showed. As good a weatherman as he is, Jack is not a news anchor. As a news reader he was stiff and unnatural, unlike the work he was noted for, the brilliant weather presenter and commercial pitchman.

Cindy Brucato, who began her broadcast career in Duluth, also shared the anchor desk with me for a few months, but that didn't work either. She want on to become Governor Arne Carlson's communications director and a public relations consultant.

Perhaps the most famous dual-anchor flop in television history was ABC's attempt to team Harry Reasoner with Barbara Walters. Harry had come over from CBS where he had successfully co-hosted *60 Minutes*. Barbara had been enticed away from NBC for a cool million dollars, a staggering sum in those days, becoming the first million-dollar anchor in the history of news broadcasting. The partnering of these two was doomed from the start. It's legendary how Harry couldn't stand Barbara and it showed on the air. That wasn't makeup on Harry's face, it was misery painted all over him. Barbara is still on the air and Harry is dead, buried in his native Iowa.

Another network multiple-anchor newscast that didn't work was ABC's effort at no less than three anchors. In the early 1980s, they teamed Frank Reynolds, Max Robinson and Peter Jennings. Yup, a triple-whammy. It flopped, and ABC returned to a single-anchor newscast. Peter Jennings returned solo after the death of Frank Reynolds. Max Robinson has also died.

One of the problems with the dual-anchor format is that it involves bantering back and forth for no other reason than to put two people on the desk to look friendly. The term in the industry is "warm and fuzzy," but the "conversations" usually come across as forced. Too often they sound something like this:

"Good evening, I'm Bobby Doright,"

"And I'm Cindy Smiles. Bobby, there was an ax murder over on 40th last night and police are still there collecting evidence."

"And Cindy, it looks like this could be a long investigation."

"That's right, Bobby. Police tell us they are stymied."

"Cindy, our crime reporter Lucy Leadbottom is live as the scene."

"Yes she is Bobby, let's go live to Lucy."

Then Lucy chimes in with ninety seconds of details, before tossing it back to the twosome at the anchor desk, who add more inane chatter:

"Thanks, Lucy. Well, Bobby, it sounds like the police have their hands full tonight."

"It sure does, Cindy."

See what I mean? Just tell the viewer the story. There's more time for more information without the useless banter.

Even single anchors aren't on the air very much in a thirty-minute newscast. Considering the news intro with music, commercials, news bumpers that tease the upcoming segment, and a news close, the anchor is actually seen for only three or four minutes. Out of that same thirty-minute newscast, only twelve to thirteen minutes are actual news content, and most of that time is video or live coverage from the field. The rest of the half hour is composed of weather and sports, and of course the commercials that pay our salaries.

Naturally, broadcast journalists want to get on the air as often as possible. After all, that's the reason they went into the business, to tell stories, to broadcast news, and to do that you have to be given air time.

The vast majority of broadcast journalists do not belong in the anchor seat. I know many who can sniff out a story with the best of them. They are good journalists who practice their craft with care and sincerity, and they do a first-class job of telling that story on the air. They are masters at what they do, but that doesn't automatically make them a good anchor.

Anchoring a newscast is more than reading. It is understanding the news of the day, and making sure that what the anchor understands is transferable to the audience. It is about being comfortable in front of a large audience, albeit unseen. It is about mastering the language. It is making the newscast flow. It is being calm even in the face of calamity.

A television audience will not warm up to an anchorperson who is stiff, nervous, makes reading blunders, speaks poorly, or uses poor grammar. You'd be surprised at the number of young men and women who come out of college and can't write a simple declarative sentence. More than anything, journalists, including anchors, need to be good writers, story tellers par excellence.

The greatest satisfaction I get is when the closing video tape comes up at the end of the newscast and the announcer's voice intones, "More people get their news from *Eyewitness News* than from any other station."

∞

Besides dual anchors, I have plenty of other pet peeves. We all have things that bug us, and some are more serious than others. Some of these are guy things, others professional anxieties, and some don't mean a hill of beans in the big picture, but they still bug me.

At the risk of offending some of you, I'll tell you here and now that I don't like football much, especially professional football. Pro sports, in my opinion, can no longer be classified as sports, but are big business instead.

Pro athletes are demanding and getting such exorbitant salaries that they have turned stadium audiences into an elitist crowd. You not only pay for a pricey ticket, you still have the $6 hot dog, a $5 cup of beer, popcorn that will set you back several bucks, and there might be four or five of you in the family. You get the picture. The average working stiff can't afford to take his family to the ball game, which is pretty sad.

Yet there is nothing more fun than watching high school or college football, basketball, and hockey. Kids play their hearts out, for no other reason than the thrill of the game.

Here are more of my pet peeves, in no particular order:

1. Inattentive drivers.

2. Tailgating drivers.

3. Drivers who pull out in front of on-coming traffic.

4. Drivers who shift from one lane to the next trying to get ahead of others.

5. Inattentive drivers.

6. The news going on late following an ABC sports broadcast (e.g., Monday Night Football). It's not because I'm tired, but because the news audience shrinks dramatically the moment a game ends, so our work is seen by few people.

7. Journalists who say "totally destroyed." Come on, folks, it's either destroyed or damaged.

8. Journalists who tag every police story with the words, "The incident is under investigation." Of course it is, that's why police were called in the first place.

9. Journalists who wear their politics on their sleeve.

10. Inattentive drivers

11. Unbalanced checkbooks.

12. Public office holders who are cooperative with the media only at election time.

13. Sports stadiums with commercial names: Xcel Energy Center, Target Center, Miller Stadium, U.S. Cellular One Stadium. (You get the idea. If I were a sportscaster, I would never mention the commercial name of a sports stadium.)

14. Hallmark holidays—events that greeting card companies must have invented in order to sell more greeting cards. You know, Grandparents' Day, Mother's Day, Father's Day,

Retirements, a new job, get well, St. Valentine's Day, happy birthday, congratulations on whatever.

15. Inattentive drivers.

16. Folks who play judge and jury about another person's spiritual life.

17. Telephone solicitation.

18. Computer pop-ups.

19. Toilet paper draped the wrong way on the roller. (The paper should hang forward, Judy, not draped against the wall.)

20. Did I mention inattentive drivers?

See, I'm human after all, not just another pretty face on the tube. Actually, there are a few more pet peeves that could be listed. For instance, please don't ask me to "try this, you'll like it." That should have been on the list. I do like most foods, with the exception of Chinese food, foods from India, and some vegetables like asparagus, broccoli, cauliflower, Brussels spouts, and cabbage. My wife does have me drinking tea, something I associate with having the flu as a little boy.

And here's another thing: most of us born and raised on the Iron Range are fiercely proud of our heritage, but the Range is not another country, as some non-Rangers would have you believe. Not everyone drives around with a beer can in one hand and a rifle mounted in the back window of a pickup truck. But away from the Range, those stereotypes are hard to break.

Anyway, I asked my wife to guess what was listed here and wouldn't you know, she got most of them right. Even the one about the toilet paper.

∞

All this talk about pet peeves has me thinking about another important one of mine: the public is missing out on a major government function that should be seen by anyone who is interested. Television cameras should be allowed in the courtroom. They are long overdue, and their absence is just not right.

Television is many things: movies, history, art, home remodeling, sports, fine dining, news, medical miracles, home shopping, weather information, biographies, and other facets of life that help define who we are. Television should also be an open window to the court system.

The Court TV network has opened that window a little, but only in high-profile cases and only where allowed. Judges arbitrarily exclude cameras from their courts, and here at home there have been many cases that would have benefited the public had they been seen. Cameras and tape recorders in Minnesota courtrooms have been blocked by an impenetrable wall.

Forty-seven states allow television cameras in the courtroom with the judge's discretion. There is an outright ban on courtroom television cameras in Washington, D.C., South Dakota, Mississippi, and Indiana. The U.S. Judicial Conference, which is the policy arm of our federal courts, rejected a move in 1994 to allow cameras in those federal courtrooms on a permanent basis. That action has effectively banned cameras from federal courts for now, another loss for the American people.

The Northland and all parts of the country should be allowed to see their justice system at work, in federal, state, and county courts. Given that we are now in the twenty-first century, it is long overdue. It's a different story in Wisconsin, where a single TV camera, providing pool coverage to all stations, has been allowed for years and hasn't caused the problems feared by many in the legal system. One fear was that over-zealous lawyers would play to the camera or try to enhance courtroom drama. It hasn't happened locally. To my recollection, there has not been one foul-up on the part of the media that should cause our arrangement to be reversed.

Television news cameras are permitted in the Minnesota Supreme Court, but try taking cameras into the U.S. Supreme Court. Justice David Sauter said that would only occur "over his dead body."

The argument that members of the public are allowed to attend tri
als in person are old and worn. Courtrooms were not built for large
numbers of spectators, with just a half-dozen or so church-like benches
on each side of a middle aisle. Granted, many trials don't draw a crowd,
but if it has even a smidgen of public interest, you'd better get there early.
Once the benches are full, you don't get in. There is no such thing as
standing-room-only in a courtroom.

Television serves the public, and the public is best served when it is
included in its government. Let me repeat that: *the public is best served
when it is included in its government.* The court system is a large part of
government, which is composed of the executive, the legislative, and the
judicial branches, something we learned in high school. I've mentioned
before that our government is bloated, having become so large and powerful that it often forgets that it's working for us, not the other way
around. We must never lose sight of that fact. It is not enough to allow
twenty-five to thirty people to squeeze into a courtroom and say the public is being well-served. The public is being shortchanged when cameras
are excluded.

Chapter 20

IN THE LINE OF DUTY

Duluth's last police officer killed in the line of duty was Sergeant Gary Wilson. A few minutes into the ten o'clock news on Monday, April 9, 1990, an agitated reporter ran into the studio during a commercial break and with a breathless voice told me, "Two police officers were just involved in a shooting."

I asked, "Do you mean they did the shooting, or were they shot?"

"They were shot, and two ambulances have been called. Police are coming in from all over the place."

I told the reporter to "confirm the shootings, then run back and tell me what you know." Moments later he was back in the studio, just off camera, handing me several notes. Now I had a decision to make; should I go on the air immediately with what we knew, or should I hold off for a few minutes? After all, off-duty police officers and other cops' families were probably watching the news, and this is how they would get their first information that two of their "brothers in blue" had been shot.

I ran to the newsroom during a commercial break and listened to the police scanners as officers called for additional help at the Seaway Hotel at Twentieth Avenue West and Superior Street. They were on the scene demanding ambulances and telling their radio dispatcher and other approaching squads that they had confirmed two officers were down.

It's not my usual policy to grab information right off the scanner and put it on the air, but this was absolute. You could hear the excitement in their voices, as part of the incident was being played out over the police radio. I knew instantly that this was no false alarm, this was not a "maybe" call, but the real thing.

All available squads raced Code-3 to the Seaway Hotel, lights flashing and sirens wailing. An "Officer down" call brings police from every agency. St. Louis County squads and State Patrol lead-footed their way to Duluth's West End to help the city police. This was a cop, one of their own, part of the thin blue line, that had fallen. Hurt one, you hurt them all, and they don't take it lightly. Even firefighters roared up in fire trucks.

I ran back into the studio with a breaking news bulletin the moment Steve LePage ended his sports segment. Knowing that families of Duluth police officers were likely tuned in didn't make it any easier on me.

One of my sons-in-law is a police officer, so I know how worrisome it is for their families. I worry too and often tell him to be careful. News director Steve Goodspeed's father was a career police officer in Minneapolis, and Steve has a brother who is a sheriff's deputy in the metro area, so he too has personal knowledge of what officers are up against when they leave the house.

Ray Higgins, who was one of our sports anchors at the time, and Karen Sunderman, a member of our news staff, both rushed to the scene. It didn't take long before they were broadcasting live, with me on the news set talking back and forth in a forty-five minute news special that was riveting in terms of information and video. One of our competitors reported erroneous information that one officer was already dead. It would end up that way, but his death didn't occur until the next day in the hospital. We in the news business *must* get it right.

Sergeants Gary Wilson and John Hartley were attempting to arrest Lawrence Montanaro, a forty-seven-year-old man who had moved to Duluth just a month earlier looking for work. The shootings came as police converged outside Montanaro's second floor room at the Seaway to question him about another shooting two hours earlier, a block away outside the Midway Bar. A man had been shot in the chest, and police were told that the suspect lived at the Seaway.

A half-dozen officers went to Montanaro's room, and while standing outside in the hall they shouted for him to come out. That's when Montanaro began shooting. His bullets tore through a wall hitting Wilson and Hartley. With guns blazing, other officers charged into the room. One police bullet struck Montanaro in the leg while another grazed his face.

Wilson was shot in the chest and in the head, while Hartley was hit in the arm. The bullet that hit Hartley tore through the arm, by now in a raised position, and continued on into his chest. Neither officer was wearing a bullet-proof vest, but in this case a vest may not have helped either man, especially Wilson. Montanaro had used a high-powered rifle against them, while police at the time carried .38 caliber pistols. Two other guns were found in Montanaro's room.

Gary Wilson died the next day in St. Luke's hospital without regaining consciousness, forever thirty-four years old. His father, Bozo Wilson, is one of the nicest guys you'd ever want to meet. He worked for years as a Rice Lake Township constable. Hartley, age forty-seven, returned to work after recovering from his wounds, then retired a short time later.

Hundreds of police officers, sheriff's deputies, and state patrol from five or six states attended Wilson's funeral service, which had to be moved from St. John's church in Woodland to the much larger Cathedral to better accommodate the crowd. Even so, a few dozen people stood outside on the stairs.

Bette Midler's "Wind Beneath My Wings," whose chorus includes the words "Did you ever know that you're my hero, and everything I would like to be?" was sung before the funeral started. After the service, a long line of cars followed the hearse to the cemetery, lead by dozens of police cars, all with red lights flashing. When the first car got into the cemetery, the last car was leaving the church, the longest procession I've ever seen.

It was the first fatal shooting of a Duluth police officer in twenty-four years, and the seventh in the city's long history. Prior to Sergeant Wilson's death, Sergeant Carl R. Root was beaten and shot by two teenagers in the one hundred block of West Second Street. One kid was sixteen and the other nineteen, and they hit him with a jack handle then shot him three times with his own service revolver. Root, who had a cabin just a few doors from where Judy and I would eventually have ours, died on August 18, 1966, two months after he was attacked. He was fifty-one. I was working radio in Virginia at the time and covered the story from beginning to end.

Other Duluth policemen killed in the line of duty included patrolman Harry A. Chesmore, who was shot to death by two sixteen-year-olds who held up a clerk at Duluth's McKay Hotel in January 1911. Officer Chesmore had captured the two the day after the hold-up, and, after neglecting to search them, he placed them aboard a trolley car for the ride downtown. One of them drew a gun and shot Chesmore in the head, killing him instantly, according to information provided by the police department.

Patrolman Neil Mooney was shot to death in Gary-New Duluth on January 6, 1914. Officer Mooney searched a suspect and found a gun, but failed to realize the suspect was carrying another weapon. His assailant went to prison for life.

A department release to the media, given at a memorial service for fallen officers, told how Patrolman John Callahan had been walking his beat near the Spalding Hotel on Superior Street when he came across a man who moments earlier had smashed a jewelry store window. He gave chase, and the suspect, Levi Tarbell, shot Callahan with a sawed-off rifle, killing him instantly. Tarbell confessed at trial and spent the rest of his life in Stillwater. Officer Callahan died on August 16, 1918.

Fifteen years would pass before Sergeant David Butchart was killed by a hit-and-run driver. That happened on October 6, 1933, again in Gary-New Duluth; police records indicate Butchart was trying to stop the car, "in an effort to locate a possible kidnap victim." Butchart was struck down, and the assailant's car smashed into a parked police car. The driver was later found in Wisconsin, tried, and found not guilty. Officer Butchart was a senior member of the police department, killed in the line of duty at age seventy.

Lieutenant Oscar G. Olson responded to a gun call in the twenty-two hundred block of West First Street late on the night of December 1, 1941, just days before America's entry into World War II. Olson and two other officers entered the house and were shot at almost immediately, with Olson taking a bullet in the chest and in the arm. He still managed to squeeze the trigger of his police revolver, shooting his assailant three times. Olson died on the way to the hospital and his killer died eight hours later.

Chapter 21

MY HEART ATTACK

Every life has a milestone or two that makes a difference in how we live, and some are bumps in the road that jar us into a dose of reality. One such bump in my journey was a heart attack in the summer of 1997.

Three weeks earlier, my kids and I got to ride our personal watercraft for the first time. This was the latest toy in our arsenal of boats, snowmobiles, and four-wheelers that help us enjoy Minnesota's multiple seasons. As one of my friends occasionally reminds me, "He who dies with the most toys is still dead."

Winters in our neck of the woods are long, and waiting for the ice to go out in the spring is like being a child waiting for Christmas morning. The sun climbing higher in the sky each day is mother nature giving the Northland a gentle embrace, as if to say to us, "See, I'm here; I didn't leave you."

By late May, the weather had finally warmed sufficiently to put the Jet-Ski in Caribou Lake for the first time. We took turns buzzing around that beautiful body of water, acclimating ourselves to this newfound freedom. I'm sure the constant droning of the machine was an irritant to our neighbors, something we were oblivious to that unseasonably warm afternoon.

Rather than spend the night at the cabin with the rest of the family, I had planned to drive north to Virginia and stay with mother, who was becoming frail with age and from multiple health problems. Ever since dad had died in 1991, three or four times a month I would spend a night with her, then the two of us would go out for lunch the next day, a ritual neither of us tired of.

I had no more stepped out of the cabin when a sharp pain in the chest got my attention, especially when it moved to my left arm while I walked to my truck. Pausing for a few seconds to try and rub the pain away, I passed it off as muscle strain caused by hanging onto the jet-ski all afternoon. It couldn't be my heart; after all, fifty-three isn't old.

The pain subsided for a few minutes before it returned slightly stronger. This wasn't a heart problem, was it? No way, I reasoned, that's something for older folks. This was a beautiful late afternoon, the sun was shining, temperatures were magnificent, birds were singing, and all seemed well with the world. Maybe if I ignored it, the pain will go away. It did, some forty minutes later.

By the time the truck rolled into Virginia, everything was fine. So good, in fact, that I drove right over to Rose's Pizza and bought a large beef-and-sausage double-cheese for Mom and me. See, I felt great. In fact, there wasn't another chest pain for days.

The next time the pain hit, I contemplated a visit with the doctor, but with a vacation coming up and so many things to get done before a week off, I again passed the trouble off to sore muscles from a day on the water. I had mentioned the pains to my wife only in passing and called them muscle spasms, telling her that I must be out of shape. She said something like, "Don't fool around, get it checked." So I did the next best thing—I didn't complain to her again.

Our vacation arrived in the middle of June, and Hutchinson, Minnesota, where a daughter and her family lived, was the perfect place to spend a long weekend. Our youngest, Chris, by then twenty years old, joined Judy and me for the two-hundred-mile drive to Hutch, right after the ten o'clock Friday night news.

For a while that night, I wasn't sure I'd make it out of the television station alive. Usually the nine and nine-thirty news updates are taped a few minutes before they are broadcast, but this night I would do them live. I sat down at the news desk in front of the studio cameras, and at about three minutes before air time, chest pains struck again.

These pains just didn't feel right, and the pain in my left arm was becoming more noticeable. By the time the floor director gave me a "standby," I was consciously hoping that I wouldn't drop dead on the air. The update is just thirty seconds in length, but that night it seemed to take forever to read. The walk back to the newsroom was slow and brought a definite feeling of exhaustion. Back at my desk, I explained these odd chest pains to my producer, but didn't make it sound like a big deal. I know what you're thinking: "What does it take to wake this guy up?"

Thousands of people flock to Hutchinson each June for a water carnival second to none. Hutch is a river town about sixty miles due west of the Twin Cities, and folks there know how to put on a celebration. Even the weather cooperated beautifully. Of course, they can plan without having to worry about temperatures that become "colder by the lake."

Judy and I took advantage of that gorgeous Saturday afternoon with a walk in the park. That's when the pain hit again, stronger then ever. In fact, it sapped all my strength after walking just a few steps, and I sat down on the grass for a couple minutes before wobbling over to a park bench, finally admitting to not feeling well.

My son-in-law Jason, a Hutchinson police officer, happened to drive through the park in his squad car, and Judy told him that his strong-willed father-in-law was having another round of chest pains. Jason asked if he should call an ambulance, but stubborn me passed it off again— nothing more than being out of shape. You get the picture. Talk about ignoring all the classic warning signs: two weeks of chest pains. Several nurses told me later, that "it's a man thing, and you're lucky to be alive."

It's been said that a doctor trying to treat himself has a fool for a patient. Well, I was a fool for not becoming a patient. All this time I knew something was wrong, but this was a vacation. I promised to get the pains checked out when we got back to Duluth the following week. Who wants to run to the doctor while on vacation, even though heart trouble runs in the family? Mother and Dad both died of heart disease. So did two grandparents and an uncle.

Sunday came and everything went well. So good in fact that standing to watch a three-hour parade was no trouble at all. By bedtime, I hadn't had a pain all day, which lulled me into a false sense of security.

Monday morning, June 16, 1997, dawned sunny, with a warm, slight westerly wind already caressing Hutchinson at 7 A.M. It looked like a beautiful day in the making, a chance to do nothing at all, or, if we chose, to return to Duluth or some other destination. After all, this was our first day of vacation, a time to play, relax, read, nap, fish, nap some more, and explore. Oh, did I mention nap? I had become increasingly sleepy over the past couple of months, passing it off as part of the aging process. All these signs, and it still didn't register.

Then it hit. At five minutes past seven o'clock, while lying there in bed minding my own business, I had a heart attack. The pain was intense in the center of the chest, and it radiated down to my left hand, and to my right elbow, with pain in the left neck area. Sitting up with both feet on the floor, I hunched my shoulders inward to catch each breath and sat that way for the next hour and twenty minutes. Twice I walked to the bathroom feeling nauseated, yet nothing came. Finally Judy awakened and the first words out of her mouth were, "What's wrong?"

"I'm having a heart attack," I finally admitted quietly, not wanting to panic myself, her, or the rest of the family. Too late. My son-in-law heard me and hollered, "What? I'm calling an ambulance."

"No ambulance," I insisted, but agreed to have Chris drive his mother and me to the hospital. Jodi and Jason stayed home with their infant son Cameron.

The Hutchinson hospital is a newer one-story building not all that far from my daughter's apartment. While Chris parked the car outside the ambulance entrance, Judy ran to get a nurse. Moments later they came back with a wheel chair, rolling me into an emergency bay.

Mention heart attack and people scramble. A doctor slipped into the room behind the nurse and gave me a nitro pill, hoping to reduce my pain and open the arterial system to better blood flow. It didn't work. Neither did a second, nor a third, given about five minutes apart. Nitroglycerin is a small pill or spray that has a history of great success in dilating the system, but leaves its user with a headache—which is no big deal, considering the alternative.

By now my blood pressure was dropping too low, so the nitros were put away and the morphine came out. A number of morphine shots failed to substantially reduce the pain, and there's a limit on those, too. While all of that was going on, and the morphine made me a bit confused and sick, I was hooked to an electrocardiogram machine.

Then came a strange decision. After a couple of hours in the emergency room I was discharged and told to see my regular doctor. They said their tests showed nothing. Suffice it to say, we got back to my daughter's apartment, packed the car, and headed straight for Duluth.

The next morning, Judy actually had to talk me out of mowing the lawn and into getting my butt down to the clinic. Thank God I got there. Pains returned to my chest and left arm moments after sitting down in the third-floor waiting room. They were so sharp at times that I actually looked for a place to fall if I passed out. As soon as the nurse came to get me, I told her about the pain and she wasted no time getting me on an examination table. Another electrocardiogram followed, and within minutes I was being taken by wheelchair to the cardiac intensive care unit in St. Mary's hospital.

I can be stubborn at times, and insisted that my trip to the clinic be alone, so Judy had gone shopping. For those not familiar with the Duluth Clinic and St. Mary's, the two are located across the street from each other, accessible by a skywalk system, three floors above Third Street. After so many years on television, people stare wherever I go, and riding across the skywalk in a wheelchair brought more attention than desired. That's when I asked a nurse if we could use the back elevators, to avoid additional attention. One of the drawbacks of having a familiar face.

Cardiac intensive care is an interesting place. All sorts of monitoring and support gadgets are hooked up, and the room gets exceedingly busy. This is where the rubber hits the road and you realize that your condition is serious. It's when you start thinking about the possibility of dying and wonder how many people have died in this very bed. For people of faith, it's also a time to communicate with the Fellow upstairs. While I was getting all that attention from the medical people, God was getting attention from me, a lot of it.

Any dreams of enjoying the rest of the week fishing were now dashed. It didn't take long for my family to rally at St. Mary's, but they were still not allowed into the cardiac unit. After all, there was plenty for the medical staff to accomplish in those first many minutes. Eventually, two family members at a time were allowed in, but only after getting permission through a telephone outside the cardiac center.

The cardiologist on call came in to talk with me and Judy about the situation and suggested an angiogram, a procedure in which a device is inserted into the arterial system near the groin and fed up into the heart area to determine if there are blockages that require bypass surgery. Let's face it, the heart needs blood.

There I was, on a beautiful summer day with temperatures in the seventies, in the hospital wondering if I would ever get outside again, alive. The angiogram showed four blockages that would need immediate attention. One was ninety-nine percent blocked, a second had ninety-eight percent blockage, a third was ninety-six percent, and a fourth was forty-five percent blocked. After explaining his findings, the doctor said, "But of immediate concern are the three blood clots near the heart, and if one of them moves just this much further..."—he held his right thumb and index finger a half-inch apart—"...we've lost you. Will you consent to immediate surgery?" Within seconds, he had a surgery consent form in my hands, which was signed without hesitation.

By late in the day, all my children spent time in the unit trying to bolster my spirits. Jodi and Jason had driven up from Hutchinson. Sally and Rob, Chris and Aerin, and Cindy and Jesse all live in Duluth, so they got to spend a little more time.

That night my pastor, Father Jon Wild, came to see me and heard my confession. I was also visited by Fathers Dale Nau and David Tuschar, which meant a lot to me. Faith also meant a lot. I was actually quite calm and relaxed, with the nurse telling Judy that I was "doing well." Choking back tears, we said our goodbyes, as they wheeled me into pre-op.

One more prayer before the operation and this one got right to the point. While being wheeled into the operating room, I silently thanked God for the gift of life and for medical people. I prayed that I would survive the surgery and get well, thankful for the fifty-three years I had already enjoyed. I knew that if I didn't survive, I would be taken care of. At this point, everything was out of my control. I had to turn it over to God, the doctors, nurses, and technicians. There was no sense of panic, no real fear. It wouldn't have helped anyway. There was nothing more to do but to allow Dr. Per Wickstrom and his highly skilled team to go to work.

The last thing I remember was the anesthesiologist telling me to put my arm on a narrow board-like device on the side of the operating table. That was around twelve noon. In the next instant, I was waking up in recovery in what is best described as a foggy confusion. What a trip.

The operation had taken longer than my family expected. The medical team cut open my left leg from groin to ankle to harvest the blood vessels that were used to make the bypasses.

It was now between seven and eight o'clock in the evening, and in this daze I remember someone calling my name, barking an order to "wake up." As you might imagine, the brain is trying to figure out this odd experience it's never had before. Plus the respirator was still in the throat doing the breathing. That's another thing.

The respirator was the worst part of the entire affair. Any attempt to cough would stop the air flow and bring on a sense of choking. Then about the time panic would set in, the choking would stop and breathing settled down.

There is a memory of Judy asking me to squeeze her hand, and while the eyes remained shut and most of that time is a blur, it was now a few minutes before ten and the nurse was suggesting that I try to watch the late edition of the news. Sure enough, the story of my heart surgery led the broadcast that night, and Channels 3 and 6 also included mentions of the operation in their newscasts.

The *Duluth News-Tribune* gave it front page attention in the morning. In the story, station manager George Couture paid me a wonderful compliment, calling me the "heart and soul of our news operation." It was through that newspaper story that I learned it would be eight weeks before returning to work.

Recuperation time in the hospital wasn't bad, but getting up to walk for the first time was more than a little painful. And the hallucinations from one of the pain killers were rather interesting. In one vision, my family was sitting in chairs around my bed, all of them headless. Another incident forced Judy to call a nurse: apparently I started talking about the giant M&Ms that were walking out of the wall, each of them wearing brightly colored rubber boots; reds, blues, yellows, and greens. They changed my meds. And to think, some people actually like such a trip.

I went home six days after open heart surgery, admittedly a little nervous about leaving the safety of the hospital. Thankfully, there was no period of depression that doctors said often follows such surgeries. Ah, it's great to be alive.

There is a moral to this story, folks. Chest pains need attention, not weeks after they start, but as soon as possible. You may not have weeks, or even days, or hours to delay. Recent radio ads warn that eighty-two thousand men each year will discover they have heart disease—and one in three of us don't survive our first heart attack. It's called death.

Chapter 22

LABOR AND UNIONS

Early settlers had few choices when it came to picking a career: iron mining, lumbering, or something in service industries. Those who chose to live in the Twin Ports saw potential in railroading or in Lake Superior transportation. The big lake was immediately a means of travel to faraway markets. These were insightful people, focusing on their futures, knowing full well that that the work would be grueling and sometimes nearly impossible.

Duluth's seven Merritt brothers discovered iron ore near Mountain Iron. It was the first good quality ore to be found, and they needed a railroad and ore docks to get their product to eastern steel mills. They put together the Duluth, Missabe & Northern Railway Company, but they went to John D. Rockefeller, the super wealthy oil king, for additional funding help. That was a mistake.

Rockefeller foreclosed on the Merritts due to the Panic of 1893 when a shortage of cash forced the "seven iron men" to pledge their mines and their railroad to the man who was later dubbed "the greatest of the robber barons."

Rockefeller had invested about $3 million in the Merritt venture (a $2 million loan and a $900,000 buyout), and walked away with Merritt property and other assets valued then at around $335 million. That was a whopping amount of money in the late nineteenth century, more like $6.5 billion dollars today, according to some inflation calculators.

The Duluth, Missabe & Northern Railway eventually became the Duluth, Missabe & Iron Range, most often called the DM&IR, headquartered out of Proctor. In 2004, it was sold to the Canadian National, ending one hundred years of history and chopping seventy-six jobs in Duluth and Proctor, including clerks, dispatchers, electricians, machinists, and seventeen management positions.

∞

Northern Minnesota is very much a labor community, and sadly we've seen an erosion of jobs that has forced people to move away to seek the bare necessities of life. Duluth has lost many large labor pools with the closing of the steel plant, the cement plant, the Air Force base, Litten Industries, the Coolerator plant, Chun King, and others.

The 2001 closing of the LTV taconite operations in Hoyt Lakes took a bite of out prosperity when about 1,300 employees, including 980 hourly workers, lost their jobs. Senator Paul Wellstone made an appearance at Mesabi East High School in Aurora the day after LTV Steel announced that its forty-three-year history in Hoyt Lakes would end immediately.

With our cameras rolling, those students challenged Wellstone to do something and challenged politicians in general to save jobs before they're lost. One of the students said the only time the politicians came to town was after the fact, seldom before. There would be no last-second reprieve, and our reporters captured the hurt in the people, their eyes almost hollow in disbelief. And to make matters worse, LTV announced on December 6 that they would actually close six months earlier than the original intent.

In a news release sent to Minnesota media, LTV's president Richard J. Hipple said, "We had expected to operate the mine until the middle of 2001, but the extremely difficult business conditions now facing LTV and the domestic steel industry, have made this action (early closing) unavoidable."

Governor Jesse Ventura met with Hipple in Duluth, and the governor left convinced that the quality of the ore being processed in Hoyt Lakes didn't justify the spending of huge sums of money to modernize the plant. Ventura said, "It's important to face reality."

The day after LTV announced that the plant would close early was Pearl Harbor day, and three weeks before Christmas. Union leader Jerry Fallos told us, "Even Scrooge had some compassion during Christmas. All of a sudden [foreign steel makers] didn't just drop a pile of steel. They [LTV] have known about this forever." Employee Bruce Riddle said, "It's like a Pearl Harbor to us. A lot of people thought they had a half-year yet."

Even after the plant closed, employees had other issues with the company, like health insurance, pensions, and vacations. Now, four years after LTV shut down its Hoyt Lakes business, there is hope for the plant site as a non-ferrous operation processing nickel, copper, and similar minerals.

∞

I was twelve years old when I first began to realize there was a rift between management and union in the mining industry—that there was a constant tug of war that was almost relentless on both sides. In 1956 my dad and thousands of other steelworkers were locked in a labor strike, costing them any meager savings they may have put away. It went on for months, and I could see the hurt and humiliation on Mom and Dad the day a deputy sheriff brought a summons forcing them to pay their milk bill.

That was the year Dad, while trying to make ends meet working for a roofing contractor, fell off the roof of a building in downtown Virginia. He also shot deer out of season to put food on the table that year, and he and Mother quadrupled the size of their garden.

It has always been feast or famine in Northern Minnesota's mining industry. There were good times and bad, growth and shrinkage, and steelworkers hung on. It says something for the labor force. The passage of the Taconite Amendment brought hope and prosperity for a while, but as the good times rolled, dark clouds started forming again on the horizon, and today's mining industry is but a shadow of its former self.

The Taconite Amendment was approved by Minnesota voters in 1964, to guarantee that taconite industry taxes would go no higher than taxes on any other industries in the state. Critics say the promise was not kept, pointing to reduced employment across the Range.

Take an airplane ride across the Iron Range and see the number of open pit mines that were abandoned years ago. They are now small lakes—watery graves, if you will, to the past.

The stories of these hardy people have been told and retold on my newscasts, and because I am a product of the Range, I feel a bond with them. When they talk about frustration and uncertainty, I hear my father all over again wondering if he and Mom would be able to hang on. When today's people of the Range express fear for the future, I recall how Dad and Mom talked about their future and whether it would be better to move, as so many ended up doing. In the end, they stuck it out.

There is an upward swing in taconite orders again, keeping jobs going, but thousands fewer than a couple of decades ago. What is the future of the mining industry? If I knew, I'd be making millions working for industry analysts. I'm convinced that someday there will be only two or three taconite plants operating, and direct reduced iron will provide some future work. A half-century from now the Range will be as different as it was in 1945, when it was booming during the peak of World War II. If you can be certain about one thing on the Iron Range, it's the resiliency of its people.

∞

Even though I have that bond with the Range, not every story I put on the air is well received. Take for example the 1989 labor dispute in International Falls, which resulted in a large fire, several people injured, cars overturned, and more than thirty people arrested.

I personally answered a number of phone calls from people criticizing us for trying to, as they put it, "make a fool of union workers." They thought our story was slanted against them, but in reality, nothing could be further from the truth.

Television news differs from newspapers in several ways, the most obvious being that television is a picture medium, and pictures tell stories, sometimes far better than words. That's why TV reporters are taught and often reminded to "write to video." Reporters generally have a good idea what video is available to tell their story, so when a car fire is mentioned we should see the car burning. If the reporter's talking about a robin pulling a worm out of the earth, let's see the tug-of-war and not a picture of a cloud floating overhead.

The International Falls riot is a good example. A crowd estimated at five-hundred strong gathered outside the I-Falls Boise Cascade paper mill on the morning of September 9. They were there to protest Boise's expansion project being built by nonunion labor. This was a major expansion, more than $500 million being reinvested in Boise's commitment to the city.

International Falls is a union town, and the use of nonunion workers angered the rank and file. Protesters showed up from around Minnesota, and a busload came in from Michigan. Some of them were armed with baseball bats and lead pipes. Just after seven o'clock that morning, they knocked down a chain-link fence and stormed the housing camp outside the paper mill, in which nonunion people were living. Security guards were assaulted and an ambulance was rushed to the scene.

Dressed in riot helmets, Koochiching County Sheriff's deputies and International Falls police were overwhelmed, and before the hour was up, the housing unit known as "Mancamp" was burning. The Federal Bureau of Alcohol, Tobacco, and Firearms called to see if they should send a unit, and a call went out for the National Guard, which did not respond. Governor Rudy Perpich took plenty of flak for that, and he was forced to defend his decision not to send in the Guard. He called the criticism that he hesitated to act against the unions, "an outrageous lie."

The news media didn't escape either. Rampaging protestors threatened photographers, and mud was smeared on camera lenses. Phone calls to our newsroom criticized our reporting as "anti-union," and "pro-business," as if the media should be pro- or anti- anything. This was a classic case of "Don't make us look bad." More police were called to the scene, including manpower from St. Louis County, Beltrami County, Itasca County, and agents from the Bureau of Criminal Apprehension. Their people were armed with video cameras, taking pictures of protestors to use in possible legal action against them.

Of the nearly three dozen people arrested, a half-dozen were from International Falls, and at least fifteen were from out of state. It wasn't a pretty picture, and the union blamed Boise while Boise blamed the union. At least one union official said this riot showed that the unions were "not going to roll over and let nonunion shops take over the state." Eventually, union leaders denounced the violence, saying frustration lead to the riot.

Chapter 23

LOCAL FAME

A young newspaper photographer once asked if I went into television to "meet chicks." He said it looked like the perfect career to be a "chick-magnet," a term these ears hadn't heard before.

I was asked to be the master of ceremonies for the Miss Minnesota Universe Pageant in 1968. The extravaganza was in Hibbing that year to help the city celebrate its Diamond Jubilee, and being chosen emcee was both an honor and frightening. The bio alongside my picture in the printed program touted a broadcast career still in its infancy. By 1968, I had seven years on the radio and only a few months' experience anchoring the Saturday night news on TV. Hibbing is also where Judy and I had enjoyed our one-night honeymoon, but I don't think my honeymoon performance had anything to do with getting the job.

One time a female reporter showed some interest in me on an overnight assignment in Hibbing, asking if I wanted to swim with her "in the raw." I'm watching my choice of words here, folks, this is a family publication. Just in case you're wondering, I turned her down. Actually, I've been propositioned several times, but Judy always burst my bubble telling me it was "only because you're on television."

∞

I got my first taste of local prominence during an Easter break from school when I was fifteen years old. The *Mesabi Daily News* published a picture on the front page of me sitting atop a pole, with one leg wrapped around to hold on, and reaching down to pick up a bag lunch from my friend Gloria Nozal. My buddy LeRoy "Puttsy" Anderson is looking on from his bicycle.

It was Puttsy who bet me twenty-five cents, a decent wager in those days, that I wouldn't sit on that twelve-foot pole for four hours. He lost. Unfortunately, I may have lost a little too—my dignity. Anyway, there we were, hanging out in the playground at James Madison School, when Gloria's mother felt sorry for me and packed a lunch for her daughter to deliver. The newspaper photographer in tow grabbed a quick shot and got it printed the next day. As I said before, my kids have told me, "Dad, you were such a nerd."

∞

I remember the first time I saw a TV star in person. The city of Virginia celebrated an anniversary in the mid-1950s, complete with a parade that wound through the downtown area for the better part of three hours. It drew a crowd of thousands, thanks in part to Herb Taylor, better known to television viewers as "Mr. Tolliver," an after-school favorite of thousands of kids. Ulysses X. Tolliver was an old man in a small room who built a magic screen on which he showed Crusader Rabbit cartoons.

With local television still in its infancy, anyone who worked on the small screen was as famous as any big-screen Hollywood star to us, and Mr. Tolliver was the star attraction of that parade. I stood, cheered, and waved at him, thinking to myself, "Wow, an honest-to-goodness movie star." I shared that story with Herb years later, after I was well on my way in television.

Herb lost his life in March 2004, in Cape Girardeau, Missouri, where he had settled long ago. According to his obituary, Herb retired in 1990 after a career in university broadcasting and as a member of the faculty. Memories come flooding back at the mention of his name.

Herb also played the part of "Dr. Macabre," on Channel 3's *Shock Theatre*, sponsored by Old Mold cigarettes (a parody of Old Gold cigarettes) which were displayed on the program in coffin-shaped cartons.

∞

Jack McKenna is another local TV pioneer and celebrity. He's a dear friend, and although we see each other just a few times a year, we speak frequently on the phone. Jack's been retired for about a decade now, and is feeling well after a heart attack in 2003. He's living in an apartment in Superior, after losing his wife, Marge, a lady both Judy and I loved.

Years ago Jack played "Professor Fantastic" on WDIO, an effort to duplicate the success Channel 3 had with *Shock Theatre*. Even earlier, he helped a generation of children grow up as "Captain Q."

The Captain, a loveable, bearded old sea salt who had a brick fireplace in his ship's stateroom—with a monkey and a parrot on opposite ends of the mantel—would descend on a ladder into the vessel's wheelhouse. This was the only ship I've ever heard of where you didn't climb up into the wheelhouse. Oh well, this was television, and what did kids know about sailing vessels and wheelhouses?

Ray Paulson was also a children's entertainer on TV, playing a variety of different characters including "Sparky," a ship's radio operator, and "Mr. Toot," a clown. Those programs ran for many years, and when they died off, it was the end of those types of programs, not only locally, but across the country.

Captain Kangaroo, Pinky Lee before that, and Buffalo Bob Smith and Howdy Doody are now but a memory. Pinky Lee suffered a heart attack on live TV and survived to entertain for a few more years wearing his checkered jacket and hat. The good captain finally retired after a successful run which started on CBS and ended on PBS, and Buffalo Bob ended early, even before color television.

∞

There's another local fellow who made a name for himself, but perhaps not a name or face you would recognize. He was Lorenzo Music, the voice of Carlton the doorman on the old *Rhoda* television show and of the cartoon cat Garfield. He was heard more often than seen.

Lorenzo moved to Duluth as a child and graduated from Central High. Eventually, he and his Duluth bride, Henrietta—whom he met in the UMD theater department—headed for sunny California, where he struck the big time. Lorenzo started out doing voices on *The Jetsons* cartoon, then moved along into writing for *The Smothers Brothers Comedy Hour, Love, American Style*, and *The Mary Tyler Moore Show*. Next, he co-developed and wrote for *The Bob Newhart Show* and the *Mary Tyler Moore* spin-off, *Rhoda*, which brought him true stardom as the elusive Carlton the doorman, who appeared only as a voice on an intercom. But it was enough to get the country talking about him, and wondering if they would ever see this character's face. They never did. But Lorenzo wasn't completely invisible. He had performed on *The Smothers Brothers Comedy Hour* and he and his wife even had a short-lived variety show, *The Lorenzo and Henrietta Music Show*, which lasted for about a month in 1976. Lorenzo passed away from cancer in 2001.

Actor Telly Savalas also married a Duluth woman. His resume includes a long list of movies from cinema blockbusters to the bald-headed New York TV cop, Kojak. He too was an interesting character in person, and I mean that in the kindest sense. He mentioned that he had seen me on television a number of times, but never offered if he liked my work. I did a story on Telly filming a promo for Glensheen, the Congdon estate, and after the shoot we talked about how much he regretted shaving his head. His baldness had become a trademark, and he told me what a pain it was to have to scrape every bit of hair off every day.

∞

The infamous serial killer Henry Lee Lucas allegedly had a Duluth connection. He confessed to murdering a Duluth woman in the late 1950s, which would have been one of the earliest killings for which he took credit. Local police believe that could have been the 1958 stabbing death of Marie Hoidman, which remains a cold case crime.

I never met Lucas, but I certainly broadcast enough stories about him, making it feel as if I'd known him personally. I even got a letter from a man who called me every name in the book for giving Lucas "publicity."

Police can't agree on how many crimes this man committed. Some believe he got most of his information from the legal system itself, allowing him to take credit for many unsolved murders. He admitted to as many as five hundred killings, eventually recanting most of them. He had his death sentence pardoned for lack of evidence, but he still could not escape the call that all of us face. He died in prison of natural causes.

∞

It's flattering to be recognized, because it's an indication that people are watching. Many people just stare, wanting to respect my privacy. Most folks are decent and genuinely happy to meet me. Just recently a man came up to me in a local hospital hallway, shook my hand, and said he has watched me for years, but had never seen me before in person. That conversation happens multiple times every day.

One man got a little carried away with the bear hug he gave me, and accidentally blew his nose on my ear during his impromptu embrace. Another fellow nearly cracked my ribs doing the same thing. Others get overly talkative, giving me a long version of the last forty years of their life. This celebrity thing isn't all it's cut out to be.

But it did help me move quickly through the security line the last time the president was in town, and there have been times when Judy and I haven't had to stand in line waiting for a table. But never, not once, have I asked for a special favor from anyone. And just like you, I have to take my shoes off at airport security, even in Duluth, with the security agent chatting amicably that she watches me every night.

I've been recognized in the strangest places. Just as Judy and I reached the top of Mt. Diamond Head in Honolulu, a young honeymooning couple recognized me. It turned out they were from Aurora, and in conversation we learned that the fellow's mother used to baby sit Judy when she was a kid. Several folks from Minnesota and Wisconsin have spotted me in Cancun and Akumal, Mexico. Not once have we gone on vacation and not been recognized, even in San Francisco, Washington, D.C., Phoenix, downtown Cody, Wyoming, and dozens of places in between, including a small hole-in-the-wall restaurant in rural Missouri.

But rest assured, I am not known by everyone, not even here in the Northland, not even in Duluth. One day I was in conversation with four women, three of whom said they were faithful watchers, never missing a ten o'clock broadcast. The fourth woman asked one of her friends, "Who's he?"

"Why, that's Dennis Anderson," the friend said. "Don't you watch him on Channel 10?"

"No, I've never heard of him. I always watch Channel 3."

∞

On August 18, 2003, Judy and I were driving home from Minneapolis on I-35 near Forest Lake when traffic began to slow, and we saw a news helicopter flying to an area about a mile ahead of us. When the chopper began hovering, I told Judy that there was probably a serious accident.

As we got closer, we could see a body lying in the median, covered with a blue tarp. A short distance away, just off the south-bound blacktop, was a Toyota minivan, heavily damaged and back on its wheels after an obvious rollover. It was clear this wreck had killed at least one person.

Back home two hours later, we learned that the person killed in the crash was famed hockey coach Herb Brooks, who had coached the U.S. Olympic hockey team to a gold medal over the Soviet Union in 1980 (Kurt Russell portrayed Brooks in the 2004 movie *Miracle*). He had spent his last weekend on the Iron Range and was returning home from a golf game at Giants Ridge near Biwabik. The night before, Herb was at a dinner at the U.S. Hockey Hall of Fame in Eveleth, honoring Bobby Hull.

Herb had coached the Minnesota Gophers in the 1970s, and spent time with the Minnesota North Stars, the New York Rangers, and the Pittsburgh Penguins, all in the National Hockey League. His last several years were spent as a scout for the Penguins.

Eventually, the state patrol confirmed that Herb had fallen asleep at the wheel. We reported on Channel 10 that "he had not been drinking, speeding, talking on a cell phone, nor did he have a health problem. There was no evidence that he had been wearing a seatbelt."

A few days after the crash, the sports world gathered at his funeral to pay Herb homage. Tom Micheletti, the Hockey Hall of Fame's board chairman said on our air, "Herb was a giver, he was never a taker. He would do anything we ever asked him to, and it's sort of, in a way, ironic that his last official act was up here (on the Range) doing something again for the Hall, helping us out."

Author Ross Bernstein was working on a book with Brooks at the time Herb died. The book was going to be part autobiographical and part inspirational. Bernstein said, "Brooks always had a passion for growing the sport, whether it be through USA Hockey or specifically here in Minnesota."

∞

With fame comes both praise and criticism, and there are times when I'm not prepared for either. No one likes to be criticized, and yet it's part of the territory that comes with reporting. Here's how I look at it. A third of the people like me, a third of the people don't like me, and the remaining third don't care one way or another. Taking that attitude keeps my feet grounded and my head out of the clouds.

Another thing that keeps my feet grounded is reminding myself of a time I looked quite foolish on air. A young man from Virginia once called program director Dave Poirier asking for a tour of the TV station. That fellow carried a gym bag during Dave's tour. In the last two minutes of the six o'clock news, he dashed into the studio, reaching into the gym bag. Blinded by the studio lights, I thought this was someone running toward the news desk to hand me a late-breaking bulletin. Instead, he tossed a fresh cream pie right in my kisser. From that moment on, much greater care was given to the safety of the people on the air, and the doors to the television station were locked.

Chapter 24

POLITICS

Paul Wellstone met Sheila, his high school sweetheart from Kentucky, during her junior year. They both attended high school in Arlington, Virginia, just outside Washington, D.C. He invited Sheila to a beach party, fell in love, and in 1963 they were married. Their fortieth anniversary was coming up in 2003.

I spent the morning of October 24, 2002, sitting in front of the fireplace at home, preparing for that evening's Wellstone-Coleman debate at St. Scholastica. Senator Wellstone was running for re-election, with strong competition from Republican Norm Coleman, the former mayor of St. Paul. As one of the panelists for the debate, I was studying the issues and drafting a list of potential questions.

Coleman was in Grand Rapids that morning looking for votes, while Wellstone flew to the Iron Range to attend a funeral for the father of state senator Tom Rukavina. The weather was a mix of drizzle, snow flurries, and low clouds.

We expected to have a large audience for the debate, which would be broadcast live on two local television stations, plus Minnesota Public Radio was going to plug into the proceedings for statewide radio coverage. In addition, television crews from national networks were expected. This was going to be a big deal, and I wanted to make certain we were up to the assignment.

The ringing of the telephone broke my concentration. Assistant news director Ray Higgins told me that a plane had gone down near Eveleth and that Senator Wellstone may have been aboard. The phone rang again before I could leave home and this time Ray said that there were definitely fatalities and it was still believed that this was Wellstone's plane.

By the time I drove the five miles to the television station, morning anchor Steve Long had called Wellstone headquarters and questioned them about the senator's trip north. They confirmed that he was flying in a chartered Beechcraft King Air, headed for a funeral in Virginia, via the Eveleth airport.

The newsroom also touched base with the company that leased the plane to Wellstone's re-election effort. This particular model King Air, an eleven-seat turboprop made by the Raytheon Corporation, had a solid, safe, and stable record. The plane was often used on charter flights. Unfortunately, everything matched up, including the N-number stenciled on the outside of the aircraft. Flames consumed the plane, which dropped into a swampy area off the Bodas Road two miles southeast of the airfield. The site would become the focal point of a federal investigation and of news stories sent around the country.

We went live on the air even before knowing the fate of the senator and his party, a marathon broadcast that didn't end until 10:35 that night. Once again, I was the main anchor for this special report, seated at the news desk in the studio. Steve Long took up a position in front of the newsroom camera, and together we carried on an educated conversation about Wellstone and his political career. Reporters Julie Moravchik and Colleen Mahoney were sent to Eveleth with our satellite truck to provide live coverage from there. Five o'clock anchor Dan Shutte went to DFL headquarters with another live truck, while a host of our people went to work on the telephones.

It was the White House that confirmed there were no survivors. Killed in the crash were Paul and Sheila Wellstone; their daughter Marcia; three campaign staffers, Will McLaughlin, Tom Lapic, and Mary McEvoy; and the two pilots, Richard Conry and copilot Michael Guess. All died on impact or moments later.

Eveleth airport manager Gary Ulman took a news photographer from KSTP, our sister station in the Twin Cities, for a quick flyover of the crash site. What they got turned out to be the only video of the destroyed airplane that day, since federal authorities soon closed off the airspace around the crash.

Being a retired private pilot, the Eveleth airport is familiar ground for me, having flown into that airfield many times. I was able to describe to our viewers the layout of the airport and how the plane would have been coming in while flying in instrument weather.

The first report of the plane down was at 10:50 A.M., with first responders confirming the crash just after eleven o'clock. Plane crashes are not unusual in this part of the country, where pilots fly for business and pleasure. Firefighters from Fayal township responded, as did the FBI, the Bureau of Criminal Apprehension, the State Patrol, and the National Transportation Safety Board, which promised to be there by eight o'clock the next morning. The FBI told us they were there to protect the integrity of the site; after all, Senator Wellstone was not an average citizen.

Mayor Doty joined me in the studio for some ninety minutes of dialogue, telling viewers that he had a chance to work with Wellstone on numerous occasions and he liked the spirit that Wellstone brought to each issue. However, the mayor made it clear what we already knew, that he and the senator were in different ballparks politically.

Long-time Republican activist and former Hermantown mayor Dan Urshan echoed those sentiments. Like the rest of us, community leaders were stunned by Wellstone's death and many of them gladly came on the air to talk about the life and the loss of this man. We received similar reactions from Governor Jesse Ventura, Lieutenant Governor Mae Shunk, and former Democratic governor Wendell Anderson, who all appeared on our broadcast.

Our reporting crew was set up for live reports from the Eveleth airport by the time we were an hour into the story. That's where much of the organizational action took place, the gathering spot for those involved in the crash investigation.

Julie and Colleen fed us constant live stories, while others were put on tape for later playback. Airport manager Ulman went on tape with Colleen talking about the crash site, what it looked like at the time of the accident, the weather, and the final words from the pilot over the plane's radio. He said visibility was down to about two miles in light snow. The weather was not ideal, but pilots have flown in much worse conditions.

When senate-hopeful Coleman heard the news while sitting in his airplane in Grand Rapids, he told us that he and his family "hugged and prayed." Coleman and Wellstone were locked in a tight race with the election just days away, and Coleman issued a statement announcing the suspension of all his campaign activities for a time. Obviously, the political debate scheduled for that night was cancelled, and the crash story played out on local and national television for several days.

Former Vice President Walter Mondale was recruited by his party to replace Wellstone as a candidate, giving him only days to prepare. The DFL thought Mondale would beat Norm Coleman, after all the Veep was the party's senior statesman and well respected in most circles.

Some Republicans feared that if Mondale won the six-year term, he would resign after a couple years in office, with a younger Democrat appointed to fill out the term. Mondale said he would remain for all six years.

Three days before the election, Mondale made a campaign appearance at UMD to a crowd of several hundred people, a large share of them college students. Then he did a one-on-one interview with me. We had not seen each other for about ten years; the former vice president asked me if I was still involved in church ministry. We talked at length about the Wellstone memorial service that had gone sour when it turned into a political rally. The service, which was telecast statewide, angered a lot of voters, Republicans and Democrats alike.

The night before Mondale's Duluth appearance, I was a member of a panel of journalists who appeared on a statewide telecast of a debate between the senate candidates, but Mondale chose not to be there. Instead, he did a bus tour of the state, stumping in person hoping to appeal directly to voters. He missed a chance to talk to hundreds of thousands of voters by not appearing on the debate, which was broadcast live on five television stations and rebroadcast several times in the Twin Cities market. So Norm Coleman debated two lesser known candidates that Friday night, and Coleman won the election the following Tuesday.

Eventually, our news staff and I were honored by our professional peers with two separate Emmy awards for our stories on the Wellstone plane crash, both for best newscast, two years running. Suffice it to say, I was honored by the accolades but it took a lot of people both in front of and behind the cameras to get it done right. My two Emmys sit on a mantel at home, a reflection of the hard work that went into our coverage of this local, yet national, tragedy.

Thirteen months after the crash, federal investigators ruled that pilot error was to blame.

∞

This paragraph is being written during the 2004 presidential race between President George W. Bush and Senator John F. Kerry, and there has been some nasty mud-slinging. It was hoped the so-called "527" groups, which, at least on paper, are independent from political parties and candidates, would provide some relief. In 2004, however, these groups spent many millions of dollars on what critics called "in-your-face ads"—the candidates, although they did not approve the ads, also did nothing to stop them. Republican senator John McCain, writing in a *Newsweek* opinion piece, said the ads were "negative and nasty, and threaten to bring politics to a new low."

I've noticed for some time that politicians who run for state offices no longer campaign in front of people, but in front of television cameras that have been set up in some airport lounge. That way they can hit a half-dozen cities in a day, never seeing a voter with the exception of the reporters and photographers, some of whom are so disillusioned that they have quit voting. Half of our politicians wouldn't recognize a constituent if they bumped into one on the street. If the media chose, it could stop that practice, which would force office seekers to get back on the streets and shake hands with those who went to the polls.

The Radio-Television News Directors Association publishes the *RTNDA Communicator*, what they call "The magazine for electronic journalists." They reported that in 2002, the Annenberg School for Communication at the University of Southern California, found that "only 44 percent of television stations in the nation's Top 50 media markets provided any campaign coverage at all."

Unless politicians stop tossing muck and if the media doesn't work to cover the issues instead of the personality of a campaign, more and more Americans will abandon their voting privilege. There is a growing disillusionment among the populace and with some media outlets. It would be a shame if we didn't nip this erosion in the bud right now.

∞

State politics used to be a part-time job in Minnesota, with the legislature meeting every other year. We have allowed them to create a bureaucracy that is cumbersome and wasteful. Our current system is exceedingly expensive for what comes out of it.

I'm like a lot of other people, Democrats, Republicans, and Independents alike, who favor just two terms for every politician. If two terms is good enough for the President of the United States, it's good enough for members of city and county government, state legislative bodies, and the Congress. One could argue that we already have term limits, which are called elections. But we all know that incumbents have a way of staying forever, thanks to name recognition and an illness called citizen apathy. Many don't vote, tossing up their hands instead and asking, "What's the use?"

Some politicians do a good job, but the system wasn't meant to have them stay in office for twenty to forty years. That's not a citizen government; it's a professional government. We have drifted from being a government of the people, by the people, and for the people to a government that is bloated and wasteful, going through taxpayers' money with little accountability. I'm sure most of you will agree that the government wastes billions of dollars each year.

Dealing with government agencies is often frustrating for the very people the government is there to serve. That's wrong—very wrong. Are they spending your money wisely? Are they making government agencies more people-friendly? It's my job as a journalist to keep an eye on our government, but you need to do the same.

Chapter 25

THE GLENSHEEN MURDERS

January 2004 found me standing outside the main gate of Perryville Prison on the far southwest edge of Phoenix, Arizona. It wasn't cold enough for a jacket, but the day dawned cool as the first signs of life began to stir in the Valley of the Sun. The announcer on the car radio predicted 71 degrees for later in the day, and my thoughts flashed back to the deep below-zero wave hitting Duluth and the rest of that region.

I was not alone at Perryville. With me was Dean Vogtman, my award-winning news photographer, who was checking his lenses and microphones. We also had the company of Gail Feichtinger of Minneapolis, author of *Will to Murder*, and her Duluth publisher, Tony Dierckins. They came to Phoenix for the same reason we did. A reporter and a photographer from a Minneapolis television station also showed up.

The six of us were camped outside Perryville, hoping to film Marjorie Caldwell Hagen as she left prison, ending a fifteen-year sentence for attempted arson after serving just ten years. Marjorie was one of the central figures in the Glensheen murders, but ironically it was this other felony that put her away.

∞

Early on the morning of June 27, 1977, I was standing someplace else watching the sun come up, a long way from Arizona. Grandma Ida had died a few days earlier, and with the funeral now behind us, Judy and I packed up the kids for a week of fishing in Canada, with friends Ernie and Judy Shelton and their children.

The day dawned crisp at Eagle Lake, and after a couple of hours of early morning worm-drowning, we would head home rested and with our taste for fresh walleye well satisfied. Little did I know the surprise waiting back in Duluth.

About the time Ernie and I were pushing the boat away from the dock for another crack at those tasty fish, the bodies of Elisabeth Congdon and her nurse Velma Pietila were being discovered at Glensheen, the Congdon family estate on Duluth's fashionable London Road.

It was widely believed that Elisabeth had a net worth in excess of $50 million and several relatives stood to gain from her death. Elisabeth's adopted daughter Marjorie Caldwell and her second husband Roger had a history of lousy money management and the two quickly became the prime suspects—the only suspects. A week and a half after the killings, Roger was arrested. He stood trial and was convicted of murder. Marjorie too was arrested but she beat the rap. Five years later, the Minnesota Supreme Court overturned Roger's conviction on legal technicalities, and rather than try him again the prosecution worked out a deal with the defense. Roger pleaded guilty to second-degree murder for time served and became a free man. He was free in the physical sense, but he must have been mentally imprisoned, for six years later, in his hometown of Latrobe, Pennsylvania, he committed suicide. Caldwell left a note declaring his innocence.

DNA testing wasn't even a dream when Mrs. Congdon and Mrs. Pietila were so savagely killed, but now the use of DNA testing as a biological fingerprint can eliminate 99.9999 percent of the population from matching a given genetic sample. Prosecutor John DeSanto had the presence of mind to save some of the evidence from the trials, including an envelope mailed the day of the murders from Duluth to Roger Caldwell in Colorado. DNA testing, while not conclusive, eliminated 99.44 percent of the population from matching the DNA in the saliva that sealed the envelope. Caldwell denied being in Duluth, but he was a member of that .46 percent—less than one half of a percent—who could have licked the envelope closed. It was a key piece of evidence that has almost positively cinched his guilt all these years later. As Gail Feichtinger wrote in *Will to Murder*, the DNA evidence was a "statistical smoking gun" that essentially confirmed Caldwell's conviction and casts doubt over Marjorie Caldwell's acquittal.

∞

So there I was, still chasing Marjorie around the country. While Roger had cooled his heels in prison, Marjorie married Wally Hagen without first getting a divorce. Wally's wife died mysteriously in a nursing home the day after Marjorie visited her and hand-fed her dinner (in 1974 the Congdon family had suspected Marjorie of attempting to poison her mother).

Marjorie had also become an arsonist. After she spent nearly two years in prison in Shakopee for setting fire to a house she had just sold, she and Wally moved to Ajo, Arizona, a small desert town located about halfway between Phoenix and Yuma. Ajo suffered a terrible economic depression when the town's copper mine closed, and today the community is but a shadow of its former self.

The town became plagued with a series of arson fires, and once again Marjorie was the prime suspect. She was chased down after attempting to torch a neighbor's house with a kerosene-soaked rag. She apparently thought the house's resident was asleep, but he had awakened three hours earlier when she had first stuck the rag in his window. Now he had a deputy in his bedroom, and four more covered the alley outside. Marjorie was caught red-handed. The legal system sentenced her to be locked away in the Arizona prison system for fifteen years. She was even suspected of murdering her husband Wally, who died under suspicious circumstances on the very day she went to prison. Suspicion was one thing—proof was another. And investigators had no proof of murder.

And there we were outside Perryville Prison, waiting for the lady of the day to taste freedom—no more being told what to do and when to do it. At Perryville, a women's prison, all inmates dress in bright orange jumpsuits, easy to see against the desert brown. Uniformed guards stand everywhere, keeping order inside. Many had no idea who Marjorie really was, other than her name and her inmate number: 098685. To them she was just another prisoner, much older than the rest, many of whom are in their early twenties.

Finally, we got a glimpse of Marjorie, one of three women who would be released on that particular morning. Perryville has no gate at its main entrance, but deeper inside this sprawling compound the yard and living quarters are lined with heavy-duty fencing and razor wire. And believe me, there is a gate inside. This is a foreboding institution, which almost seems out of place in the beauty of the desert, just a stone's throw from a mountain range. As the sun crept higher in the sky, the mountains turned three different shades of purple, and the temperature inched up from where the mercury spent the night, in the mid-40s. A guard casually mentioned that it was just twenty-eight degrees that morning on the north rim of the Grand Canyon. He's the first guard we saw who seemed friendly, dropping his intimidating posture while spending a few seconds with us.

Marjorie had cast her eyes on those mountains a thousand times, and one can only imagine how she dreamed of someday getting on the highway that meanders through them, hoping to get as far away from this place as possible. Tucson would be her choice.

We watched with cameras rolling as her chauffer-driven car, reportedly rented by an attorney friend, drove up to near where she was undergoing her final processing, and in clear view. This place is a far cry from growing up in the paneled halls of Glensheen, where her every whim was attended to by a cadre of servants. No buzzers to summon a butler here.

Looking younger than her seventy years and still dressed in prison orange, she stepped into an outdoor booth to change clothes. It's a tiny one-room device that looks more like a Porta Potty than anything else. A few moments later, we watched as Marjorie stepped out in civilian clothing. She must have felt like a human being again.

Her driver put three boxes of personal belongings into the car, and minutes later they drove toward the gate. At the last moment they spotted the waiting TV cameras, never realizing that they had been taped the entire time. Marjorie ducked down, and the driver made a sharp left turn toward another gate, hoping to avoid the nightly news. I can only imagine Marjorie shouting at him to "turn, turn!" Too late. We captured the entire event on video, including their car speeding down the highway, its tires letting out a bit of a squeal at one point. We got what we had come to Arizona to cover.

One high prison official told me they believed Marjorie will re-offend. In fact, Marjorie's only sister told the *Minneapolis Star-Tribune*, "I'm worried that she will do something awful again."

The prison's warden, Mary Hennessy, granted four of us—Feichtinger, Dierckins, photographer Vogtman, and myself—a tour of Perryville, a chance to see and videotape anything we wanted, setting no limits. We even went inside the cell that Marjorie had occupied during her many years of captivity. Her living conditions could best be described as bleak in that tiny room—just a bed, a toilet, and a desk. This was no country club, not by any stretch of the imagination. Warden Hennessy said Marjorie had been well-behaved over the past couple of years, but copies of Arizona Department of Corrections files in my possession indicate that she had some minor infractions during her stay. Those records, which are public information, show that in 1999 Marjorie had wrongly accused prison staff of inappropriate inmate/staff sexual relations.

One of the guards who was working the compound which housed Marjorie recognized me from television. He was surprised to see me there, then identified himself as a man from Superior who had grown up watching me on the news. It's a small world.

Our work done at Perryville, Dean and I drove into downtown Phoenix to write, edit, and broadcast reports live that night during all three evening newscasts, at five, six, and ten. I reported what one prison official said on the record, "You can't treat someone who can't admit what they have done, and Marjorie never owned up to any responsibility for starting those fires [in Ajo]."

That same official said that anything that was contrary to what Marjorie wanted would "set her off, but that she adapted well to prison life." Former friends in Ajo, told me, "We are wondering if she will adapt to life outside of prison."

There was a strange coincidence in the aftermath of Marjorie's release from Perryville. Hours after she got out, there was a fire at the Catholic church in Ajo, the church the Hagens attended. Marjorie had had a dispute with the parish priest years earlier, so for a brief time people wondered. In fact, there were three fires in Ajo within twenty-four hours of Marjorie's release, more fires than the small town would normally see in such a short span. Fire Chief Jim Bush told me that all three fires were accidents related to candles, weren't suspicious, and Marjorie had nothing to do with them.

I've been watching the comings and goings of Marjorie Caldwell Hagen since 1977, and who knows if she will be back in the news. She is certainly one of the most interesting characters I've covered as a reporter.

Chapter 26

LETTERS AND QUESTIONS

Back in 1969, when I was hired by WDIO, program director Larry Clamage offered some sage advice, "Denny, be yourself on television and you will succeed. Try to be someone you're not, and you're doomed to failure." Larry was making it clear that an audience can spot a phony. I never forgot his advice, and constantly work to give you the real me.

To be honest, it's difficult to be myself on the air, which forces me to strip away the protective veneer, inviting all sorts of comment and criticism—and we get it.

Consider, for example, how I've been working undercover for more than thirty years. Some people are born with a full head of hair that lasts from the cradle to the grave. Others aren't so lucky. By my midtwenties, those locks of mine were getting mighty thin. That hadn't mattered on the radio; I had a strong voice and couldn't be seen.

Then WDIO came along. All of a sudden appearance was more important. During my seven-year stint at WHLB, just one suit had hung in the closet. There was hardly a demand to dress in a three-piece suit while reading newscasts on radio, but television invites you into strangers' houses. Today there are nineteen crammed in there, along with 162 neckties and who knows how many shirts. After I was named the station's primary newscaster, someone, Jack McKenna I think, mentioned a hair piece. So in 1972, I began working undercover.

Management knew that wearing a toupee would be a major change, and there was no sense in having me magically appear one night with a full head of hair, pretending nothing had happened. Manager Frank Befera came up with the idea of having the hairpiece applied on the air for all the Northland to watch. The station worked out a plan, bought the toupee (they still pay for my hairpieces), and chose *The Peggy Chisholm Show* as the perfect vehicle. It was a local noontime program patterned after Dottie Becker's successful *Town and Country*, seen on Channel 3.

Weeks before the installation, my head was measured, and the hairpiece was constructed and trimmed, so that by the time the TV show rolled around, my newfound hair was ready for placement. That week, *The Peggy Chisholm Show* had a special night version.

Over a thirty-minute period, and live on camera, the barber gave me a haircut then applied the bonding tape, plopping the hair down for its very first appearance. That early toupee didn't have the quality of today's hairpieces, but it was a start.

Today, thirty-three years and many toupees later, it's no big deal. My children and grandchildren all know that I have a toupee, since it's often not worn around the house or at our cabin. But imagine the confusion while the grandkids are young; one minute they see grandpa with a full head of hair, and the next moment he's as bald as a rock. In fact, I often have fun with it while playing with my younger grandkids, putting it on their heads and having them look in a mirror. They laugh and laugh, sometimes singing, "Grandpa has a wig, grandpa has a wig!" The first time they see me take it off, some of them get scared. Who can blame them? I get scared too.

Apparently my first toupee frightened a viewer from Crane Lake. He wrote:

> Did you read Dear Abby's views on men's hairpieces? You should have. You would look better if you transplanted the hair on your upper lip to your bald pate and get rid of that goat hair toupee from Sam Donaldson's goat farm. You and he are one of the same. [All you do is] rip conservatives and give liberals softballs.

∞

I still cringe at hate mail, even after all these years. Nevertheless, good journalism should inspire and incite, and that it does. I try hard to keep a close contact with those who write us, either via the more modern e-mail or through what has become known as snail mail. I enjoy writing back even if the mail is mean, as long as a return address is available.

But I will not put up with someone swearing at me over the phone. The moment a foul word comes out of a caller's mouth, I hang up. Some have called back again, angrier than ever because they got slammed. It doesn't matter, I'll hang up a second time. There is no way that I will accept such abuse.

Speaking of abuse, that same viewer from Crane Lake took me to task on several occasions, one of many viewers taking a stab at figuring out my political bend:

> The news media turns a blind eye to the lies and deceit of [President] Clinton, Hilary, and their cohorts. You are one of them. I've never heard one word from your mouth against the present administration or its record of indictments of criminal wrong doing.

That letter, by the way, was written long before the Monica Lewinski affair was exposed, after which there were plenty of stories taking the president to task. But it is not our job to promote agendas. We are not public relations agents, though we are often criticized for failing to support some popular push, such as the Duluth smoking ban. While voters and the city council passed the ban, the issue of government intervention was just as big a part of the story. Some people didn't see it that way, but again, that's my job.

Personally, I disagree with the ban. We all carry a personal bias. That's what makes us individuals, and that's why we have rules and laws to regulate our differences and to keep order amongst the globe's six billion inhabitants. We need to have give and take, but sometimes I think the

American public has given up too much. For a long while now, I have watched our rights and privileges slip away. Don't get me wrong: I am not anti-government. However, there are times when the government sticks its nose were it doesn't belong. If I don't want to wear a helmet while riding a motorcycle, that's my business. If I don't want to wear a seat belt while driving my car with me alone in the automobile, that's my business. Please know that my seatbelt is always tightly fastened, and I wouldn't think of hopping on a motorcycle without a helmet, but the government should not dictate such policy for adults. If I owned a restaurant or a bar in this city, I wouldn't want the government telling me that patrons can't smoke in my private establishment. That's the owner's business, not the government's. If customers don't want to patronize a bar or restaurant that permits smoking, good for them. They have that right. Little by little the government is nicking away at individual freedoms, and as a journalist and as a citizen of Minnesota, that bothers me.

This next letter put me on the other side of the political aisle:

> Anderson, you take the cake. Your Republican colors are showing again. Everyone knows you despise democrats. How can you sit there on television spewing stories night after night that favor your conservative wing? You are not doing much honor to your father, who was a staunch democrat and damn proud of it.

Another letter I tucked away for posterity also came from far Northern Minnesota. This writer put me back on the left:

> Mr. Anderson, I'll bet my bottom dollar that you are one of the draft dodgers along with 99% of the dominant liberal news media that we see on the tube today, that never served in our armed forces, and are doing everything they can to keep the tax and spend [Democrats] in power. . . . [You are] turning the big guns against the Republicans with all the lies and dirt [you] can muster. You are one of them, you can see it on your faces while you sing the praises of this liar [Bill Clinton]. You end your news commentary with "and be kind," then broadcast such programs. Don't make me laugh.

Since the letter writer signed his name, I wrote back:

Dear Mr. _____,

Over the past decades of broadcasting the news to the Northland, I have been accused of being a Republican and I have been accused of being a Democrat, but your letter is the granddaddy of them all.

P.S., I served proudly in the military. And be Kind.

This letter arrived one morning with some career advice:

Dear Anderson. You have been on the news a long time. You need a change. Don't you get tired saying "this is Dennis Anderson" over and over again? Maybe you should try Hardees. Change would do you good.

∞

I got more e-mail and snail mail about Duluth's Ten Commandments Monument than any other issue in a long, long time—the issue surfaced in the summer of 2003, polarizing Christians and non-Christians in Duluth, and carried over into the following year.

This monument occupied a small parcel of land on City Hall property for more than forty-five years. It was a 1957 gift to the city from the Fraternal Order of Eagles, Aerie 79. When the American Civil Liberties Union filed suit to get the religious monument removed from city land, even the faith community became divided. Some church people agreed that the monument violated the separation of church and state, while others worked to save it.

Even a petition drive couldn't keep the monument on city land, and former mayor Gary Doty raised almost $17,000 in donations to fight the suit. A federal judge made the final decision, and on May 14, 2004, the Ten Commandments were lifted off city property; the monument's new home is in front of the Comfort Suites Hotel in Canal Park, where it's even more visible than before.

Personally, I was disappointed that the Ten Commandments monument was moved from city hall property. You recall from your history books that the Pilgrims left a land where they were persecuted to establish a colony where they could worship God as they chose. While the Separatists on the *Mayflower* didn't want the government to dictate how they worshipped God, they had to live by a set of rules in this new land. Quoting from the book *The Rebirth of America*, published by the Arthur S. DeMoss Foundation: "At the heart of the [Mayflower] Compact lay an undisputed conviction that God must be at the center of all law...." America is a great melting pot of nations coming together to live in a land of freedom, a land of choice, a land that allows the free expression of thought and ideas. But I believe it was built on a foundation of faith that our forefathers planted deep into the ground. All these years later, that foundation is fighting erosion.

Do strong opinions such as this and my views on the smoking ban influence how I report on these topics? If you've read this far, you know the answer: Nope. Because of course, it's not just me reporting the news. We have teams of reporters and a news director that also shape what goes on the air, and they all have diverse opinions on the matter. Our job is to explain every side of the story, not voice our opinions. That's for talk shows and the opinion page of newspapers—and personal memoirs, such as the book you're reading.

∞

Sometimes, while going after a potential story, something happens along the way that eclipses journalism. Scattered throughout the WDIO newsroom are scanners which help us keep tabs on the work of police, fire, and other emergency agencies. A call of a possible drowning came across the scanner one afternoon, so a photographer and I drove to the scene just behind the DECC. There we found a man in his late forties or early fifties sitting dazed on the ground while firefighters probed the dark water trying to find the body of his adult son.

They pulled him out of the harbor a few minutes later and began CPR, hoping to jump start the heart. The father and son had spent the day fishing when the younger man, who couldn't swim, fell off the railing into the water.

The distraught father's eyes fell on mine, and without so much as a single word he rushed over and threw his arms around my shoulders in a tight embrace, sobbing. He was dripping wet from making his own rescue attempt, and his soaked clothing saturated the front of my suit, which at that point didn't seem to matter. He recognized my face from television and needed comfort from the only one in the crowd he knew. Together we watched as paramedics tried in vain to restore life to his son. Days later he sent a note thanking me for being there.

Please understand that I don't rush from the newsroom to tragedies to comfort suffering people, but a similar incident happened while searching for a missing girl on the Iron Range who drowned in a swamp. These incidents remind me how influential we can be on television. And every once in a while we do get mail from people who actually make sense and appreciate what we are doing, such as this:

> Dear Dennis,
>
> I am a regular viewer of your six and ten PM news programs. When you say "be kind" at the end of the broadcast, it really means something. At least to me. One month ago I was beginning to commit suicide, and your news program (6 P.M.) was on my TV at the time. At the end of the newscast you said "be kind." I heard you and decided to be kind to myself. Thank you for your genuine concern for viewers of your newscasts. And thank you Dennis. God works in mysterious ways.

See what I mean about inciting and inspiring?

❦

"Laugh and the world laughs with you." That's what it says under my high school graduation picture in the 1962 *Rohian*, the Virginia High

School yearbook. Maintaining a sense of humor in a world that is often problematic is my prescription to better mental health. So efforts are made to bring a little laughter into each day.

Nearly each newscast ends with a light story, something from the ridiculous to the zany. A softer story with a humorous twist isn't a bad way to tuck people in for the night. My co-workers learned long ago that I'm an easy guy to break up; Steve LePage and Collin Ventrella don't have to try hard to get me going. One of the questions I'm most often asked is, "What were you guys laughing about on television last night?" Most often it's something silly said by one of them just seconds before the camera and microphones are turned on.

The three of us are often asked to speak to different groups and organizations, where we usually end with a question-and-answer period. Here's what people usually ask me:

WHAT'S BEEN YOUR MOST EMBARRASSING MOMENT ON THE AIR?
Two things: a pie thrown at me at the end of a newscast, and a little green thing that flew out of my nose and landed on my chin while trying to hold back a laugh. A viewer mailed me a handkerchief.

DO YOU DARE TO REALLY TELL IT LIKE IT IS?
Absolutely, but keep in mind broadcasting the news isn't a matter of daring to tell a story accurately. Accuracy is the main thing, personal feelings are left out. And no, we don't bow to pressure to keep details out of a story. I once had an Iron Range attorney ask me to keep his client's name off the news, for fear it would hurt his mother. While sympathizing, I suggested he tell his client to stop committing crimes. That's the best way to keep your name out of the news. Incidentally, that same criminal is now in prison for attempted murder.

WHAT'S THE BIGGEST STORY YOU COVERED?
That's hard to say, there have been so many. Certainly the aftermath of September 11 ranks right up there, along with the con-

tinuing threat of terrorism. My breaking the story of the
Edmund Fitzgerald sinking was huge, as was the Paul Wellstone
plane crash. The Northwest Airlink crash in Hibbing was the
worst plane disaster in Minnesota history, a major story. There
was the double murder in Glensheen, the Congdon mansion in
Duluth. The benzene spill and the Halloween blizzard are close
to the top. So was the assassination of President Kennedy. And
integration and race riots were colossal, as was Vietnam. It's difficult to put one single story at the pinnacle.

HAVE NEWS VALUES CHANGED SINCE YOU FIRST BECAME A
JOURNALIST?
Yes, without a doubt. We are reporting stories today that the
mainstream media would not have touched years ago. For example, politicians are more carefully scrutinized than ever before,
especially candidates for president. Sexual abuse cases were
rarely if ever in the news, not because they didn't happen, but
because they were just not talked about. We see more personal-
ity-driven news and less investigative stories. I'm not at all interested in what television and movie personalities are doing. I
don't care if they're having babies, getting divorced, or spending
time in a recovery center for drug abuse.

WHAT SUBJECTS INTEREST YOU?
I'm enthralled with politics, with a passion for stories that are
political in nature, especially Minnesota's political machinery.
History is another subject dear to my heart. I've always said,
"How can you know where you are going, if you don't know
where you've been?" The history of this area amazes me. Take
a walk through Ironworld and see the faces of the men and
women who took a monumental risk by coming here from
Europe to start a new life. That took guts. So did the founding of this country, the wars we fought, the struggles our
ancestors faced to get us to where we are today. History puts a
perspective on life.

HOW DO YOU WANT TO BE REMEMBERED?

That's a difficult question because it forces me to look at the future without my job and perhaps without my life. Actually, two words come to mind: honest and fair. If twenty years from now someone said, "Remember Dennis Anderson? He was an honest man when it came to the news. He was fair in his reporting." That would be sufficient. However, I hope my friends and family would remember me as striving to be kind, gentle, loving, helpful, approachable.

DO YOU HAVE ANY HEROES?

We are living in a time when heroes have become old fashioned, out of vogue. And that's too bad. Comic book heroes were big in my youth, as were sports heroes who didn't drink, didn't indulge in drugs, weren't hopped-up on steroids, weren't arrested for shooting their wife or girlfriend, or tried for rape. "Hero" used to mean something. My real heroes were my mother and father. They taught me right from wrong, the difference between love and hatred, and they demonstrated compassion which rubbed off on others they knew. And my wife is my greatest hero. She keeps my feet grounded and my heart in the right place. Her gift of love to me is magnificent and generous. Talk about finding the right soul mate.

YOU LOOKED RELAXED ON TELEVISION;
ARE YOU NERVOUS OR UPTIGHT BEFORE GOING ON THE AIR?

Not at all. After all these years, the job comes without jitters. But there are still stories that make me anxious and get the adrenaline pumping, so there remains an excitement about the job.

WHAT TYPE OF TRAINING OR EDUCATION
IS BEST FOR BROADCAST JOURNALISM?

Almost no news organization will hire a reporter today without a college degree. I got started before going to college, which is just not the case anymore. So did Peter Jennings, who didn't even graduate from high school. Large numbers of broadcast journalists have degrees in political science, history, or law, and maybe a minor in journalism. I studied business administration in junior college, then went back to the classroom in 1978 to study for the ministry. I also went to UMD as an adult in the 1980s to get a little more knowledge in psychology, but I am not a UMD graduate.

WHAT DO YOU LIKE MOST ABOUT YOUR CAREER?
No two days are the same. News is forever changing and stories evolve. One day you get to cover the President of the United States, and the next day you may be on the scene of some disaster, or investigating a story about graft. There have been travels to far-off lands throughout the United States, Mexico, Canada, Panama, and more. Journalism allows reporters to sample first-hand what is taking place on the world stage.

WHAT DO YOU LIKE LEAST ABOUT YOUR CAREER?
The same thing other journalists would say, the hours. It's difficult to constantly work the night shift, missing out on family activities and school projects. Lost family time can not be replaced. And this may sound strange, but constant recognition isn't all that fun. With notoriety comes the fish-bowl lifestyle that can get annoying at times.

IF YOU HAD TO DO IT ALL OVER AGAIN, WOULD YOU?
Yes, without a doubt. It will be emotionally difficult to retire because of my commitment to journalism and the belief that an informed person is an educated person. Information is a powerful tool. At least two other careers would also have brought much joy to my life: a surgeon or an airline pilot.

DO YOU CONSIDER YOURSELF AN INSTITUTION OR A LEGEND?
Goodness no. I hope I've brought some dignity to this profession we call journalism, but I too will be forgotten someday, which is what happens in life.

Chapter 27

Television,
Now and in the Future

On a normal day, I arrive at the station on Observation Road at four in the afternoon and usually leave at 10:45, a few minutes after the late broadcast. Since mine is the Monday-through-Friday evening shift, I try to grab a power nap every work day (remember, I also spend time each weekday in another office for my work as a deacon). Twenty to forty minutes on the couch will do wonders, and it's a rare day the nap is missed.

Dan Shutte now anchors the five o'clock news, replacing Pam Fish who had anchored that broadcast since its inception. There are two live cut-ins from me during that newscast; my segments originate from the newsroom.

Shortly after settling at my desk, I get into the computer to begin reviewing the lineup and the scripts written for the six o'clock news. Since I'm the one who must read them, it's common for me to rewrite them into my style and correct any grammatical errors. If a story is confusing to the anchor, it will be confusing to the viewer, so there are times when scripts are changed dramatically, at least the portion that I will read.

The entire newscast is displayed on teleprompters, a system of mirrors that reflects an image from a small television set, mounted on the front of the TV camera, directly in front of the camera lens. That allows a newscaster to look right into the lens and read the script as it rolls. It's more comfortable for both the anchor and the viewer when the news-caster is looking directly at the people to whom he is speaking.

Invariably, whenever I'm out making a speech to some civic group, the question comes up of how we decide what goes into a newscast. We work a beat system in our newsroom; for example, one reporter has the responsibility of the port and Lake Superior. Folks generally agree that the lake has as many different stories as there are people living around it. Other reporters are assigned to the Iron range, local politics, etc.—you get the picture.

I ask myself a series of questions to determine which stories to include: Is this story relevant? Can we learn something from this story? Does it impact the community? Is this nothing but a time-filler?

Too many crime stories, especially ones that have minimal impact on the community, find their way into the news. And there are segments within newscasts that aren't really news, but time-fillers—stories like meatball dinners, buffalo chip-tossing contests, pizza cook-offs, and the like. Real news has many elements, but acceptable stories are unusual, dramatic, have human interest—and are even, to some degree, filled with suspense. I've always believed that a story without relevance does not have an audience.

What's it like sitting in the anchor chair knowing that in a few min-utes tens of thousands of people will be staring at you and hanging on every word? There are times when I get a little anxious before a broad-cast, hoping we'll be able to cover an event well when there are a num-ber of technical challenges to pull off. That's especially true if we've spent a great deal of money or invested time and energy on a big story that requires live time from the field.

We face a lot of challenges in this business, the biggest of which is to grab and hold an audience in this time of multiple-channel news organ-izations. Once we've attracted a viewer, we have to hold their interest, and that's not easy. Ten or more years ago, there were only three networks delivering the news, none of which was seen twenty-four hours a day. On top of that, we now have to worry about channel surfing. Millions of us watch television with munchies in one hand and a clicker in the other. Make one misstep on the air and there they go…click, click, click.

I believe some of the nationwide loss of TV news viewers can be attributed to us not listening to our customers. All businesses must listen to what their customers are telling them. It doesn't matter if we are selling widgets, funerals, used cars, or TV programming.

Linda Ellerbee, the one-time co-anchor of two NBC shows—*NBC Overnight* and *Weekend*—is one of the best writers in the business. In her book, *And So It Goes*, she wrote, "We who work in television believe that we are smarter than the people who watch television…. Television news producers often turn down certain stories, because they say the stories are too complicated or too dull to mean anything." Producing a newscast is a difficult, demanding job, but you can't think you're too smart for your viewers. Viewers just want solid, relevant stories on their news shows. Good producers are worth their weight in gold, and can often find work in larger markets even before news anchors or reporters.

One of our best was a Duluth native by the name of David Gower, who was hired away by a TV station in Austin, Texas, where he remains today, many years later. He knew a story when it bit him, unlike other producers who have come and gone. Some become so worried about the technical aspect of building a newscast, they lose sight of the journalistic value of stories.

Our current producer is John Ellis, a talented man who came out of a radio background and has a good head for news. John is not only responsible for putting the six and ten o'clock newscasts together, but also for arranging all the technical work that goes into a broadcast: satellite usage, including arranging for live reports from the field, the technical aspect of each page of news script, and arranging for any and all visual effects. Those include what we in the business call "supers," which are superimposed on the bottom of the screen, like the names of people, sports scores, locater effects, and all other wording that is part of the visual. Once John determines what will be used and where, he gives those supers to the graphics artist who actually programs the effects on a computer.

The producer is also responsible for timing, and newscasts must be timed to the second. When things go wrong on his watch, it's his neck that's in the noose. John knows television like I know television—how to gather and present the news without all the flash and glitter of *Inside Edition*.

My role in the news business has been one of great enjoyment, and as I grow older and reflect on where it has carried me, I couldn't be happier. There are some things that could have been done differently, but by and large this profession has been life-enriching, and I hope it has meant something to the thousands who have tuned in each night to get a glimpse of the world in which they live.

Ken Auletta's book, *Three Blind Mice: How the TV Networks Lost Their Way*, addresses the anchor, specifically how CBS's Dan Rather sees himself as a "symbol." He quotes Rather as saying, "When you're a reporter you're not a symbol. You take responsibility for your own work, but you don't have to take responsibility for other people's work." An anchor does.

Rather was reminded of his own words recently when *60 Minutes Two* broadcast a so-called investigative piece on President George W. Bush's National Guard record. Using sources that provided unsubstantiated information, CBS ran with the report just before the 2004 election. That was a monumental mistake. The story had no merit because it had no confirmation, no truthful attribution. In the end, three CBS news executives and a producer were fired. Dan Rather had egg on his face and felt the wrath of his critics, but with his retirement from the anchor desk looming, Rather escaped pretty much unscathed. Actually, Rather had little to do with the preparation of the story, including its investigative work. He was the front man, the anchor who presented the piece, proving that the anchor too, can get tarred with the same brush.

Every once in a while I'm put in a position of having to apologize on the air for a story that contained erroneous information. By the time it gets into the evening news lineup and the scripts are printed, I must have confidence that the information about to be presented is factual, well-investigated, and is fair and balanced.

Sometimes errors are caught too late, which can completely change the meaning of a story. Here's an example. When Bob Beaudin was mayor of Duluth, we ran a late-breaking story in which a reporter quoted the mayor, not by title but by name only, and spelled his last name Bodin. This was a case where I went on the air without first seeing the script, which had been inserted in the broadcast after the news got started. I quoted a Bob Bodin (Bo-deen), not Bob Beaudin, which not only didn't make sense, it was wrong.

All journalists have made mistakes, it comes with the territory. We've all learned that speed for the sake of being first with a story can not replace accuracy. Three words ring in my mind thirty minutes before each broadcast: careful, careful, careful.

Several times a year I'm lambasted through either a phone call or a letter for something we have had on the air, and even though I had nothing to do with the story's research and writing, I'm caught up like Dan Rather. The public sees the anchor as the voice of that news operation, and in their mind, it had better be right. I couldn't agree more. News director Steve Goodspeed's mantra is accuracy, accuracy, accuracy. I've said it before, accuracy builds credibility, and as journalists, that's all we have. A reporter carries much responsibility and power, which, if not careful, can be wielded like a stick clubbing people on the head. Some have done that, but most of my peers have worked diligently, fairly, and honestly to tell stories that have an impact, stories that are relevant and necessary.

If any of you are considering a try at journalism, go for it. Grab the ring and run. It's a lot of hard work, irregular hours, low pay at the beginning, much criticism, and even threats of lawsuits. All that aside, there is much satisfaction that will carry you through if you have it in your blood.

Don't go into journalism to be a star, that's totally the wrong reason. I'll give you the same advice I got so long ago: People can spot a phony.

∞

Is my future secure at Channel 10? I like to think so, and I've been careful not to become overly demanding of my bosses. WDIO management has treated me well, and I've tried to return that respect at every chance.

I like to think that an older—perhaps wiser—journalist should be in every newsroom—broadcast or print. Long-time journalists who stay in one place for many years are walking history books. But journalists tend to move on after spending a few years in a city the size of Duluth, hoping to reach the pinnacle of their career in a much larger city, reporting to a much larger audience.

We've been fortunate though to have had several great reporters remain with us for many years, some as long as ten years or more. People like Julie Moravchik, Colleen Mahoney, Leonard Lee, Dana Larson, Mike Kahlstad, the late Linda Peinovich, the late Stu Stronach, the late Dick Gottschald, and many others. They are true assets to the operation when they stay that long.

Some of our best reporters eventually either moved to larger markets or got out of the business or retired to take on motherhood. We no longer live in a day and age when everyone stays in a lifetime career, with some people switching professions several times. Just the other day I was talking with an emergency-room doctor who said he would love to be a farmer. On the other hand, news departments in big cities employ journalists who have had other careers in the past. They include doctors, lawyers, accountants, retired military officers, and former police. Each of them bring their areas of expertise into the stories they tell.

The goal of many reporters is to climb high and climb fast, hoping to get out of smaller markets and into the big time. Those who are aiming for New York, Chicago, and Los Angeles may want to take note that there are network people who crave for smaller markets and are bailing out of the big ten.

Desmond Smith, writing for *Washington Journalism Review*, reported on network stars who decided the big time wasn't all it was cut out to be. In an article called "You Can Go Home Again," he told how ABC's Steve Bell, a long-time journalist who cut his network teeth reporting from Vietnam and Atlanta, eventually landed the morning news anchor job on "Good Morning America." It was a prestigious, high-visibility position that some would die for. Then Baltimore called, and Bell jumped ship for reasons of job security.

Other network stars who returned to local television include Morton Dean, a twenty-year veteran with CBS, who called it quits and became a nightly anchor at WPIX-TV in New York, and ABC's Spencer Christian, the well-liked weatherman from "Good Morning America," who left after thirteen years to work for a local San Francisco station. (Spencer broadcast from Duluth once, giving Collin Ventrella the opportunity to appear on the show. WDIO held a reception for Spencer and, with advanced notice that he was a wine connoisseur, gave him a fine bottle of wine.)

Certain network journalists believe there will be a constant exodus of top talent moving into the ranks of local news, recognizing that there will be an immense shift in the way TV news will be gathered in the future, especially at the local level.

Not too many years ago ABC, CBS, and NBC, were the dominating news sources. Today, there are many other choices, not the least of which are newscasts produced by local stations using the same technology as the big guys in New York.

There was a time in the late 1960s and up to the mid-1970s when Channel 3, then known as KDAL (now KDLH), gave WDIO a run for its money during the six o'clock news. It wasn't unusual for KDAL to be number one at six and WDIO number one at ten. Then something happened.

Channel 3 went through several ownership changes, and it was as if they stopped spending money on news; they were slow to get modern technology. Channels 6 and 10 purchased live trucks, allowing reporters to broadcast live via microwave technology. Channel 3 got their first live capabilities many years after Channels 6 and 10, years during which the size of their news audience eroded, a costly ratings loss. With Channel 3's news in the ratings tank for so many years, it gave Channel 6 a shot at increasing their audience as they vastly improved their product. As of this writing Channel 3 news is still in third place.

While not as good as satellite equipment, microwave trucks do allow line-of-sight broadcasts from up to several miles away. That means the truck's sending dish must be pointed directly at the receiving dish at the TV station, mounted high on the broadcast tower, or the signal can't be received. We still use a well-equipped microwave truck, plus a portable microwave unit, in addition to our huge satellite truck. That means we can broadcast live shots from three different locations in a newscast, which is a great deal of mobility. Some stations would give anything to have that much equipment.

Having the very same equipment as the networks allows us to plug into live and taped reports from anywhere in the world. And with independent reporters working around the globe, they can tailor-make a report on an African famine specifically for WDIO. We can take our satellite truck anywhere on the face of the earth and broadcast live on Channel 10.

∞

There is an entirely different breed of news outlets in existence today, compared with the early days of broadcasting, and that's how it should be. The industry grew, and with growth came change. Today's multiple twenty-four-hour news outlets are clamoring for ratings as are all TV channels—after all, there is only so much of the pie to divide.

As I watch cable news it's clear that they are often short on information and strong on analysis. I call them "screamers." Often it's not even intellectual analysis, but pure bias. The pundits have taken over cable news, not afraid to show their political stripes, and that bothers me. They are shouters and screamers, and are boring to watch. The public is not well-served when there is more analysis from blatantly conservative and liberal contributors than there is news information. A television consultant once told me that Walter Cronkite wouldn't be a success on television today. To that I say, "BS." Uncle Walter didn't become the most trusted man in America by voicing his personal agenda or taking sides in shallow debate.

The late Fred Friendly, the former CBS newsman from the Edward R. Murrow era and one of the industry's giants, said, "Sadly, I must tell you the television networks of which I was once a part are mercantile shadows of what they once were. Those in Congress, those in the FCC [Federal Communications Commission], and people like myself who stand idly by are as guilty as the Wall Street traders who have changed something once licensed 'in the public interest, convenience and necessity,' into a midway of junk entertainment and headline news." Friendly didn't pull his punches. He also called for top news anchors to take pay cuts—men like Jennings, Brokaw, and Rather, who were multimillion-dollar-a-year stars.

In *A Reporter's Life*, Walter Cronkite boldly wrote, "Press freedom is essential to our democracy, but the press must not abuse this license. We must be careful with our power." He also said, "Above all else, however, the press itself must unwaveringly guard the First Amendment guarantees of a free press." He called it "the central nervous system of a democratic society."

That's why Mr. Cronkite is my journalism hero (if that sounds juvenile, so be it), and that's why there is such a great need to get young people interested again in watching the news and caring about local and world events. Some of you, like me, lived the bulk of your life in the last century. Now the twenty-first century has dawned as the twentieth century did—full of hope, full of belief that mankind really is trying to put its knowledge and abilities to work for the betterment of today and for future generations. Young people desperately need to discover the passion that they used to have when significant news seemed so vital.

The *Los Angeles Times* reported in 2002 that, according to Nielson research, the median age for Tom Brokaw's NBC viewers stood at 56.7 years (Brokaw has since retired, replaced by Brian Williams); Peter Jennings over at ABC has an audience median age of 58.7; Dan Rather's audience at CBS was 60.3 (Rather is no longer the anchor, and his replacement at the time of this writing was Bob Schieffer); CNN's is 63.

The former president of NBC News, Reuven Frank, wrote a guest commentary in *Electronic Media Magazine* in which he asked, "How can you expect young people to be interested [in watching the news]? The school system we taxpayers pay for has not equipped them to be. If you are really concerned about young people being interested in news, get after your local school board. Go to PTA meetings. Do something!"

∞

The playing field for the media has changed a great deal since my entry into the business in 1961. There was a time when broadcast companies could have no more than one property in any given market, which was true for both radio and television. Today that has all changed, and owners and operators play by a new set of rules.

For example, larger newspapers and publishing chains are buying up smaller weeklies and profitable dailies. In Duluth, Knight-Ridder, the parent company of the *News-Tribune*, purchased the *Duluth Budgeteer* and all other Murphy-McGinnis newspapers. It now owns the vast majority of newspapers throughout the region.

Also in Duluth, one company owns four radio stations, KKCB (B-105), KLDJ (Kool-101.7), KUSC ("The Point" 107.7), and WEBC (AM-560). Another company owns five Duluth radio stations, KDAL (AM-610), KDAL (FM-96 Lite), KRBR (FM-102.5), KTCO (FM-98.9) and KXTP (Radio Disney).

And television is not exempt from deregulation. In March of 2005, Malara Broadcasting bought KDLH-TV (channel 3) for $10.8 million. Malara swiftly all but eliminated its operations in Duluth, with the exception of a newscast at 5:30 P.M., an eight-minute "news capsule" at 10 P.M., and regular CBS programming (*The CBS Evening News* now airs at 6 P.M.). The Florida-based company also entered into a management agreement with KBJR-TV (channel 6) to run what is left of channel 3 out of KBJR's Canal Park studios, leaving KDLH's highly-visible Superior Street building closed. More than fifty KDLH employees lost their jobs, and the news department was gutted. News content on KDLH will now all originate from KBJR's newsroom. This is further complicated by the *Duluth News-Tribune's* role as a "news partner" with KDLH; at the time this book went to press, the *News-Tribune* said it will "have to reassess" that relationship.

I see a danger in the ownership of multiple outlets in one market when it comes to the way news is covered. It could be tempting for a mega-outlet to become one voice, giving one slant to how news is covered (or omitted) and how opinions are written and editorial decisions made.

The competitive battle faced by independent news sources better serves the public than a conglomerate of same-owned radio and television stations and newspapers in a single town.

∞

So, where do we go from here? What lies ahead for WDIO and the hundreds of other television stations involved in broadcast news?

I believe the future is good for television news, but I'm also convinced that it's going to change. Don't think for one minute that TV news twenty-five years from now will look like it does today. Future broadcasts will be as different as today's news programs are from John Cameron Swayze's *Camel News Caravan* of the 1950s.

For example, I'm convinced that news anchors are dinosaurs. Future news watchers will get their stories as "selective news" seen on computer-system televisions. Click and get the story of the mayor signing a proclamation. Click to get the story of the big fire that hit the town. Click to satisfy your needs regarding a certain murder trial. Selecting only the stories you want will eliminate the anchor.

There is a downside to such news delivery. An anchor gives the viewer a cohesive synopsis of the day's important events; selective viewing won't provide that. Pick-and-choose viewing will leave the viewer ignorant about other subjects that helped shape the day.

I also think newspapers will change radically. Already, huge numbers of daily papers have died. Even in a large city it's almost impossible for more than one daily paper to exist. Newsprint is costly. Discarded newspapers are an environmental headache. Home delivery is expensive and the carrier is paid a pittance—just look at the want ads and you'll see a constant call for carriers.

Like television, newspaper publishers will be turning to the internet—many major papers are already available online. I believe the newspaper as we know it will cease to exist, and will come into our homes only on the computer. That will certainly change the way we enjoy our first cup of morning joe.

Whatever changes are forthcoming will not end the need for reporters and photographers. The method of delivery will change, not the need for those who do the digging, the writing, and the telling. My heart will always be in this business we call journalism, despite our occasional failings. It's my hope that journalists of the future will feel some of the enthusiasm that has enthralled this reporter, and that they too will stick it out for many decades, honing a craft that must never be lost. Storytelling is freedom, not only of the press, but of the country.

RETIREMENT?

Whatever happens to the state of journalism, I probably won't be behind the news desk when the big changes occur. Age is catching up with me. I should have gotten suspicious that Father Time was up to no good when Judy and I went to my fortieth high school reunion a few years ago, and a bunch of old people showed up.

You see, I don't have a twenty-year-old body anymore. I have a few aches and pains. I'm not an athlete, and I eat some of the wrong foods. I've been subscribing to *AARP Magazine* for a while, and it's clear that many of their ads are geared toward helping fix body functions that aren't working like they once did. You know what I mean: this pill for your sex life, that pill for memory function, smaller hearing aids, and better reading glasses. And there are tons of articles about saving for retirement. If you haven't saved by the time *AARP Magazine* reaches your mailbox, it's too late.

You know you're getting old when your surprise birthday party is held in a funeral home. Honest, my sixtieth was in a funeral chapel. Judy is a master of surprises, and I am easily fooled. My beautiful bride tossed me a grand surprise party when I turned forty and again at fifty, so it was only natural to expect a blowout when sixty rolled around. But turning the big Six-O happened in Mexico, while Judy was back in Duluth. I happened to be in Akumal, Mexico, on a business trip the day I turned sixty, January 18, 2004. After getting out of bed, I glanced at the mirror and noticed an old man looking back. My hair wasn't on, television makeup wasn't hiding the wrinkles, and a couple of days' growth was screaming for a shave. It's a good thing you can't see me in the morning, before I get straightened out. After ten minutes of feeling sorry for myself, it was time to jump into the Caribbean Sea for a swim, which magically erased any thoughts of old age. After all, it was eighty-two degrees in Akumal and twenty below back in Duluth. Come on, folks, that's 102 degrees warmer on the white sand beaches of the Yucatan, which helped cure my birthday blues. All of a sudden I was a youth again. Okay, let's not get carried away. I felt a little younger.

Judy joined me a few days later in Mexico, so we celebrated with a big dinner and night out, so I though that was it—no surprise party at this milestone. Little did I know that she had concocted this huge party at the funeral home with which I'm associated. She invited dozens of friends, including the WDIO-TV staff, the funeral home staff, and many others to celebrate my becoming a senior citizen. My buddy Joe Green, the manager of the funeral home, asked me if I would go with him to make a removal of a deceased and help him bring the body to the mortuary. So that's what we did. I've been on a couple thousand removals over the past twenty-five years, so for me this was nothing out of the ordinary. Once we placed the body in the embalming room, we walked to the far end of the funeral home, where Joe asked me to help him with another project. I opened the doors to the reception room and imagine my shock. Judy had pulled off another surprise birthday party.

So we had a great party, but it also served to remind me that I was sixty, and there was no warm blue sea nearby to wash the age away. The good news is that I don't smoke or drink, and I don't have a twenty-year-old brain either. With older age comes wisdom. My curiosity about the world, my desire to get beyond the obvious, has not dimmed. It will take many more candles on the birthday cake for that to happen. My competitive spirit is alive and well, providing me with encouragement to face the future.

Actually, it's still fun to go to work. There is no need to try and rein-
vent myself as so many folks do when they hit that magic number known
as sixty. Unproductive at my age? That's a myth folks, don't even think
it. I like being sixty. I go on the air each night filled with confidence,
even when it's obvious that something could and sometimes does go
wrong. Confidence helps me return night after night. It helps me set a
purpose to what I'm doing, and a person without a purpose is like a ship
without a rudder.

There's a great book in my home library called *Success Over Sixty*. I'm
holding tight to one chapter, "How Not To Be Your Own Worst
Enemy." Authors Albert Myers and Christopher Andersen say we "have
been lead to believe that the golden years should be a time of benign resignation." They don't believe that for one moment, and neither do I. As
they say, "We've got to stop believing those lies about age."

Sixty is not old, and neither is eighty if you're healthy, alert, and
energetic. There is success waiting around the corner, but it's not enough
to sit and dream. We must get up from the easy chair and mold our des-
tiny, since it's unlikely to drop into our lap.

Success can not and should not be measured in terms of income,
but rather in terms of happiness. If that's the case, I'm the most successful guy around. And that's the exciting part of moving into the senior
citizen stage of life—there is still more to enjoy, even work if you
choose.

Does retirement sound appealing? Yes, someday. But I will not be
plunked down in a soft chair twiddling my thumbs. Rather, it's going
to be a busy time of travel, fishing, volunteering, and spending time
with my wife, kids, and grandchildren. Winters will be spent in
Arizona. Judy and I have made many January trips to the Southwest,
where her parents spent nineteen winters away from our northern
Minnesota cold.

We attended Sunday Mass at a variety of churches down there. One
day I was caught up in trying to explain purgatory to a non-Catholic.

Purgatory is a place between Heaven and Hell. It's like your stuck between floors on an elevator, and this elevator is jammed full of people who have just been to Taco Bell for lunch. You're going to get to the top floor eventually, but it's not going to be a pleasant ride. We also discovered that it's hard for churches in Arizona to motivate people with thoughts of an afterlife. That's because it's so beautiful there in the winter that Heaven has no attraction. And it's so hot there in the summer that Hell doesn't scare them.

I will stay in church ministry and in the funeral business, now with my dear friend Joe Green, who manages the Cremation Society of Minnesota. He and I are fortunate to be a part of the Society, which was brought to Duluth by Mark and Kevin Waterston. Eventually the undertaker comes for all of us, and even though several of my good friends are morticians, I'm trying to stay one step ahead of those rascals.

∞

A couple of days after hearing that I got the job at WHLB radio, I was riding in a Northern Transportation bus returning home after a weekend with friends in Cook. I seated myself directly behind the driver for the twenty-six-mile ride to Virginia on a cold November night.

I believe the driver's name was Chet, and he had the radio turned down low but loud enough that I could tell he was listening to WHLB. I sat proudly in that bus, knowing that in a few days it would be my voice that Chet and the rest of the Northland would be listening to.

I was but seventeen years old, and now I'm in my sixties. I've been privileged to be invited into thousands of homes every night, several million over the span of a month. For that I say, "thank you." Without you, I'd be pursuing another line of work—I've entertained thoughts of being a doctor, a pastor, a funeral director, an airline pilot, an over-the-road truck driver, a Greyhound bus driver, and even a nice quiet librarian surrounded by the books I love—equally important perhaps, but maybe not as rewarding. I'd have to live another three hundred years to squeeze all those in before permanent retirement. We can sit and dream, but we can't change what's already been lived.

Scientists tell us that the earth is at least 4.6 billion years old, perhaps as old as 7 billion. Your life, and mine, is but a split second in the grand scheme of things. Even so, each of us is part of the big story, the story of life itself which unfolds a little more each day. That's where I come in as a storyteller.

The last century will forever be measured by historians because people like me, journalists, kept a record. Each achievement, each step forward, can be measured against our failures, each step backward. That's what makes my job so exciting, so valuable. We journalists have made a written and pictorial record, which can be studied to keep us from making the same mistakes while propelling ourselves through time.

Bear with me while I get philosophical for a moment—the chance doesn't come around too often. Some people are satisfied with achieving average results in what they do, while others seek a stronger purpose. That's true not only in their professional lives, but in their marriage, their faith, their family relationships, hobbies, and goals. Every one of us has been given the chance to change some of the circumstances of life, if we get off our duff and start doing a little creative thinking and less worrying.

Dr. Charles Mayo, co-founder of Rochester's Mayo Clinic once said, "Worry affects the circulation—the heart, the glands, the whole nervous system. I have never known a man who died from overwork, but many who died from doubt."

Not a single one of us can be guaranteed that we have a future, not one more day let alone more years. So preoccupation with the future can prevent us from enjoying today. It took me a long time to learn that, and I'm thrilled that it finally sunk in. We must learn to enjoy the moment, for in reality, that is all we have.

And that's why Judy and I are enjoying our children and their spouses. They have made us the proud grandparent of a baker's dozen, thirteen blessings, including our newest, Aubrie, born as work on this book came to an end. What more could we ask for? They all live in Duluth. Christmas at our house is a real family celebration, as are most weekends.

Someday this career of mine will come to an end, and it certainly is a lot closer than when I started on December 1, 1961. That's a long time on the air, but upon reflection it feels like just a few minutes. God willing, there will be more.

Have a good night, everybody...and be kind.

PHOTO GALLERY

My great-grandparents from Sweden, Axel Aronsson and Hulda Augusta Aronsson, stand on either side of Grandma Ida's sister. (Photo taken about 1912.)

Grandpa Frank and Grandma Ida, 1947.

My parents, Arthur and Florence Anderson, 1964.

In 1947, age three (far left), with my father, brother Jim, and sister Donna.

Also in 1947, with my mother, Jim, and Donna.

Climbing a tree at age 4.

With brother Jim, 1948.

Already an avid outdoorsman at age five.

With Jim, 1949.

Jim and I pose with our dog Skippy and Grandma Caroline, early 1950s.

With sister Donna, 1952.

Donna and me on a fire truck in
Cook, Minnesota, 1952.

Outside a rented cabin in Grand
Marais during a family vacation, 1953.

Serenading friends at age 11.

My friend Gloria (r) brings me lunch as I pole sit to win a 25¢ bet with Puttsy (l).

At age 15 with Pokey, a friend's dog.

Camping at Kendal Lake, age 15 or 16.

Our high school radio broadcast club, which started me on the road to radio and television journalism (that's me in the back, top center, with the glasses).

My high school yearbook photo.

The night of my high school graduation, 1962.

WHLB-Radio in Virginia, Minnesota, where I began my broadcasting career.

At WHLB, 1963.

Behind the microphone, 1965.

Judy and I get married, January 15, 1966.

The Cloquet Pine Knot captured Cloquet airport manager Arne Odegaard congratulating me on passing my pilot's test in 1976.

Judy and me flying our plane over West Duluth bound for Grand Rapids, 1976.

PAULUCCI MAUSOLEUM

TALES FROM THE CRYPT

November 24, 1993

Dennis Anderson
Director of News
WDIO - TV
10 Observation Road
Duluth, MN 55811

Sorry, Dennis, to disappoint...

...some of your audience, but the rumor of my death ... as
they say ... is grossly exaggerated.

However, thanks for your concern as well as "nose for news".

As an old friend and supporter, I promise I will let you know
before I change residence.

For now I have too much to do to take time to die!

Kindest personal regards,

Jeno F. Paulucci

JFP/kl
JFP93.1015

Forest Hill Cemetery   2516 Woodland Ave., Duluth, MN   218-724-6743   Fax 218-723-5580
"For the dead who want to be kept informed."

"LONGEVITY" IS OUR MOTTO

Please Leave Message...It Will be Answered; One Way or Another

Jeno Paulucci's 1993 tongue-in-cheek letter in response to my premature report of his demise. Note the stationery, created just for the occasion.

At the WDIO anchor desk, 1978.

With WDIO weathercaster Ken Chapin, 1978.

With Collin Ventrella at the anchor desk, 2004.

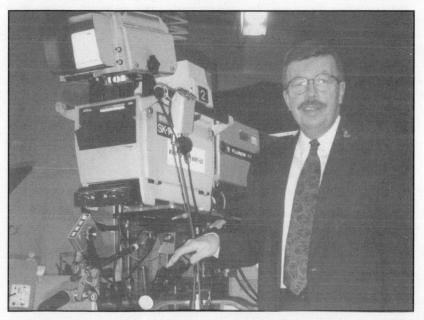

In the WDIO studio, 1998.

Snapped by a coworker while at my desk in 2003.

With retired weathercaster Jack McKenna, 2004.

With then-President Jimmy Carter in a visit to the White House in the late 1970s.

With Vice President Walter Mondale in Washington, D.C., 1979.

One of my favorite photos of Judy, taken in 1979 in Walter and Joan Mondale's dining room in the "Admiral's House," the vice presidential estate.

With ABC World News Tonight *anchor Peter Jennings, 2002.*

Celebrating our twenty-fifth wedding anniversary in Hawaii in 1991, serenaded by Charo.

With polka legend Lawrence Welk, 1978.

My ordination by Bishop Paul Anderson, June 1982.

In my deacon vestments, 1993.

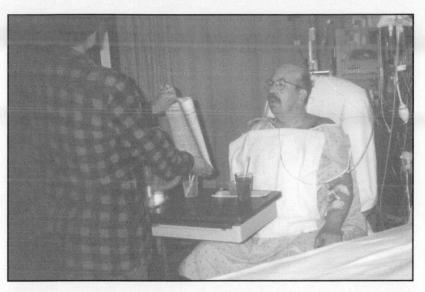

The day after triple-bypass surgery in June 1997, Judy holds the newspaper for me to read.

At our home in 2001.

Our children (l to r) Cindy, Sally, Jodi, and Christian (seated), 2004.

Our grandchildren, Halloween 2004.

INDEX